Containerization with LXC

Get acquainted with the world of LXC

Konstantin Ivanov

BIRMINGHAM - MUMBAI

Containerization with LXC

Copyright © 2017 Packt Publishing

First published: February 2017

Production reference: 1220217

Published by Packt Publishing Ltd.
Livery Place
35 Livery Street
Birmingham
B3 2PB, UK.

ISBN 978-1-78588-894-6

www.packtpub.com

Credits

Author

Konstantin Ivanov

Reviewer

Jay Payne

Commissioning Editor

Kartikey Pandey

Acquisition Editor

Mansi Sanghavi

Content Development Editor

Radhika Atitkar

Technical Editors

Devesh Chugh
Bhagyashree Rai

Copy Editor

Tom Jacob

Project Coordinator

Kinjal Bari

Proofreader

Safis Editing

Indexer

Mariammal Chettiyar

Graphics

Kirk D'Penha

Production Coordinator

Aparna Bhagat

About the Author

Konstantin Ivanov is a Linux systems engineer, an open source developer, and a technology blogger who has been designing, configuring, deploying, and administering large-scale, highly available Linux environments for more than 15 years.

His interests include large distributed systems and task automation, along with solving technical challenges involving multiple technology stacks.

Konstantin received two MS in Computer Science from universities in Bulgaria and the United States, specializing in system and network security and software engineering.

In his spare time, he loves writing technology blogs and spending time with his two boys. He can be reached on LinkedIn at `https://www.linkedin.com/in/konstantinivanov` or on his blog at `http://www.linux-admins.net/`.

About the Reviewer

Jay Payne has been a database administrator 5 at Rackspace for over 10 years, working on the design, development, implementation, and operation of storage systems.

Previously, Jay worked on billing and support systems for hosting companies. For the last 20 years, he has primarily focused on the data life cycle, from database architecture, administration, operations, reporting, disaster recovery, and compliance. He has domain experience in hosting, finance, billing, and customer support industries.

www.PacktPub.com

For support files and downloads related to your book, please visit www.PacktPub.com.

Did you know that Packt offers eBook versions of every book published, with PDF and ePub files available? You can upgrade to the eBook version at www.PacktPub.com and as a print book customer, you are entitled to a discount on the eBook copy. Get in touch with us at service@packtpub.com for more details.

At www.PacktPub.com, you can also read a collection of free technical articles, sign up for a range of free newsletters and receive exclusive discounts and offers on Packt books and eBooks.

https://www.packtpub.com/mapt

Get the most in-demand software skills with Mapt. Mapt gives you full access to all Packt books and video courses, as well as industry-leading tools to help you plan your personal development and advance your career.

Why subscribe?

- Fully searchable across every book published by Packt
- Copy and paste, print, and bookmark content
- On demand and accessible via a web browser

Customer Feedback

Thanks for purchasing this Packt book. At Packt, quality is at the heart of our editorial process. To help us improve, please leave us an honest review on this book's Amazon page at `https://www.amazon.com/dp/1785888943`.

If you'd like to join our team of regular reviewers, you can e-mail us at `customerreviews@packtpub.com`. We award our regular reviewers with free eBooks and videos in exchange for their valuable feedback. Help us be relentless in improving our products!

I dedicate this book to my uncle Radoslav, who took me to his work when I was 8 years old in a computer manufacturing facility and sparked a life-long passion for technology and science, and to my parents, Anton and Darinka, who sold the family car to buy me my first computer.

Table of Contents

Preface

Not too long ago, we used to deploy applications on a single server, scaling up by adding more hardware resources—we called it "the monolith approach." Achieving high availability was a matter of adding more single purpose servers/monoliths behind load balancers, more often than not ending with a cluster of under-utilized systems. Writing and deploying applications also followed this monolithic approach—the software was usually a large binary that provided most, if not all of the functionality. We either had to compile it from source and use some kind of installer, or package it and ship it to a repository.

With the advent of virtual machines and containers, we got away from the server monolith, fully utilizing the available compute resources by running our applications in isolated, resource-confined instances. Scaling up or down applications become a matter of adding more virtual machines or containers on a fleet of servers, then figuring a way to automatically deploy them. We also broke down the single binary application into microservices that communicate with each other through a message bus/queue, taking full advantage of the low overhead that containers provide. Deploying the full application stack is now just a matter of bundling the services into their own containers, creating a single, fully isolated, dependency-complete work unit that is ready to deploy. Using continuous integration patterns and tools such as Jenkins allowed us to automate the build and deploy process even further.

This book is about LXC containers and how to run your applications inside them. Unlike other container solutions such, as Docker, LXC is designed to run an entire Linux system, not just a single process, though the latter is also possible. Even though an LXC container can contain an entire Linux filesystem, the underlined host kernel is shared, no hypervisor layer needed.

This book takes a direct and practical approach to LXC. You will learn how to install, configure, and operate LXC containers along with multiple examples explaining how to run highly scalable and highly available applications inside LXC. You will use monitoring and deployment applications and other third-party tools. You will also learn how to write your own tools that extend the functionality provided by LXC and its various libraries. Finally, you will see a complete OpenStack deployment that adds the intelligence to managing a fleet of compute resources to easily deploy your application inside LXC containers.

What this book covers

Chapter 1, *Introduction to Linux Containers*, provides an in-depth exploration of the history of containers in the Linux kernel, along with some fundamental terminology. After going through the basics, you will have a detailed view of how kernel namespaces and control groups (cgroups) are implemented and will be able to experiment with some C system calls.

Chapter 2, *Installing and Running LXC on Linux Systems*, covers everything that is needed to install, configure, and run LXC on Ubuntu and Red Hat systems. You will learn what packages and tools are required along with different ways of configuring LXC. By the end of this chapter, you will have a Linux system with running LXC containers.

Chapter 3, *Command-Line Operations Using Native and Libvirt Tools*, is all about running and operating LXC on the command line. The chapter will cover various tools from a list of packages and demonstrate different ways of interacting with your containerized application. The focus will be on the functionality that libvirt and the native LXC libraries provide in controlling the full life cycle of an LXC container.

Chapter 4, *LXC Code Integration with Python*, will show examples of how to write tools and automate LXC provisioning and management using Python libraries. You will also learn how to create a development environment using Vagrant and LXC.

Chapter 5, *Networking in LXC with the Linux Bridge and Open vSwitch*, will be a deep dive into networking in the containerized world—connecting LXC to the Linux bridge, using direct connect, NAT, and various other methods. It will also demonstrate more advanced technics of traffic management using Open vSwitch.

Chapter 6, *Clustering and Horizontal Scaling with LXC*, builds upon the knowledge presented in earlier chapters to build a cluster of Apache containers and demonstrate how to connect them using GRE tunnels with Open vSwitch. The chapter also presents examples of running single process applications inside minimal root filesystem containers.

Chapter 7, *Monitoring and Backups in a Containerized World*, is about backing up your LXC application containers and deploying monitoring solutions to alert and trigger actions. We are going to see examples of using Sensu and Monit for monitoring, and iSCSI and GlusterFS for creating hot and cold backups.

Chapter 8, *Using LXC with OpenStack*, demonstrates how to provision LXC containers with OpenStack. It begins by introducing the various components that make OpenStack and how to use the LXC nova driver to automatically provision LXC containers among a pool of compute resources.

`Appendix`, *LXC Alternatives to Docker and OpenVZ*, ends the book by demonstrating how other popular container solutions, such as Docker and OpenVZ, came to be and the similarities and differences between them. It also explores practical examples of installing, configuring, and running them alongside LXC.

What you need for this book

A beginner-level knowledge of Linux and the command line should be enough to follow along and run the examples. Some Python and C knowledge is required to fully understand and experiment with the code snippets, though the book is not about software development and you can skip `Chapter 4`, *LXC Code Integration with Python* altogether, if not interested.

In terms of hardware and software requirements, most examples in the book have been tested in virtual machines utilizing various cloud providers such as Amazon AWS and Rackspace Cloud. We recommend using the latest version of Ubuntu, given Canonical's involvement with the LXC project, though we provide examples with CentOS whenever the installation/operation methods diverge.

Who this book is for

This book is for anyone who is curious about Linux containers, from Linux administrators who are looking for in-depth understanding of how LXC works, to software developers who need a quick and easy way to prototype code in an isolated environment without the overhead of a full hypervisor. A DevOps engineer is most likely the best job title for those who want to read the book from cover to cover.

Conventions

In this book, you will find a number of text styles that distinguish between different kinds of information. Here are some examples of these styles and an explanation of their meaning.

Code words in text, database table names, folder names, filenames, file extensions, pathnames, dummy URLs, user input, and Twitter handles are shown as follows: "Manually building the root filesystem and configuration files using tools such as `debootstrap` and `yum`."

A block of code is set as follows:

```
#define _GNU_SOURCE
#include<stdlib.h>
#include<stdio.h>
```

```
#include<signal.h>
#include<sched.h>

staticintchildFunc(void *arg)
{
  printf("UID inside the namespace is %ld\n", (long) geteuid());
  printf("GID inside the namespace is %ld\n", (long) getegid());
}
```

When we wish to draw your attention to a particular part of a code block, the relevant lines or items are set in bold:

```
<head>
#define _GNU_SOURCE
#include
#include
#include
#include

staticintchildFunc(void *arg)
{
  printf("UID inside the namespace is %ld\n", (long) geteuid());
  printf("GID inside the namespace is %ld\n", (long) getegid());
}
```

Any command-line input or output is written as follows:

```
root@ubuntu:~# lsb_release -dc
Description:    Ubuntu 14.04.5 LTS
Codename:       trusty
root@ubuntu:~#
```

New terms and **important words** are shown in bold. Words that you see on the screen, for example, in menus or dialog boxes, appear in the text like this: "Navigate to **Networking support** | **Networking options** | **802.1d Ethernet Bridging** and select either **Y** to compile the bridging functionality in the kernel, or **M** to compile it as a module."

Warnings or important notes appear in a box like this.

Tips and tricks appear like this.

Reader feedback

Feedback from our readers is always welcome. Let us know what you think about this book-what you liked or disliked. Reader feedback is important for us as it helps us develop titles that you will really get the most out of. To send us general feedback, simply e-mail feedback@packtpub.com, and mention the book's title in the subject of your message. If there is a topic that you have expertise in and you are interested in either writing or contributing to a book, see our author guide at www.packtpub.com/authors.

Customer support

Now that you are the proud owner of a Packt book, we have a number of things to help you to get the most from your purchase.

Downloading the example code

You can download the example code files for this book from your account at http://www.packtpub.com. If you purchased this book elsewhere, you can visit http://www.packtpub.com/support and register to have the files e-mailed directly to you.

You can download the code files by following these steps:

1. Log in or register to our website using your e-mail address and password.
2. Hover the mouse pointer on the **SUPPORT** tab at the top.
3. Click on **Code Downloads & Errata**.
4. Enter the name of the book in the **Search** box.
5. Select the book for which you're looking to download the code files.
6. Choose from the drop-down menu where you purchased this book from.
7. Click on **Code Download**.

Once the file is downloaded, please make sure that you unzip or extract the folder using the latest version of:

- WinRAR / 7-Zip for Windows
- Zipeg / iZip / UnRarX for Mac
- 7-Zip / PeaZip for Linux

The code bundle for the book is also hosted on GitHub at `https://github.com/PacktPubl ishing/Containerization-with-LXC`. We also have other code bundles from our rich catalog of books and videos available at `https://github.com/PacktPublishing/`. Check them out!

Downloading the color images of this book

We also provide you with a PDF file that has color images of the screenshots/diagrams used in this book. The color images will help you better understand the changes in the output. You can download this file from `https://www.packtpub.com/sites/default/files/down loads/ContainerizationwithLXC_ColorImages.pdf`.

Errata

Although we have taken every care to ensure the accuracy of our content, mistakes do happen. If you find a mistake in one of our books-maybe a mistake in the text or the code-we would be grateful if you could report this to us. By doing so, you can save other readers from frustration and help us improve subsequent versions of this book. If you find any errata, please report them by visiting `http://www.packtpub.com/submit-errata`, selecting your book, clicking on the **Errata Submission Form** link, and entering the details of your errata. Once your errata are verified, your submission will be accepted and the errata will be uploaded to our website or added to any list of existing errata under the Errata section of that title.

To view the previously submitted errata, go to `https://www.packtpub.com/books/conten t/support`and enter the name of the book in the search field. The required information will appear under the **Errata** section.

Piracy

Piracy of copyrighted material on the Internet is an ongoing problem across all media. At Packt, we take the protection of our copyright and licenses very seriously. If you come across any illegal copies of our works in any form on the Internet, please provide us with the location address or website name immediately so that we can pursue a remedy.

Please contact us at `copyright@packtpub.com` with a link to the suspected pirated material.

We appreciate your help in protecting our authors and our ability to bring you valuable content.

Questions

If you have a problem with any aspect of this book, you can contact us at questions@packtpub.com, and we will do our best to address the problem.

1
Introduction to Linux Containers

Nowadays, deploying applications inside some sort of a Linux container is a widely adopted practice, primarily due to the evolution of the tooling and the ease of use it presents. Even though Linux containers, or operating-system-level virtualization, in one form or another, have been around for more than a decade, it took some time for the technology to mature and enter mainstream operation. One of the reasons for this is the fact that hypervisor-based technologies such as KVM and Xen were able to solve most of the limitations of the Linux kernel during that period and the overhead it presented was not considered an issue. However, with the advent of kernel namespaces and **control groups** (**cgroups**) the notion of a *light-weight virtualization* became possible through the use of containers.

In this chapter, I'll cover the following topics:

- Evolution of the OS kernel and its early limitations
- Differences between containers and platform virtualization
- Concepts and terminology related to namespaces and cgroups
- An example use of process resource isolation and management with network namespaces and cgroups

The OS kernel and its early limitations

The current state of Linux containers is a direct result of the problems that early OS designers were trying to solve – managing memory, I/O, and process scheduling in the most efficient way.

In the past, only a single process could be scheduled for work, wasting precious CPU cycles if blocked on an I/O operation. The solution to this problem was to develop better CPU schedulers, so more work can be allocated in a *fair* way for maximum CPU utilization. Even though the modern schedulers, such as the **Completely Fair Scheduler (CFS)** in Linux do a great job of allocating fair amounts of time to each process, there's still a strong case for being able to give higher or lower priority to a process and its subprocesses. Traditionally, this can be accomplished by the `nice()` system call, or real-time scheduling policies, however, there are limitations to the level of granularity or control that can be achieved.

Similarly, before the advent of virtual memory, multiple processes would allocate memory from a shared pool of physical memory. The virtual memory provided some form of memory isolation per process, in the sense that processes would have their own address space, and extend the available memory by means of a swap, but still there wasn't a good way of limiting how much memory each process and its children can use.

To further complicate the matter, running different workloads on the same physical server usually resulted in a negative impact on all running services. A memory leak or a kernel panic could cause one application to bring the entire operating system down. For example, a web server that is mostly memory bound and a database service that is I/O heavy running together became problematic. In an effort to avoid such scenarios, system administrators would separate the various applications between a pool of servers, leaving some machines underutilized, especially at certain times during the day, when there was not much work to be done. This is a similar problem as a single running process blocked on I/O operation is a waste of CPU and memory resources.

The solution to these problems is the use of hypervisor based virtualization, containers, or the combination of both.

The case for Linux containers

The hypervisor as part of the operating system is responsible for managing the life cycle of virtual machines, and has been around since the early days of mainframe machines in the late 1960s. Most modern virtualization implementations, such as Xen and KVM, can trace their origins back to that era. The main reason for the wide adoption of these virtualization technologies around 2005 was the need to better control and utilize the ever-growing clusters of compute resources. The inherited security of having an extra layer between the virtual machine and the host OS was a good selling point for the security minded, though as with any other newly adopted technology there were security incidents.

Nevertheless, the adoption of full virtualization and paravirtulization significantly improved the way servers are utilized and applications provisioned. In fact, virtualization such as KVM and Xen is still widely used today, especially in multitenant clouds and cloud technologies such as OpenStack.

Hypervisors provide the following benefits, in the context of the problems outlined earlier:

- Ability to run different operating systems on the same physical server
- More granular control over resource allocation
- Process isolation – a kernel panic on the virtual machine will not effect the host OS
- Separate network stack and the ability to control traffic per virtual machine
- Reduce capital and operating cost, by simplification of data center management and better utilization of available server resources

Arguably the main reason against using any sort of virtualization technology today is the inherited overhead of using multiple kernels in the same OS. It would be much better, in terms of complexity, if the host OS can provide this level of isolation, without the need for hardware extensions in the CPU, or the use of emulation software such as QEMU, or even kernel modules such as KVM. Running an entire operating system on a virtual machine, just to achieve a level of confinement for a single web server, is not the most efficient allocation of resources.

Over the last decade, various improvements to the Linux kernel were made to allow for similar functionality, but with less overhead – most notably the kernel namespaces and cgroups. One of the first notable technologies to leverage those changes was LXC, since kernel 2.6.24 and around the 2008 time frame. Even though LXC is not the oldest container technology, it helped fuel the container revolution we see today.

The main benefits of using LXC include:

- Lesser overheads and complexity than running a hypervisor
- Smaller footprint per container
- Start times in the millisecond range
- Native kernel support

It is worth mentioning that containers are not inherently as secure as having a hypervisor between the virtual machine and the host OS. However, in recent years, great progress has been made to narrow that gap using **Mandatory Access Control** (**MAC**) technologies such as SELinux and AppArmor, kernel capabilities, and cgroups, as demonstrated in later chapters.

Linux namespaces – the foundation of LXC

Namespaces are the foundation of lightweight process virtualization. They enable a process and its children to have different views of the underlying system. This is achieved by the addition of the unshare() and setns() system calls, and the inclusion of six new constant flags passed to the clone(), unshare(), and setns() system calls:

- clone(): This creates a new process and attaches it to a new specified namespace
- unshare(): This attaches the current process to a new specified namespace
- setns(): This attaches a process to an already existing namespace

There are six namespaces currently in use by LXC, with more being developed:

- Mount namespaces, specified by the CLONE_NEWNS flag
- UTS namespaces, specified by the CLONE_NEWUTS flag
- IPC namespaces, specified by the CLONE_NEWIPC flag
- PID namespaces, specified by the CLONE_NEWPID flag
- User namespaces, specified by the CLONE_NEWUSER flag
- Network namespaces, specified by the CLONE_NEWNET flag

Let's have a look at each in more detail and see some userspace examples, to help us better understand what happens under the hood.

Mount namespaces

Mount namespaces first appeared in kernel 2.4.19 in 2002 and provided a separate view of the filesystem mount points for the process and its children. When mounting or unmounting a filesystem, the change will be noticed by all processes because they all share the same default namespace. When the CLONE_NEWNS flag is passed to the clone() system call, the new process gets a copy of the calling process mount tree that it can then change without affecting the parent process. From that point on, all mounts and unmounts in the default namespace will be visible in the new namespace, but changes in the per-process mount namespaces will not be noticed outside of it.

The clone() prototype is as follows:

```
#define _GNU_SOURCE
#include <sched.h>
int clone(int (*fn)(void *), void *child_stack, int flags, void *arg);
```

An example call that creates a child process in a new mount namespace looks like this:

```
child_pid = clone(childFunc, child_stack + STACK_SIZE, CLONE_NEWNS |
SIGCHLD, argv[1]);
```

When the child process is created, it executes the `childFunc` function, which will perform its work in the new mount namespace.

The `util-linux` package provides userspace tools that implement the `unshare()` call, which effectively unshares the indicated namespaces from the parent process.

To illustrate this:

1. First open a terminal and create a directory in /tmp as follows:

    ```
    root@server:~# mkdir /tmp/mount_ns
    root@server:~#
    ```

2. Next, move the current `bash` process to its own mount namespace by passing the mount flag to `unshare`:

    ```
    root@server:~# unshare -m /bin/bash
    root@server:~#
    ```

3. The `bash` process is now in a separate namespace. Let's check the associated inode number of the namespace:

    ```
    root@server:~# readlink /proc/$$/ns/mnt
    mnt:[4026532211]
    root@server:~#
    ```

4. Next, create a temporary mount point:

    ```
    root@server:~# mount -n -t tmpfs tmpfs /tmp/mount_ns
    root@server:~#
    ```

5. Also, make sure you can see the mount point from the newly created namespace:

    ```
    root@server:~# df -h | grep mount_ns
    tmpfs            3.9G      0  3.9G    0% /tmp/mount_ns

    root@server:~# cat /proc/mounts | grep mount_ns
    tmpfs /tmp/mount_ns tmpfs rw,relatime 0 0
    root@server:~#
    ```

As expected, the mount point is visible because it is part of the namespace we created and the current `bash` process is running from.

6. Next, start a new terminal session and display the namespace inode ID from it:

```
root@server:~# readlink /proc/$$/ns/mnt
mnt:[4026531840]
root@server:~#
```

Notice how it's different from the mount namespace on the other terminal.

7. Finally, check if the mount point is visible in the new terminal:

```
root@server:~# cat /proc/mounts | grep mount_ns
root@server:~# df -h | grep mount_ns
root@server:~#
```

Not surprisingly, the mount point is not visible from the default namespace.

In the context of LXC, mount namespaces are useful because they provide a way for a different filesystem layout to exist inside the container. It's worth mentioning that before the mount namespaces, a similar process confinement could be achieved with the `chroot()` system call, however `chroot` does not provide the same per-process isolation as mount namespaces do.

UTS namespaces

Unix Timesharing (UTS) namespaces provide isolation for the hostname and domain name, so that each LXC container can maintain its own identifier as returned by the `hostname -f` command. This is needed for most applications that rely on a properly set hostname.

To create a `bash` session in a new UTS namespace, we can use the `unshare` utility again, which uses the `unshare()` system call to create the namespace and the `execve()` system call to execute `bash` in it:

```
root@server:~# hostname
server
root@server:~# unshare -u /bin/bash
root@server:~# hostname uts-namespace
root@server:~# hostname
uts-namespace
root@server:~# cat /proc/sys/kernel/hostname
```

```
uts-namespace
root@server:~#
```

As the preceding output shows, the hostname inside the namespace is now uts-namespace.

Next, from a different terminal, check the hostname again to make sure it has not changed:

```
root@server:~# hostname
server
root@server:~#
```

As expected, the hostname only changed in the new UTS namespace.

To see the actual system calls that the unshare command uses, we can run the strace utility:

```
root@server:~# strace -s 2000 -f unshare -u /bin/bash
...
unshare(CLONE_NEWUTS)                   = 0
getgid()                                = 0
setgid(0)                               = 0
getuid()                                = 0
setuid(0)                               = 0
execve("/bin/bash", ["/bin/bash"], [/* 15 vars */]) = 0
...
```

From the output we can see that the unshare command is indeed using the unshare() and execve() system calls and the CLONE_NEWUTS flag to specify new UTS namespace.

IPC namespaces

The **Interprocess Communication** (**IPC**) namespaces provide isolation for a set of IPC and synchronization facilities. These facilities provide a way of exchanging data and synchronizing the actions between threads and processes. They provide primitives such as semaphores, file locks, and mutexes among others, that are needed to have true process separation in a container.

PID namespaces

The **Process ID (PID)** namespaces provide the ability for a process to have an ID that already exists in the default namespace, for example an ID of 1. This allows for an init system to run in a container with various other processes, without causing a collision with the rest of the PIDs on the same OS.

To demonstrate this concept, open up `pid_namespace.c`:

```
#define _GNU_SOURCE
#include <stdlib.h>
#include <stdio.h>
#include <signal.h>
#include <sched.h>

static int childFunc(void *arg)
{
    printf("Process ID in child  = %ld\n", (long) getpid());
}
```

First, we include the headers and define the `childFunc` function that the `clone()` system call will use. The function prints out the child PID using the `getpid()` system call:

```
static char child_stack[1024*1024];

int main(int argc, char *argv[])
{
    pid_t child_pid;

    child_pid = clone(childFunc, child_stack +
    (1024*1024),
    CLONE_NEWPID | SIGCHLD, NULL);

    printf("PID of cloned process: %ld\n", (long) child_pid);
    waitpid(child_pid, NULL, 0);
    exit(EXIT_SUCCESS);
}
```

In the `main()` function, we specify the stack size and call `clone()`, passing the child function `childFunc`, the stack pointer, the `CLONE_NEWPID` flag, and the `SIGCHLD` signal. The `CLONE_NEWPID` flag instructs `clone()` to create a new PID namespace and the `SIGCHLD` flag notifies the parent process when one of its children terminates. The parent process will block on `waitpid()` if the child process has not terminated.

Compile and then run the program with the following:

```
root@server:~# gcc pid_namespace.c -o pid_namespace
root@server:~# ./pid_namespace
PID of cloned process: 17705
Process ID in child  = 1
root@server:~#
```

From the output, we can see that the child process has a PID of 1 inside its namespace and 17705 otherwise.

 Note that error handling has been omitted from the code examples for brevity.

User namespaces

The user namespaces allow a process inside a namespace to have a different user and group ID than that in the default namespace. In the context of LXC, this allows for a process to run as root inside the container, while having a non-privileged ID outside. This adds a thin layer of security, because braking out for the container will result in a non-privileged user. This is possible because of kernel 3.8, which introduced the ability for non-privileged processes to create user namespaces.

To create a new user namespace as a non-privileged user and have root inside, we can use the unshare utility. Let's install the latest version from source:

```
root@ubuntu:~# cd /usr/src/
root@ubuntu:/usr/src# wget
https://www.kernel.org/pub/linux/utils/util-linux/v2.28/util-linux-2.28.tar
.gz
root@ubuntu:/usr/src# tar zxfv util-linux-2.28.tar.gz
root@ubuntu:/usr/src# cd util-linux-2.28/
root@ubuntu:/usr/src/util-linux-2.28# ./configure
root@ubuntu:/usr/src/util-linux-2.28# make && make install
root@ubuntu:/usr/src/util-linux-2.28# unshare --map-root-user --user sh -c
whoami
root
root@ubuntu:/usr/src/util-linux-2.28#
```

We can also use the `clone()` system call with the `CLONE_NEWUSER` flag to create a process in a user namespace, as demonstrated by the following program:

```c
#define _GNU_SOURCE
#include <stdlib.h>
#include <stdio.h>
#include <signal.h>
#include <sched.h>

static int childFunc(void *arg)
{
    printf("UID inside the namespace is %ld\n", (long)
    geteuid());
    printf("GID inside the namespace is %ld\n", (long)
    getegid());
}

static char child_stack[1024*1024];

int main(int argc, char *argv[])
{
    pid_t child_pid;

    child_pid = clone(childFunc, child_stack +
    (1024*1024),
    CLONE_NEWUSER | SIGCHLD, NULL);

    printf("UID outside the namespace is %ld\n", (long)
    geteuid());
    printf("GID outside the namespace is %ld\n", (long)
    getegid());
    waitpid(child_pid, NULL, 0);
    exit(EXIT_SUCCESS);
}
```

After compilation and execution, the output looks similar to this when run as `root` – UID of 0:

```
root@server:~# gcc user_namespace.c -o user_namespace
root@server:~# ./user_namespace
UID outside the namespace is 0
GID outside the namespace is 0
UID inside the namespace is 65534
GID inside the namespace is 65534
root@server:~#
```

Network namespaces

Network namespaces provide isolation of the networking resources, such as network devices, addresses, routes, and firewall rules. This effectively creates a logical copy of the network stack, allowing multiple processes to listen on the same port from multiple namespaces. This is the foundation of networking in LXC and there are quite a lot of other use cases where this can come in handy.

The `iproute2` package provides very useful userspace tools that we can use to experiment with the network namespaces, and is installed by default on almost all Linux systems.

There's always the default network namespace, referred to as the root namespace, where all network interfaces are initially assigned. To list the network interfaces that belong to the default namespace run the following command:

```
root@server:~# ip link
1: lo: <LOOPBACK,UP,LOWER_UP> mtu 65536 qdisc noqueue state UNKNOWN mode
DEFAULT group default
    link/loopback 00:00:00:00:00:00 brd 00:00:00:00:00:00
2: eth0: <BROADCAST,MULTICAST,UP,LOWER_UP> mtu 9001 qdisc pfifo_fast state
UP mode DEFAULT group default qlen 1000
    link/ether 0e:d5:0e:b0:a3:47 brd ff:ff:ff:ff:ff:ff
root@server:~#
```

In this case, there are two interfaces – `lo` and `eth0`.

To list their configuration, we can run the following:

```
root@server:~# ip a s
1: lo: <LOOPBACK,UP,LOWER_UP> mtu 65536 qdisc noqueue state UNKNOWN group
default
    link/loopback 00:00:00:00:00:00 brd 00:00:00:00:00:00
    inet 127.0.0.1/8 scope host lo
       valid_lft forever preferred_lft forever
    inet6 ::1/128 scope host
       valid_lft forever preferred_lft forever
2: eth0: <BROADCAST,MULTICAST,UP,LOWER_UP> mtu 9001 qdisc pfifo_fast state
UP group default qlen 1000
    link/ether 0e:d5:0e:b0:a3:47 brd ff:ff:ff:ff:ff:ff
    inet 10.1.32.40/24 brd 10.1.32.255 scope global eth0
       valid_lft forever preferred_lft forever
    inet6 fe80::cd5:eff:feb0:a347/64 scope link
       valid_lft forever preferred_lft forever
root@server:~#
```

Also, to list the routes from the root network namespace, execute the following:

```
root@server:~# ip r s
default via 10.1.32.1 dev eth0
10.1.32.0/24 dev eth0  proto kernel  scope link  src 10.1.32.40
root@server:~#
```

Let's create two new network namespaces called ns1 and ns2 and list them:

```
root@server:~# ip netns add ns1
root@server:~# ip netns add ns2
root@server:~# ip netns
ns2
ns1
root@server:~#
```

Now that we have the new network namespaces, we can execute commands inside them:

```
root@server:~# ip netns exec ns1 ip link
1: lo: <LOOPBACK> mtu 65536 qdisc noop state DOWN mode DEFAULT group
default
    link/loopback 00:00:00:00:00:00 brd 00:00:00:00:00:00
root@server:~#
```

The preceding output shows that in the ns1 namespace, there's only one network interface, the loopback – lo interface, and it's in a DOWN state.

We can also start a new bash session inside the namespace and list the interfaces in a similar way:

```
root@server:~# ip netns exec ns1 bash
root@server:~# ip link
1: lo: <LOOPBACK> mtu 65536 qdisc noop state DOWN mode DEFAULT group
default
    link/loopback 00:00:00:00:00:00 brd 00:00:00:00:00:00
root@server:~# exit
root@server:~#
```

This is more convenient for running multiple commands than specifying each, one at a time. The two network namespaces are not of much use if not connected to anything, so let's connect them to each other. To do this we'll use a software bridge called Open vSwitch.

Open vSwitch works just as a regular network bridge and then it forwards frames between virtual ports that we define. Virtual machines such as KVM, Xen, and LXC or Docker containers can then be connected to it.

Most Debian-based distributions such as Ubuntu provide a package, so let's install that:

```
root@server:~# apt-get install -y openvswitch-switch
root@server:~#
```

This installs and starts the Open vSwitch daemon. Time to create the bridge; we'll name it OVS-1:

```
root@server:~# ovs-vsctl add-br OVS-1
root@server:~# ovs-vsctl show
0ea38b4f-8943-4d5b-8d80-62ccb73ec9ec
    Bridge "OVS-1"
        Port "OVS-1"
            Interface "OVS-1"
                type: internal
    ovs_version: "2.0.2"
root@server:~#
```

> If you would like to experiment with the latest version of Open vSwitch, you can download the source code from http://openvswitch.org/download/ and compile it.

The newly created bridge can now be seen in the root namespace:

```
root@server:~# ip a s OVS-1
4: OVS-1: <BROADCAST,UP,LOWER_UP> mtu 1500 qdisc noqueue state UNKNOWN
group default
    link/ether 9a:4b:56:97:3b:46 brd ff:ff:ff:ff:ff:ff
    inet6 fe80::f0d9:78ff:fe72:3d77/64 scope link
        valid_lft forever preferred_lft forever
root@server:~#
```

In order to connect both network namespaces, let's first create a virtual pair of interfaces for each namespace:

```
root@server:~# ip link add eth1-ns1 type veth peer name veth-ns1
root@server:~# ip link add eth1-ns2 type veth peer name veth-ns2
root@server:~#
```

The preceding two commands create four virtual interfaces eth1-ns1, eth1-ns2 and veth-ns1, veth-ns2. The names are arbitrary.

To list all interfaces that are part of the root network namespace, run:

```
root@server:~# ip link
1: lo: <LOOPBACK,UP,LOWER_UP> mtu 65536 qdisc noqueue state UNKNOWN mode
DEFAULT group default
```

```
      link/loopback 00:00:00:00:00:00 brd 00:00:00:00:00:00
2: eth0: <BROADCAST,MULTICAST,UP,LOWER_UP> mtu 9001 qdisc pfifo_fast state
UP mode DEFAULT group default qlen 1000
      link/ether 0e:d5:0e:b0:a3:47 brd ff:ff:ff:ff:ff:ff
3: ovs-system: <BROADCAST,MULTICAST> mtu 1500 qdisc noop state DOWN mode
DEFAULT group default
      link/ether 82:bf:52:d3:de:7e brd ff:ff:ff:ff:ff:ff
4: OVS-1: <BROADCAST,UP,LOWER_UP> mtu 1500 qdisc noqueue state UNKNOWN mode
DEFAULT group default
      link/ether 9a:4b:56:97:3b:46 brd ff:ff:ff:ff:ff:ff
5: veth-ns1: <BROADCAST,MULTICAST> mtu 1500 qdisc noop state DOWN mode
DEFAULT group default qlen 1000
      link/ether 1a:7c:74:48:73:a9 brd ff:ff:ff:ff:ff:ff
6: eth1-ns1: <BROADCAST,MULTICAST> mtu 1500 qdisc noop state DOWN mode
DEFAULT group default qlen 1000
      link/ether 8e:99:3f:b8:43:31 brd ff:ff:ff:ff:ff:ff
7: veth-ns2: <BROADCAST,MULTICAST> mtu 1500 qdisc noop state DOWN mode
DEFAULT group default qlen 1000
      link/ether 5a:0d:34:87:ea:96 brd ff:ff:ff:ff:ff:ff
8: eth1-ns2: <BROADCAST,MULTICAST> mtu 1500 qdisc noop state DOWN mode
DEFAULT group default qlen 1000
      link/ether fa:71:b8:a1:7f:85 brd ff:ff:ff:ff:ff:ff
root@server:~#
```

Let's assign the `eth1-ns1` and `eth1-ns2` interfaces to the `ns1` and `ns2` namespaces:

```
root@server:~# ip link set eth1-ns1 netns ns1
root@server:~# ip link set eth1-ns2 netns ns2
```

Also, confirm they are visible from inside each network namespace:

```
root@server:~# ip netns exec ns1 ip link
1: lo: <LOOPBACK> mtu 65536 qdisc noop state DOWN mode DEFAULT group
default
      link/loopback 00:00:00:00:00:00 brd 00:00:00:00:00:00
6: eth1-ns1: <BROADCAST,MULTICAST> mtu 1500 qdisc noop state DOWN mode
DEFAULT group default qlen 1000
      link/ether 8e:99:3f:b8:43:31 brd ff:ff:ff:ff:ff:ff
root@server:~#
root@server:~# ip netns exec ns2 ip link
1: lo: <LOOPBACK> mtu 65536 qdisc noop state DOWN mode DEFAULT group
default
      link/loopback 00:00:00:00:00:00 brd 00:00:00:00:00:00
8: eth1-ns2: <BROADCAST,MULTICAST> mtu 1500 qdisc noop state DOWN mode
DEFAULT group default qlen 1000
      link/ether fa:71:b8:a1:7f:85 brd ff:ff:ff:ff:ff:ff
root@server:~#
```

Notice, how each network namespace now has two interfaces assigned – `loopback` and `eth1-ns*`.

If we list the devices from the root namespace, we should see that the interfaces we just moved to `ns1` and `ns2` namespaces are no longer visible:

```
root@server:~# ip link
1: lo: <LOOPBACK,UP,LOWER_UP> mtu 65536 qdisc noqueue state UNKNOWN mode
DEFAULT group default
    link/loopback 00:00:00:00:00:00 brd 00:00:00:00:00:00
2: eth0: <BROADCAST,MULTICAST,UP,LOWER_UP> mtu 9001 qdisc pfifo_fast state
UP mode DEFAULT group default qlen 1000
    link/ether 0e:d5:0e:b0:a3:47 brd ff:ff:ff:ff:ff:ff
3: ovs-system: <BROADCAST,MULTICAST> mtu 1500 qdisc noop state DOWN mode
DEFAULT group default
    link/ether 82:bf:52:d3:de:7e brd ff:ff:ff:ff:ff:ff
4: OVS-1: <BROADCAST,UP,LOWER_UP> mtu 1500 qdisc noqueue state UNKNOWN mode
DEFAULT group default
    link/ether 9a:4b:56:97:3b:46 brd ff:ff:ff:ff:ff:ff
5: veth-ns1: <BROADCAST,MULTICAST> mtu 1500 qdisc noop state DOWN mode
DEFAULT group default qlen 1000
    link/ether 1a:7c:74:48:73:a9 brd ff:ff:ff:ff:ff:ff
7: veth-ns2: <BROADCAST,MULTICAST> mtu 1500 qdisc noop state DOWN mode
DEFAULT group default qlen 1000
    link/ether 5a:0d:34:87:ea:96 brd ff:ff:ff:ff:ff:ff
root@server:~#
```

It's time to connect the other end of the two virtual pipes, the `veth-ns1` and `veth-ns2` interfaces to the bridge:

```
root@server:~# ovs-vsctl add-port OVS-1 veth-ns1
root@server:~# ovs-vsctl add-port OVS-1 veth-ns2
root@server:~# ovs-vsctl show
0ea38b4f-8943-4d5b-8d80-62ccb73ec9ec
    Bridge "OVS-1"
        Port "OVS-1"
            Interface "OVS-1"
                type: internal
        Port "veth-ns1"
            Interface "veth-ns1"
        Port "veth-ns2"
            Interface "veth-ns2"
    ovs_version: "2.0.2"
root@server:~#
```

From the preceding output, it's apparent that the bridge now has two ports, `veth-ns1` and `veth-ns2`.

The last thing left to do is bring the network interfaces up and assign IP addresses:

```
root@server:~# ip link set veth-ns1 up
root@server:~# ip link set veth-ns2 up
root@server:~# ip netns exec ns1 ip link set dev lo up
root@server:~# ip netns exec ns1 ip link set dev eth1-ns1 up
root@server:~# ip netns exec ns1 ip address add 192.168.0.1/24 dev eth1-ns1
root@server:~# ip netns exec ns1 ip a s
1: lo: <LOOPBACK,UP,LOWER_UP> mtu 65536 qdisc noqueue state UNKNOWN group
default
    link/loopback 00:00:00:00:00:00 brd 00:00:00:00:00:00
    inet 127.0.0.1/8 scope host lo
       valid_lft forever preferred_lft forever
    inet6 ::1/128 scope host
       valid_lft forever preferred_lft forever
6: eth1-ns1: <BROADCAST,MULTICAST,UP,LOWER_UP> mtu 1500 qdisc pfifo_fast
state UP group default qlen 1000
    link/ether 8e:99:3f:b8:43:31 brd ff:ff:ff:ff:ff:ff
    inet 192.168.0.1/24 scope global eth1-ns1
       valid_lft forever preferred_lft forever
    inet6 fe80::8c99:3fff:feb8:4331/64 scope link
       valid_lft forever preferred_lft forever
root@server:~#
```

Similarly for the ns2 namespace:

```
root@server:~# ip netns exec ns2 ip link set dev lo up
root@server:~# ip netns exec ns2 ip link set dev eth1-ns2 up
root@server:~# ip netns exec ns2 ip address add 192.168.0.2/24 dev eth1-ns2
root@server:~# ip netns exec ns2 ip a s
1: lo: <LOOPBACK,UP,LOWER_UP> mtu 65536 qdisc noqueue state UNKNOWN group
default
    link/loopback 00:00:00:00:00:00 brd 00:00:00:00:00:00
    inet 127.0.0.1/8 scope host lo
       valid_lft forever preferred_lft forever
    inet6 ::1/128 scope host
       valid_lft forever preferred_lft forever
8: eth1-ns2: <BROADCAST,MULTICAST,UP,LOWER_UP> mtu 1500 qdisc pfifo_fast
state UP group default qlen 1000
    link/ether fa:71:b8:a1:7f:85 brd ff:ff:ff:ff:ff:ff
    inet 192.168.0.2/24 scope global eth1-ns2
       valid_lft forever preferred_lft forever
    inet6 fe80::f871:b8ff:fea1:7f85/64 scope link
       valid_lft forever preferred_lft forever
root@server:~#
```

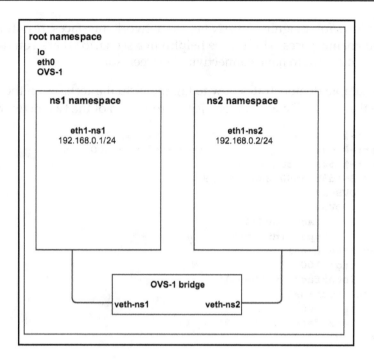

With this, we established a connection between both `ns1` and `ns2` network namespaces through the Open vSwitch bridge. To confirm, let's use `ping`:

```
root@server:~# ip netns exec ns1 ping -c 3 192.168.0.2
PING 192.168.0.2 (192.168.0.2) 56(84) bytes of data.
64 bytes from 192.168.0.2: icmp_seq=1 ttl=64 time=0.414 ms
64 bytes from 192.168.0.2: icmp_seq=2 ttl=64 time=0.027 ms
64 bytes from 192.168.0.2: icmp_seq=3 ttl=64 time=0.030 ms
--- 192.168.0.2 ping statistics ---
3 packets transmitted, 3 received, 0% packet loss, time 1998ms
rtt min/avg/max/mdev = 0.027/0.157/0.414/0.181 ms
root@server:~#
root@server:~# ip netns exec ns2 ping -c 3 192.168.0.1
PING 192.168.0.1 (192.168.0.1) 56(84) bytes of data.
64 bytes from 192.168.0.1: icmp_seq=1 ttl=64 time=0.150 ms
64 bytes from 192.168.0.1: icmp_seq=2 ttl=64 time=0.025 ms
64 bytes from 192.168.0.1: icmp_seq=3 ttl=64 time=0.027 ms
--- 192.168.0.1 ping statistics ---
3 packets transmitted, 3 received, 0% packet loss, time 1999ms
rtt min/avg/max/mdev = 0.025/0.067/0.150/0.058 ms
root@server:~#
```

Open vSwitch allows for assigning VLAN tags to network interfaces, resulting in traffic isolation between namespaces. This can be helpful in a scenario where you have multiple namespaces and you want to have connectivity between some of them.

The following example demonstrates how to tag the virtual interfaces on the ns1 and ns2 namespaces, so that the traffic will not be visible from each of the two network namespaces:

```
root@server:~# ovs-vsctl set port veth-ns1 tag=100
root@server:~# ovs-vsctl set port veth-ns2 tag=200
root@server:~# ovs-vsctl show
0ea38b4f-8943-4d5b-8d80-62ccb73ec9ec
    Bridge "OVS-1"
        Port "OVS-1"
            Interface "OVS-1"
                type: internal
        Port "veth-ns1"
            tag: 100
            Interface "veth-ns1"
        Port "veth-ns2"
            tag: 200
            Interface "veth-ns2"
    ovs_version: "2.0.2"
root@server:~#
```

Both the namespaces should now be isolated in their own VLANs and ping should fail:

```
root@server:~# ip netns exec ns1 ping -c 3 192.168.0.2
PING 192.168.0.2 (192.168.0.2) 56(84) bytes of data.
--- 192.168.0.2 ping statistics ---
3 packets transmitted, 0 received, 100% packet loss, time 1999ms
root@server:~# ip netns exec ns2 ping -c 3 192.168.0.1
PING 192.168.0.1 (192.168.0.1) 56(84) bytes of data.
--- 192.168.0.1 ping statistics ---
3 packets transmitted, 0 received, 100% packet loss, time 1999ms
root@server:~#
```

We can also use the unshare utility that we saw in the mount and UTC namespaces examples to create a new network namespace:

```
root@server:~# unshare --net /bin/bash
root@server:~# ip a s
1: lo: <LOOPBACK> mtu 65536 qdisc noop state DOWN group default
    link/loopback 00:00:00:00:00:00 brd 00:00:00:00:00:00
root@server:~# exit
root@server
```

Resource management with cgroups

Cgroups are kernel features that allows fine-grained control over resource allocation for a single process, or a group of processes, called **tasks**. In the context of LXC this is quite important, because it makes it possible to assign limits to how much memory, CPU time, or I/O, any given container can use.

The cgroups we are most interested in are described in the following table:

Subsystem	Description	Defined in
cpu	Allocates CPU time for tasks	kernel/sched/core.c
cpuacct	Accounts for CPU usage	kernel/sched/core.c
cpuset	Assigns CPU cores to tasks	kernel/cpuset.c
memory	Allocates memory for tasks	mm/memcontrol.c
blkio	Limits the I/O access to devices	block/blk-cgroup.c
devices	Allows/denies access to devices	security/device_cgroup.c
freezer	Suspends/resumes tasks	kernel/cgroup_freezer.c
net_cls	Tags network packets	net/sched/cls_cgroup.c
net_prio	Prioritizes network traffic	net/core/netprio_cgroup.c
hugetlb	Limits the HugeTLB	mm/hugetlb_cgroup.c

Cgroups are organized in hierarchies, represented as directories in a **Virtual File System (VFS)**. Similar to process hierarchies, where every process is a descendent of the init or systemd process, cgroups inherit some of the properties of their parents. Multiple cgroups hierarchies can exist on the system, each one representing a single or group of resources. It is possible to have hierarchies that combine two or more subsystems, for example, memory and I/O, and tasks assigned to a group will have limits applied on those resources.

If you are interested in how the different subsystems are implemented in the kernel, install the kernel source and have a look at the C files, shown in the third column of the table.

The following diagram helps visualize a single hierarchy that has two subsystems—CPU and I/O—attached to it:

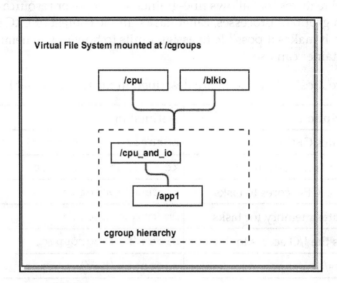

Cgroups can be used in two ways:

- By manually manipulating files and directories on a mounted VFS
- Using userspace tools provided by various packages such as cgroup-bin on Debian/Ubuntu and libcgroup on RHEL/CentOS

Let's have a look at few practical examples on how to use cgroups to limit resources. This will help us get a better understanding of how containers work.

Limiting I/O throughput

Let's assume we have two applications running on a server that are heavily I/O bound: app1 and app2. We would like to give more bandwidth to app1 during the day and to app2 during the night. This type of I/O throughput prioritization can be accomplished using the blkio subsystem.

First, let's attach the `blkio` subsystem by mounting the `cgroup` VFS:

```
root@server:~# mkdir -p /cgroup/blkio
root@server:~# mount -t cgroup -o blkio blkio /cgroup/blkio
root@server:~# cat /proc/mounts | grep cgroup
blkio /cgroup/blkio cgroup rw, relatime, blkio,
crelease_agent=/run/cgmanager/agents/cgm-release-agent.blkio 0 0
root@server:~#
```

Next, create two priority groups, which will be part of the same `blkio` hierarchy:

```
root@server:~# mkdir /cgroup/blkio/high_io
root@server:~# mkdir /cgroup/blkio/low_io
root@server:~#
```

We need to acquire the PIDs of the `app1` and `app2` processes and assign them to the `high_io` and `low_io` groups:

```
root@server:~# pidof app1 | while read PID; do echo $PID >>
/cgroup/blkio/high_io/tasks; done
root@server:~# pidof app2 | while read PID; do echo $PID >>
/cgroup/blkio/low_io/tasks; done
root@server:~#
```

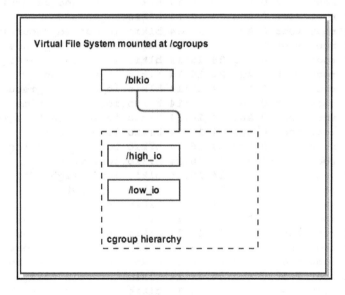

The blkio hierarchy we've created

The `tasks` file is where we define what processes/tasks the limit should be applied on.

Finally, let's set a ratio of 10:1 for the `high_io` and `low_io` cgroups. Tasks in those cgroups will immediately use only the resources made available to them:

```
root@server:~# echo 1000 > /cgroup/blkio/high_io/blkio.weight
root@server:~# echo 100 > /cgroup/blkio/low_io/blkio.weight
root@server:~#
```

The `blkio.weight` file defines the weight of I/O access available to a process or group of processes, with values ranging from 100 to 1,000. In this example, the values of `1000` and `100` create a ratio of 10:1.

With this, the low priority application, `app2` will use only about 10 percent of the I/O operations available, whereas the high priority application, `app1`, will use about 90 percent.

If you list the contents of the `high_io` directory on Ubuntu you will see the following files:

```
root@server:~# ls -la /cgroup/blkio/high_io/
drwxr-xr-x 2 root root 0 Aug 24 16:14 .
drwxr-xr-x 4 root root 0 Aug 19 21:14 ..
-r--r--r-- 1 root root 0 Aug 24 16:14 blkio.io_merged
-r--r--r-- 1 root root 0 Aug 24 16:14 blkio.io_merged_recursive
-r--r--r-- 1 root root 0 Aug 24 16:14 blkio.io_queued
-r--r--r-- 1 root root 0 Aug 24 16:14 blkio.io_queued_recursive
-r--r--r-- 1 root root 0 Aug 24 16:14 blkio.io_service_bytes
-r--r--r-- 1 root root 0 Aug 24 16:14 blkio.io_service_bytes_recursive
-r--r--r-- 1 root root 0 Aug 24 16:14 blkio.io_serviced
-r--r--r-- 1 root root 0 Aug 24 16:14 blkio.io_serviced_recursive
-r--r--r-- 1 root root 0 Aug 24 16:14 blkio.io_service_time
-r--r--r-- 1 root root 0 Aug 24 16:14 blkio.io_service_time_recursive
-r--r--r-- 1 root root 0 Aug 24 16:14 blkio.io_wait_time
-r--r--r-- 1 root root 0 Aug 24 16:14 blkio.io_wait_time_recursive
-rw-r--r-- 1 root root 0 Aug 24 16:14 blkio.leaf_weight
-rw-r--r-- 1 root root 0 Aug 24 16:14 blkio.leaf_weight_device
--w------- 1 root root 0 Aug 24 16:14 blkio.reset_stats
-r--r--r-- 1 root root 0 Aug 24 16:14 blkio.sectors
-r--r--r-- 1 root root 0 Aug 24 16:14 blkio.sectors_recursive
-r--r--r-- 1 root root 0 Aug 24 16:14 blkio.throttle.io_service_bytes
-r--r--r-- 1 root root 0 Aug 24 16:14 blkio.throttle.io_serviced
-rw-r--r-- 1 root root 0 Aug 24 16:14 blkio.throttle.read_bps_device
-rw-r--r-- 1 root root 0 Aug 24 16:14 blkio.throttle.read_iops_device
-rw-r--r-- 1 root root 0 Aug 24 16:14 blkio.throttle.write_bps_device
-rw-r--r-- 1 root root 0 Aug 24 16:14 blkio.throttle.write_iops_device
-r--r--r-- 1 root root 0 Aug 24 16:14 blkio.time
-r--r--r-- 1 root root 0 Aug 24 16:14 blkio.time_recursive
-rw-r--r-- 1 root root 0 Aug 24 16:49 blkio.weight
```

```
-rw-r--r-- 1 root root 0 Aug 24 17:01 blkio.weight_device
-rw-r--r-- 1 root root 0 Aug 24 16:14 cgroup.clone_children
--w--w--w- 1 root root 0 Aug 24 16:14 cgroup.event_control
-rw-r--r-- 1 root root 0 Aug 24 16:14 cgroup.procs
-rw-r--r-- 1 root root 0 Aug 24 16:14 notify_on_release
-rw-r--r-- 1 root root 0 Aug 24 16:14 tasks
root@server:~#
```

From the preceding output you can see that only some files are writeable. This depends on various OS settings, such as what I/O scheduler is being used.

We've already seen what the `tasks` and `blkio.weight` files are used for. The following is a short description of the most commonly used files in the `blkio` subsystem:

File	Description
`blkio.io_merged`	Total number of reads/writes, sync, or async merged into requests
`blkio.io_queued`	Total number of read/write, sync, or async requests queued up at any given time
`blkio.io_service_bytes`	The number of bytes transferred to or from the specified device
`blkio.io_serviced`	The number of I/O operations issued to the specified device
`blkio.io_service_time`	Total amount of time between request dispatch and request completion in nanoseconds for the specified device
`blkio.io_wait_time`	Total amount of time the I/O operations spent waiting in the scheduler queues for the specified device
`blkio.leaf_weight`	Similar to `blkio.weight` and can be applied to the **Completely Fair Queuing (CFQ)** I/O scheduler
`blkio.reset_stats`	Writing an integer to this file will reset all statistics
`blkio.sectors`	The number of sectors transferred to or from the specified device
`blkio.throttle.io_service_bytes`	The number of bytes transferred to or from the disk
`blkio.throttle.io_serviced`	The number of I/O operations issued to the specified disk

`blkio.time`	The disk time allocated to a device in milliseconds
`blkio.weight`	Specifies weight for a cgroup hierarchy
`blkio.weight_device`	Same as `blkio.weight`, but specifies a block device to apply the limit on
`tasks`	Attach tasks to the cgroup

One thing to keep in mind is that writing to the files directly to make changes will not persist after the server restarts. Later in this chapter, you will learn how to use the userspace tools to generate persistent configuration files.

Limiting memory usage

The `memory` subsystem controls how much memory is presented to and available for use by processes. This can be particularly useful in multitenant environments where better control over how much memory a user process can utilize is needed, or to limit memory hungry applications. Containerized solutions like LXC can use the `memory` subsystem to manage the size of the instances, without needing to restart the entire container.

The `memory` subsystem performs resource accounting, such as tracking the utilization of anonymous pages, file caches, swap caches, and general hierarchical accounting, all of which presents an overhead. Because of this, the `memory` cgroup is disabled by default on some Linux distributions. If the following commands below fail you'll need to enable it, by specifying the following GRUB parameter and restarting:

```
root@server:~# vim /etc/default/grub
RUB_CMDLINE_LINUX_DEFAULT="cgroup_enable=memory"
root@server:~# grub-update && reboot
```

First, let's mount the `memory` cgroup:

```
root@server:~# mkdir -p /cgroup/memory
root@server:~# mount -t cgroup -o memory memory /cgroup/memory
root@server:~# cat /proc/mounts | grep memory
memory /cgroup/memory cgroup rw, relatime, memory,
release_agent=/run/cgmanager/agents/cgm-release-agent.memory 0 0
root@server:~#
```

Then set the `app1` memory to 1 GB:

```
root@server:~# mkdir /cgroup/memory/app1
root@server:~# echo 1G > /cgroup/memory/app1/memory.limit_in_bytes
root@server:~# cat /cgroup/memory/app1/memory.limit_in_bytes
1073741824
root@server:~# pidof app1 | while read PID; do echo $PID >>
/cgroup/memory/app1/tasks; done
root@server:~#
```

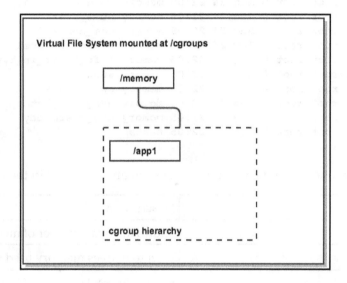

The memory hierarchy for the app1 process

Similar to the `blkio` subsystem, the `tasks` file is used to specify the PID of the processes we are adding to the cgroup hierarchy, and the `memory.limit_in_bytes` specifies how much memory is to be made available in bytes.

The `app1` memory hierarchy contains the following files:

```
root@server:~# ls -la /cgroup/memory/app1/
drwxr-xr-x 2 root root 0 Aug 24 22:05 .
drwxr-xr-x 3 root root 0 Aug 19 21:02 ..
-rw-r--r-- 1 root root 0 Aug 24 22:05 cgroup.clone_children
--w--w--w- 1 root root 0 Aug 24 22:05 cgroup.event_control
-rw-r--r-- 1 root root 0 Aug 24 22:05 cgroup.procs
-rw-r--r-- 1 root root 0 Aug 24 22:05 memory.failcnt
--w------- 1 root root 0 Aug 24 22:05 memory.force_empty
-rw-r--r-- 1 root root 0 Aug 24 22:05 memory.kmem.failcnt
-rw-r--r-- 1 root root 0 Aug 24 22:05 memory.kmem.limit_in_bytes
```

```
-rw-r--r-- 1 root root 0 Aug 24 22:05 memory.kmem.max_usage_in_bytes
-r--r--r-- 1 root root 0 Aug 24 22:05 memory.kmem.slabinfo
-rw-r--r-- 1 root root 0 Aug 24 22:05 memory.kmem.tcp.failcnt
-rw-r--r-- 1 root root 0 Aug 24 22:05 memory.kmem.tcp.limit_in_bytes
-rw-r--r-- 1 root root 0 Aug 24 22:05 memory.kmem.tcp.max_usage_in_bytes
-r--r--r-- 1 root root 0 Aug 24 22:05 memory.kmem.tcp.usage_in_bytes
-r--r--r-- 1 root root 0 Aug 24 22:05 memory.kmem.usage_in_bytes
-rw-r--r-- 1 root root 0 Aug 24 22:05 memory.limit_in_bytes
-rw-r--r-- 1 root root 0 Aug 24 22:05 memory.max_usage_in_bytes
-rw-r--r-- 1 root root 0 Aug 24 22:05 memory.move_charge_at_immigrate
-r--r--r-- 1 root root 0 Aug 24 22:05 memory.numa_stat
-rw-r--r-- 1 root root 0 Aug 24 22:05 memory.oom_control
---------- 1 root root 0 Aug 24 22:05 memory.pressure_level
-rw-r--r-- 1 root root 0 Aug 24 22:05 memory.soft_limit_in_bytes
-r--r--r-- 1 root root 0 Aug 24 22:05 memory.stat
-rw-r--r-- 1 root root 0 Aug 24 22:05 memory.swappiness
-r--r--r-- 1 root root 0 Aug 24 22:05 memory.usage_in_bytes
-rw-r--r-- 1 root root 0 Aug 24 22:05 memory.use_hierarchy
-rw-r--r-- 1 root root 0 Aug 24 22:05 tasks
root@server:~#
```

The files and their function in the memory subsystem are described in the following table:

File	Description
memory.failcnt	Shows the total number of memory limit hits
memory.force_empty	If set to 0, frees memory used by tasks
memory.kmem.failcnt	Shows the total number of kernel memory limit hits
memory.kmem.limit_in_bytes	Sets or shows kernel memory hard limit
memory.kmem.max_usage_in_bytes	Shows maximum kernel memory usage
memory.kmem.tcp.failcnt	Shows the number of TCP buffer memory limit hits
memory.kmem.tcp.limit_in_bytes	Sets or shows hard limit for TCP buffer memory
memory.kmem.tcp.max_usage_in_bytes	Shows maximum TCP buffer memory usage
memory.kmem.tcp.usage_in_bytes	Shows current TCP buffer memory
memory.kmem.usage_in_bytes	Shows current kernel memory
memory.limit_in_bytes	Sets or shows memory usage limit

`memory.max_usage_in_bytes`	Shows maximum memory usage
`memory.move_charge_at_immigrate`	Sets or shows controls of moving charges
`memory.numa_stat`	Shows the number of memory usage per NUMA node
`memory.oom_control`	Sets or shows the OOM controls
`memory.pressure_level`	Sets memory pressure notifications
`memory.soft_limit_in_bytes`	Sets or shows soft limit of memory usage
`memory.stat`	Shows various statistics
`memory.swappiness`	Sets or shows swappiness level
`memory.usage_in_bytes`	Shows current memory usage
`memory.use_hierarchy`	Sets memory reclamation from child processes
`tasks`	Attaches tasks to the cgroup

Limiting the memory available to a process might trigger the **Out of Memory** (**OOM**) killer, which might kill the running task. If this is not the desired behavior and you prefer the process to be suspended waiting for memory to be freed, the OOM killer can be disabled:

```
root@server:~# cat /cgroup/memory/app1/memory.oom_control
oom_kill_disable 0
under_oom 0
root@server:~# echo 1 > /cgroup/memory/app1/memory.oom_control
root@server:~#
```

The `memory` cgroup presents a wide slew of accounting statistics in the `memory.stat` file, which can be of interest:

```
root@server:~# head /cgroup/memory/app1/memory.stat
cache 43325       # Number of bytes of page cache memory
rss 55d43         # Number of bytes of anonymous and swap cache memory
rss_huge 0        # Number of anonymous transparent hugepages
mapped_file 2     # Number of bytes of mapped file
writeback 0       # Number of bytes of cache queued for syncing
pgpgin 0          # Number of charging events to the memory cgroup
pgpgout 0         # Number of uncharging events to the memory cgroup
pgfault 0         # Total number of page faults
pgmajfault 0      # Number of major page faults
inactive_anon 0 # Anonymous and swap cache memory on inactive LRU list
```

If you need to start a new task in the `app1` memory hierarchy you can move the current shell process into the `tasks` file, and all other processes started in this shell will be direct descendants and inherit the same cgroup properties:

```
root@server:~# echo $$ > /cgroup/memory/app1/tasks
root@server:~# echo "The memory limit is now applied to all processes
started from this shell"
```

The cpu and cpuset subsystems

The `cpu` subsystem schedules CPU time to cgroup hierarchies and their tasks. It provides finer control over CPU execution time than the default behavior of the CFS.

The `cpuset` subsystem allows for assigning CPU cores to a set of tasks, similar to the `taskset` command in Linux.

The main benefits that the `cpu` and `cpuset` subsystems provide are better utilization per processor core for highly CPU bound applications. They also allow for distributing load between cores that are otherwise idle at certain times of the day. In the context of multitenant environments, running many LXC containers, `cpu` and `cpuset` cgroups allow for creating different instance sizes and container flavors, for example exposing only a single core per container, with 40 percent scheduled work time.

As an example, let's assume we have two processes `app1` and `app2`, and we would like `app1` to use 60 percent of the CPU time and `app2` only 40 percent. We start by mounting the `cgroup` VFS:

```
root@server:~# mkdir -p /cgroup/cpu
root@server:~# mount -t cgroup -o cpu cpu /cgroup/cpu
root@server:~# cat /proc/mounts | grep cpu
cpu /cgroup/cpu cgroup rw, relatime, cpu,
release_agent=/run/cgmanager/agents/cgm-release-agent.cpu 0 0
```

Then we create two child hierarchies:

```
root@server:~# mkdir /cgroup/cpu/limit_60_percent
root@server:~# mkdir /cgroup/cpu/limit_40_percent
```

Also assign CPU shares for each, where `app1` will get 60 percent and `app2` will get 40 percent of the scheduled time:

```
root@server:~# echo 600 > /cgroup/cpu/limit_60_percent/cpu.shares
root@server:~# echo 400 > /cgroup/cpu/limit_40_percent/cpu.shares
```

Finally, we move the PIDs in the `tasks` files:

```
root@server:~# pidof app1 | while read PID; do echo $PID >>
/cgroup/cpu/limit_60_percent/tasks; done
root@server:~# pidof app2 | while read PID; do echo $PID >>
/cgroup/cpu/limit_40_percent/tasks; done
root@server:~#
```

The `cpu` subsystem contains the following control files:

```
root@server:~# ls -la /cgroup/cpu/limit_60_percent/
drwxr-xr-x 2 root root 0 Aug 25 15:13 .
drwxr-xr-x 4 root root 0 Aug 19 21:02 ..
-rw-r--r-- 1 root root 0 Aug 25 15:13 cgroup.clone_children
--w--w--w- 1 root root 0 Aug 25 15:13 cgroup.event_control
-rw-r--r-- 1 root root 0 Aug 25 15:13 cgroup.procs
-rw-r--r-- 1 root root 0 Aug 25 15:13 cpu.cfs_period_us
-rw-r--r-- 1 root root 0 Aug 25 15:13 cpu.cfs_quota_us
-rw-r--r-- 1 root root 0 Aug 25 15:14 cpu.shares
-r--r--r-- 1 root root 0 Aug 25 15:13 cpu.stat
-rw-r--r-- 1 root root 0 Aug 25 15:13 notify_on_release
-rw-r--r-- 1 root root 0 Aug 25 15:13 tasks
root@server:~#
```

Here's a brief explanation of each:

File	Description
cpu.cfs_period_us	CPU resource reallocation in microseconds
cpu.cfs_quota_us	Run duration of tasks in microseconds during one `cpu.cfs_perious_us period`
cpu.shares	Relative share of CPU time available to the tasks
cpu.stat	Shows CPU time statistics
tasks	Attaches tasks to the cgroup

The `cpu.stat` file is of particular interest:

```
root@server:~# cat /cgroup/cpu/limit_60_percent/cpu.stat
nr_periods 0        # number of elapsed period intervals, as specified in
                    # cpu.cfs_period_us
nr_throttled 0      # number of times a task was not scheduled to run
                    # because of quota limit
throttled_time 0    # total time in nanoseconds for which tasks have been
                    # throttled
root@server:~#
```

To demonstrate how the `cpuset` subsystem works, let's create `cpuset` hierarchies named `app1`, containing CPUs 0 and 1. The `app2` cgroup will contain only CPU 1:

```
root@server:~# mkdir /cgroup/cpuset
root@server:~# mount -t cgroup -o cpuset cpuset /cgroup/cpuset
root@server:~# mkdir /cgroup/cpuset/app{1..2}
root@server:~# echo 0-1 > /cgroup/cpuset/app1/cpuset.cpus
root@server:~# echo 1 > /cgroup/cpuset/app2/cpuset.cpus
root@server:~# pidof app1 | while read PID; do echo $PID >>
/cgroup/cpuset/app1/tasks limit_60_percent/tasks; done
root@server:~# pidof app2 | while read PID; do echo $PID >>
/cgroup/cpuset/app2/tasks limit_40_percent/tasks; done
root@server:~#
```

To check if the `app1` process is pinned to CPU 0 and 1, we can use:

```
root@server:~# taskset -c -p $(pidof app1)
pid 8052's current affinity list: 0,1
root@server:~# taskset -c -p $(pidof app2)
pid 8052's current affinity list: 1
root@server:~#
```

The `cpuset app1` hierarchy contains the following files:

```
root@server:~# ls -la /cgroup/cpuset/app1/
drwxr-xr-x 2 root root 0 Aug 25 16:47 .
drwxr-xr-x 5 root root 0 Aug 19 21:02 ..
-rw-r--r-- 1 root root 0 Aug 25 16:47 cgroup.clone_children
--w--w--w- 1 root root 0 Aug 25 16:47 cgroup.event_control
-rw-r--r-- 1 root root 0 Aug 25 16:47 cgroup.procs
-rw-r--r-- 1 root root 0 Aug 25 16:47 cpuset.cpu_exclusive
-rw-r--r-- 1 root root 0 Aug 25 17:57 cpuset.cpus
-rw-r--r-- 1 root root 0 Aug 25 16:47 cpuset.mem_exclusive
-rw-r--r-- 1 root root 0 Aug 25 16:47 cpuset.mem_hardwall
-rw-r--r-- 1 root root 0 Aug 25 16:47 cpuset.memory_migrate
-r--r--r-- 1 root root 0 Aug 25 16:47 cpuset.memory_pressure
-rw-r--r-- 1 root root 0 Aug 25 16:47 cpuset.memory_spread_page
```

```
-rw-r--r-- 1 root root 0 Aug 25 16:47 cpuset.memory_spread_slab
-rw-r--r-- 1 root root 0 Aug 25 16:47 cpuset.mems
-rw-r--r-- 1 root root 0 Aug 25 16:47 cpuset.sched_load_balance
-rw-r--r-- 1 root root 0 Aug 25 16:47 cpuset.sched_relax_domain_level
-rw-r--r-- 1 root root 0 Aug 25 16:47 notify_on_release
-rw-r--r-- 1 root root 0 Aug 25 17:13 tasks
root@server:~#
```

A brief description of the control files is as follows:

File	Description
cpuset.cpu_exclusive	Checks if other cpuset hierarchies share the settings defined in the current group
cpuset.cpus	List of the physical numbers of the CPUs on which processes in that cpuset are allowed to execute
cpuset.mem_exclusive	Should the cpuset have exclusive use of its memory nodes
cpuset.mem_hardwall	Checks if each tasks' user allocation be kept separate
cpuset.memory_migrate	Checks if a page in memory should migrate to a new node if the values in cpuset.mems change
cpuset.memory_pressure	Contains running average of the memory pressure created by the processes
cpuset.memory_spread_page	Checks if filesystem buffers should spread evenly across the memory nodes
cpuset.memory_spread_slab	Checks if kernel slab caches for file I/O operations should spread evenly across the cpuset
cpuset.mems	Specifies the memory nodes that tasks in this cgroup are permitted to access
cpuset.sched_load_balance	Checks if the kernel balance should load across the CPUs in the cpuset by moving processes from overloaded CPUs to less utilized CPUs
cpuset.sched_relax_domain_level	Contains the width of the range of CPUs across which the kernel should attempt to balance loads
notify_on_release	Checks if the hierarchy should receive special handling after it is released and no process are using it

`tasks`	Attaches tasks to the cgroup

The cgroup freezer subsystem

The `freezer` subsystem can be used to suspend the current state of running tasks for the purposes of analyzing them, or to create a checkpoint that can be used to migrate the process to a different server. Another use case is when a process is negatively impacting the system and needs to be temporarily paused, without losing its current state data.

The next example shows how to suspend the execution of the top process, check its state, and then resume it.

First, mount the `freezer` subsystem and create the new hierarchy:

```
root@server:~# mkdir /cgroup/freezer
root@server:~# mount -t cgroup -o freezer freezer /cgroup/freezer
root@server:~# mkdir /cgroup/freezer/frozen_group
root@server:~# cat /proc/mounts | grep freezer
freezer /cgroup/freezer cgroup
rw,relatime,freezer,release_agent=/run/cgmanager/agents/cgm-release-
agent.freezer 0 0
root@server:~#
```

In a new terminal, start the `top` process and observe how it periodically refreshes. Back in the original terminal, add the PID of `top` to the `frozen_group` task file and observe its state:

```
root@server:~# echo 25731 > /cgroup/freezer/frozen_group/tasks
root@server:~# cat /cgroup/freezer/frozen_group/freezer.state
THAWED
root@server:~#
```

To freeze the process, echo the following:

```
root@server:~# echo FROZEN > /cgroup/freezer/frozen_group/freezer.state
root@server:~# cat /cgroup/freezer/frozen_group/freezer.state
FROZEN
root@server:~# cat /proc/25s731/status | grep -i state
State:      D (disk sleep)
root@server:~#
```

Notice how the top process output is not refreshing anymore, and upon inspection of its status file, you can see that it is now in the blocked state.

To resume it, execute the following:

```
root@server:~# echo THAWED > /cgroup/freezer/frozen_group/freezer.state
root@server:~# cat /proc/29328/status  | grep -i state
State:  S (sleeping)
root@server:~#
```

Inspecting the `frozen_group` hierarchy yields the following files:

```
root@server:~# ls -la /cgroup/freezer/frozen_group/
drwxr-xr-x 2 root root 0 Aug 25 20:50 .
drwxr-xr-x 4 root root 0 Aug 19 21:02 ..
-rw-r--r-- 1 root root 0 Aug 25 20:50 cgroup.clone_children
--w--w--w- 1 root root 0 Aug 25 20:50 cgroup.event_control
-rw-r--r-- 1 root root 0 Aug 25 20:50 cgroup.procs
-r--r--r-- 1 root root 0 Aug 25 20:50 freezer.parent_freezing
-r--r--r-- 1 root root 0 Aug 25 20:50 freezer.self_freezing
-rw-r--r-- 1 root root 0 Aug 25 21:00 freezer.state
-rw-r--r-- 1 root root 0 Aug 25 20:50 notify_on_release
-rw-r--r-- 1 root root 0 Aug 25 20:59 tasks
root@server:~#
```

The few files of interest are described in the following table:

File	Description
freezer.parent_freezing	Shows the parent-state. Shows 0 if none of the cgroup's ancestors is FROZEN; otherwise, 1.
freezer.self_freezing	Shows the self-state. Shows 0 if the self-state is THAWED; otherwise, 1.
freezer.state	Sets the self-state of the cgroup to either THAWED or FROZEN.
tasks	Attaches tasks to the cgroup.

Using userspace tools to manage cgroups and persist changes

Working with the cgroups subsystems by manipulating directories and files directly is a fast and convenient way to prototype and test changes, however, this comes with few drawbacks, namely the changes made will not persist a server restart and there's not much error reporting or handling.

To address this, there are packages that provide userspace tools and daemons that are quite easy to use. Let's see a few examples.

To install the tools on Debian/Ubuntu, run the following:

```
root@server:~# apt-get install -y cgroup-bin cgroup-lite libcgroup1
root@server:~# service cgroup-lite start
```

On RHEL/CentOS, execute the following:

```
root@server:~# yum install libcgroup
root@server:~# service cgconfig start
```

To mount all subsystems, run the following:

```
root@server:~# cgroups-mount
root@server:~# cat /proc/mounts | grep cgroup
cgroup /sys/fs/cgroup/memory cgroup
rw,relatime,memory,release_agent=/run/cgmanager/agents/cgm-release-
agent.memory 0 0
cgroup /sys/fs/cgroup/devices cgroup
rw,relatime,devices,release_agent=/run/cgmanager/agents/cgm-release-
agent.devices 0 0
cgroup /sys/fs/cgroup/freezer cgroup
rw,relatime,freezer,release_agent=/run/cgmanager/agents/cgm-release-
agent.freezer 0 0
cgroup /sys/fs/cgroup/blkio cgroup
rw,relatime,blkio,release_agent=/run/cgmanager/agents/cgm-release-
agent.blkio 0 0
cgroup /sys/fs/cgroup/perf_event cgroup
rw,relatime,perf_event,release_agent=/run/cgmanager/agents/cgm-release-
agent.perf_event 0 0
cgroup /sys/fs/cgroup/hugetlb cgroup
rw,relatime,hugetlb,release_agent=/run/cgmanager/agents/cgm-release-
agent.hugetlb 0 0
cgroup /sys/fs/cgroup/cpuset cgroup
rw,relatime,cpuset,release_agent=/run/cgmanager/agents/cgm-release-
agent.cpuset,clone_children 0 0
cgroup /sys/fs/cgroup/cpu cgroup
rw,relatime,cpu,release_agent=/run/cgmanager/agents/cgm-release-agent.cpu 0
0
cgroup /sys/fs/cgroup/cpuacct cgroup
rw,relatime,cpuacct,release_agent=/run/cgmanager/agents/cgm-release-
agent.cpuacct 0 0
```

Notice from the preceding output the location of the cgroups – /sys/fs/cgroup. This is the default location on many Linux distributions and in most cases the various subsystems have already been mounted.

To verify what cgroup subsystems are in use, we can check with the following commands:

```
root@server:~# cat /proc/cgroups
#subsys_name  hierarchy  num_cgroups  enabled
cpuset  7  1  1
cpu  8  2  1
cpuacct  9  1  1
memory  10  2  1
devices  11  1  1
freezer  12  1  1
blkio  6  3  1
perf_event  13  1  1
hugetlb  14  1  1
```

Next, let's create a blkio hierarchy and add an already running process to it with cgclassify. This is similar to what we did earlier, by creating the directories and the files by hand:

```
root@server:~# cgcreate -g blkio:high_io
root@server:~# cgcreate -g blkio:low_io
root@server:~# cgclassify -g blkio:low_io $(pidof app1)
root@server:~# cat /sys/fs/cgroup/blkio/low_io/tasks
8052
root@server:~# cgset -r blkio.weight=1000 high_io
root@server:~# cgset -r blkio.weight=100 low_io
root@server:~# cat /sys/fs/cgroup/blkio/high_io/blkio.weight
1000
root@server:~#
```

Now that we have defined the high_io and low_io cgroups and added a process to them, let's generate a configuration file that can be used later to reapply the setup:

```
root@server:~# cgsnapshot -s -f /tmp/cgconfig_io.conf
cpuset = /sys/fs/cgroup/cpuset;
cpu = /sys/fs/cgroup/cpu;
cpuacct = /sys/fs/cgroup/cpuacct;
memory = /sys/fs/cgroup/memory;
devices = /sys/fs/cgroup/devices;
freezer = /sys/fs/cgroup/freezer;
blkio = /sys/fs/cgroup/blkio;
perf_event = /sys/fs/cgroup/perf_event;
hugetlb = /sys/fs/cgroup/hugetlb;
root@server:~# cat /tmp/cgconfig_io.conf
```

```
# Configuration file generated by cgsnapshot
mount {
    blkio = /sys/fs/cgroup/blkio;
}
group low_io {
    blkio {
        blkio.leaf_weight="500";
        blkio.leaf_weight_device="";
        blkio.weight="100";
        blkio.weight_device="";
        blkio.throttle.write_iops_device="";
        blkio.throttle.read_iops_device="";
        blkio.throttle.write_bps_device="";
        blkio.throttle.read_bps_device="";
        blkio.reset_stats="";
    }
}
group high_io {
    blkio {
        blkio.leaf_weight="500";
        blkio.leaf_weight_device="";
        blkio.weight="1000";
        blkio.weight_device="";
        blkio.throttle.write_iops_device="";
        blkio.throttle.read_iops_device="";
        blkio.throttle.write_bps_device="";
        blkio.throttle.read_bps_device="";
        blkio.reset_stats="";
    }
}
root@server:~#
```

To start a new process in the high_io group, we can use the cgexec command:

```
root@server:~# cgexec -g blkio:high_io bash
root@server:~# echo $$
19654
root@server:~# cat /sys/fs/cgroup/blkio/high_io/tasks
19654
root@server:~#
```

In the preceding example, we started a new bash process in the high_io cgroup, as confirmed by looking at the tasks file.

To move an already running process to the `memory` subsystem, first we create the `high_prio` and `low_prio` groups and move the task with `cgclassify`:

```
root@server:~# cgcreate -g cpu,memory:high_prio
root@server:~# cgcreate -g cpu,memory:low_prio
root@server:~# cgclassify -g cpu,memory:high_prio 8052
root@server:~# cat /sys/fs/cgroup/memory/high_prio/tasks
8052
root@server:~# cat /sys/fs/cgroup/cpu/high_prio/tasks
8052
root@server:~#
```

To set the memory and CPU limits, we can use the `cgset` command. In contrast, remember that we used the `echo` command to manually move the PIDs and memory limits to the `tasks` and the `memory.limit_in_bytes` files:

```
root@server:~# cgset -r memory.limit_in_bytes=1G low_prio
root@server:~# cat /sys/fs/cgroup/memory/low_prio/memory.limit_in_bytes
1073741824
root@server:~# cgset -r cpu.shares=1000 high_prio
root@server:~# cat /sys/fs/cgroup/cpu/high_prio/cpu.shares
1000
root@server:~#
```

To see how the cgroup hierarchies look, we can use the `lscgroup` utility:

```
root@server:~# lscgroup
cpuset:/
cpu:/
cpu:/low_prio
cpu:/high_prio
cpuacct:/
memory:/
memory:/low_prio
memory:/high_prio
devices:/
freezer:/
blkio:/
blkio:/low_io
blkio:/high_io
perf_event:/
hugetlb:/
root@server:~#
```

The preceding output confirms the existence of the `blkio`, `memory`, and `cpu` hierarchies and their children.

Once finished, you can delete the hierarchies with `cgdelete`, which deletes the respective directories on the VFS:

```
root@server:~# cgdelete -g cpu,memory:high_prio
root@server:~# cgdelete -g cpu,memory:low_prio
root@server:~# lscgroup
cpuset:/
cpu:/
cpuacct:/
memory:/
devices:/
freezer:/
blkio:/
blkio:/low_io
blkio:/high_io
perf_event:/
hugetlb:/
root@server:~#
```

To completely clear the cgroups, we can use the `cgclear` utility, which will unmount the cgroup directories:

```
root@server:~# cgclear
root@server:~# lscgroup
cgroups can't be listed: Cgroup is not mounted
root@server:~#
```

Managing resources with systemd

With the increased adoption of `systemd` as an init system, new ways of manipulating cgroups were introduced. For example, if the cpu controller is enabled in the kernel, `systemd` will create a cgroup for each service by default. This behavior can be changed by adding or removing cgroup subsystems in the configuration file of `systemd`, usually found at `/etc/systemd/system.conf`.

If multiple services are running on the server, the CPU resources will be shared equally among them by default, because `systemd` assigns equal weights to each. To change this behavior for an application, we can edit its service file and define the CPU shares, allocated memory, and I/O.

The following example demonstrates how to change the CPU shares, memory, and I/O limits for the nginx process:

```
root@server:~# vim /etc/systemd/system/nginx.service
.include /usr/lib/systemd/system/httpd.service
[Service]
CPUShares=2000
MemoryLimit=1G
BlockIOWeight=100
```

To apply the changes first reload `systemd`, then nginx:

```
root@server:~#  systemctl daemon-reload
root@server:~#  systemctl restart httpd.service
root@server:~#
```

This will create and update the necessary control files in `/sys/fs/cgroup/systemd` and apply the limits.

Summary

The advent of kernel namespaces and cgroups made it possible to isolate groups of processes in a self-confined lightweight virtualization package; we call them containers. In this chapter, we saw how containers provide the same features as other full-fledged hypervisor-based virtualization technologies such as KVM and Xen, without the overhead of running multiple kernels in the same operating system. LXC takes full advantage of Linux cgroups and namespaces to achieve this level of isolation and resource control.

With the foundation gained from this chapter, you'll be able to understand better what's going on under the hood, which will make it much easier to troubleshoot and support the full life cycle of Linux containers, as we'll do in the next chapters.

2

Installing and Running LXC on Linux Systems

LXC takes advantage of the kernel namespaces and cgroups to create process isolation we call containers, as we saw in the previous chapter. As such, LXC is not a separate software component in the Linux kernel, but rather a set of userspace tools, the `liblxc` library, and various language bindings.

In this chapter, we'll cover the following topics:

- Installing LXC on Ubuntu and CentOS using distribution packages
- Compiling and installing LXC from source code
- Building and starting containers using the provided templates and configuration files
- Manually building the root filesystem and configuration files using tools such as `debootstrap` and `yum`

Installing LXC

At the time of writing this book, there are two long-term support versions of LXC: 1.0 and 2.0. The userspace tools that they provide have some minor differences in command-line flags and deprecations, which I'll be pointing out as we use them.

Installing LXC on Ubuntu with apt

Let's start by installing LXC 1.0 on Ubuntu 14.04.5 (Trusty Tahr):

1. Install the main LXC package, tooling, and dependencies:

```
root@ubuntu:~# lsb_release -dc
Description:        Ubuntu 14.04.5 LTS
Codename:           trusty

root@ubuntu:~# apt-get -y install -y lxc bridge-utils
debootstrap libcap-dev
cgroup-bin libpam-systemdbridge-utils
root@ubuntu:~#
```

2. The package version that Trusty Tahr provides at this time is 1.0.8:

```
root@ubuntu:~# dpkg --list | grep lxc | awk '{print $2,$3}'
liblxc1 1.0.8-0ubuntu0.3
lxc 1.0.8-0ubuntu0.3
lxc-templates 1.0.8-0ubuntu0.3
python3-lxc 1.0.8-0ubuntu0.3
root@ubuntu:~#
```

To install LXC 2.0, we'll need the Backports repository:

1. Add the following two lines in the `apt` sources file:

```
root@ubuntu:~# vim /etc/apt/sources.list
deb http://archive.ubuntu.com/ubuntu trusty-backports main
restricted universe multiverse
deb-src http://archive.ubuntu.com/ubuntu trusty-backports
main restricted universe multiverse
```

2. Resynchronize the package index files from their sources:

```
root@ubuntu:~# apt-get update
```

3. Install the main LXC package, tooling, and dependencies:

```
root@ubuntu:~# apt-get -y install -y
lxc=2.0.3-0ubuntu1~ubuntu14.04.1
lxc1=2.0.3-0ubuntu1~ubuntu14.04.1
liblxc1=2.0.3-0ubuntu1~ubuntu14.04.1 python3-
lxc=2.0.3-0ubuntu1~ubuntu14.04.1 cgroup-
lite=1.11~ubuntu14.04.2
```

```
lxc-templates=2.0.3-0ubuntu1~ubuntu14.04.1bridge-utils
root@ubuntu:~#
```

4. Ensure the package versions are on the 2.x branch, in this case 2.0.3:

```
root@ubuntu:~# dpkg --list | grep lxc | awk '{print $2,$3}'
liblxc1 2.0.3-0ubuntu1~ubuntu14.04.1
lxc2.0.3-0ubuntu1~ubuntu14.04.1
lxc-common     2.0.3-0ubuntu1~ubuntu14.04.1
lxc-templates 2.0.3-0ubuntu1~ubuntu14.04.1
lxc1           2.0.3-0ubuntu1~ubuntu14.04.1
lxcfs          2.0.2-0ubuntu1~ubuntu14.04.1
python3-lxc    2.0.3-0ubuntu1~ubuntu14.04.1
root@ubuntu:~#
```

Installing LXC on Ubuntu from source

To use the latest version of LXC, you can download the source code from the upstream GitHub repository and compile it:

1. First, let's install `git` and clone the repository:

```
root@ubuntu:~# apt-get install git
root@ubuntu:~# cd /usr/src
root@ubuntu:/usr/src# git clone https://github.com/lxc/lxc.git
Cloning into 'lxc'...
remote: Counting objects: 29252, done.
remote: Compressing objects: 100% (156/156), done.
remote: Total 29252 (delta 101), reused 0 (delta 0),
pack-reused 29096
Receiving objects: 100% (29252/29252), 11.96 MiB | 12.62
MiB/s, done.
Resolving deltas: 100% (21389/21389), done.
root@ubuntu:/usr/src#
```

2. Next, let's install the build tools and various dependencies:

```
root@ubuntu:/usr/src# apt-get install -y dev-utils
build-essential aclocal automake pkg-config git bridge-utils
libcap-dev libcgmanager-dev cgmanager
root@ubuntu:/usr/src#
```

3. Now, generate the `configure` shell script, which will attempt to guess correct values for different system-dependent variables used during compilation:

```
root@ubuntu:/usr/src# cd lxc
root@ubuntu:/usr/src/lxc#./autogen.sh
```

4. The `configure` script provides options that can be enabled or disabled based on what features you would like to be compiled. To learn what options are available and for a short description of each, run the following:

```
root@ubuntu:/usr/src/lxc# ./configure –help
```

5. Its time now to run `configure`. In this example, I'll enable Linux capabilities and `cgmanager`, which will manage the cgroups for each container:

```
root@ubuntu:/usr/src/lxc# ./configure --enable-capabilities
--enable-cgmanager
...
------------------------------
Environment:
 - compiler: gcc
 - distribution: ubuntu
 - init script type(s): upstart,systemd
 - rpath: no
 - GnuTLS: no
 - Bash integration: yes
Security features:
 - Apparmor: no
 - Linux capabilities: yes
 - seccomp: no
 - SELinux: no
 - cgmanager: yes
Bindings:
 - lua: no
 - python3: no
Documentation:
 - examples: yes
 - API documentation: no
 - user documentation: no
Debugging:
 - tests: no
 - mutex debugging: no
Paths:
Logs in configpath: no
root@ubuntu:/usr/src/lxc#
```

From the preceding abbreviated output we can see what options are going to be available after compilation. Notice that we are not enabling any of the security features for now, such as `Apparmor`.

6. Next, compile with `make`:

```
root@ubuntu:/usr/src/lxc# make
```

7. Finally, install the binaries, libraries, and templates:

```
root@ubuntu:/usr/src/lxc# make install
```

As of this writing, the LXC binaries look for their libraries in a different path than where they were installed. To fix this just copy them to the correct location:

```
root@ubuntu:/usr/src/lxc# cp /usr/local/lib/liblxc.so*
/usr/lib/x86_64-linux-gnu/
```

8. To check the version that was compiled and installed, execute the following code:

```
root@ubuntu:/usr/src/lxc# lxc-create --version
2.0.0
root@ubuntu:/usr/src/lxc#
```

Installing LXC on CentOS with yum

CentOS 7 currently provides LXC version 1.0.8 in their upstream repositories. The following instructions should work on RHEL 7 and CentOS 7:

1. Install the main package and distribution templates:

```
root@centos:~# cat /etc/redhat-release
CentOS Linux release 7.2.1511 (Core)
root@centos:~# yum install -y lxc lxc-templates
root@centos:~#
```

2. Check the installed package versions:

```
root@centos:~# rpm -qa | grep lxc
lua-lxc-1.0.8-1.el7.x86_64
lxc-templates-1.0.8-1.el7.x86_64
lxc-libs-1.0.8-1.el7.x86_64
lxc-1.0.8-1.el7.x86_64
root@centos:~#
```

Installing LXC on CentOS from source

To install the latest version of LXC, we need to download it from GitHub and compile it, similar to what we did on Ubuntu:

1. Install the build utilities, `git`, and various dependencies:

```
root@centos:# cd /usr/src
root@centos:/usr/src# yum install -y libcap-devel libcgroup
bridge-utils git
root@centos:/usr/src# yum groupinstall "Development tools"
root@centos:/usr/src#
```

2. Next, clone the repository:

```
root@centos:/usr/src# git clone https://github.com/lxc/lxc.git
root@centos:/usr/src# cd lxc/
root@centos:/usr/src/lxc#
```

3. Generate the config file:

```
root@centos:/usr/src/lxc# ./autogen.sh
root@centos:/usr/src#
```

4. Prepare the software for compilation:

```
root@centos:/usr/src/lxc# ./configure
...
----------------------------
Environment:
 - compiler: gcc
 - distribution: centos
 - init script type(s): sysvinit
 - rpath: no
 - GnuTLS: no
 - Bash integration: yes
Security features:
 - Apparmor: no
 - Linux capabilities: yes
 - seccomp: no
 - SELinux: no
 - cgmanager: no
Bindings:
 - lua: no
 - python3: no
Documentation:
 - examples: yes
```

```
- API documentation: yes
- user documentation: no
Debugging:
- tests: no
- mutex debugging: no
Paths:
Logs in configpath: no
root@centos:/usr/src/lxc#
```

5. Compile and install the binaries, libraries, and distribution templates:

```
root@centos:/usr/src/lxc# make && make install
```

6. Copy the libraries to where the binaries are expecting them:

```
root@centos:/usr/src/lxc# cp /usr/local/lib/liblxc.so*
/usr/lib64/
```

7. Finally, to check the version that was compiled and installed, execute the following code:

```
root@centos:/usr/src/lxc# lxc-create --version
2.0.0
root@centos:/usr/src/lxc#
```

CentOS 7 ships with `systemd` as its init system. To start the LXC service, run the following:

```
root@centos:/usr/src/lxc# systemctl start lxc.service
root@centos:/usr/src/lxc# systemctl status lxc.service
* lxc.service - LXC Container Initialization and Autoboot
Code
Loaded: loaded (/usr/lib/systemd/system/lxc.service;
disabled; vendor preset: disabled)
Active: active (exited) since Tue 2016-08-30 20:03:58
UTC; 6min ago
Process: 10645 ExecStart=/usr/libexec/lxc/lxc-autostart-
helper start (code=exited, status=0/SUCCESS)
Process: 10638 ExecStartPre=/usr/libexec/lxc/lxc-devsetup
(code=exited, status=0/SUCCESS)
Main PID: 10645 (code=exited, status=0/SUCCESS)
CGroup: /system.slice/lxc.service
Aug 30 20:03:28 centos systemd[1]: Starting LXC Container
Initialization and Autoboot Code...
Aug 30 20:03:28 centos lxc-devsetup[10638]: Creating
/dev/.lxc
Aug 30 20:03:28 centos lxc-devsetup[10638]: /dev is devtmpfs
Aug 30 20:03:28 centos lxc-devsetup[10638]: Creating
```

```
/dev/.lxc/user
Aug 30 20:03:58 centos lxc-autostart-helper[10645]: Starting
LXC autoboot containers:   [  OK  ]
Aug 30 20:03:58 nova systemd[1]: Started LXC Container
Initialization and Autoboot Code.
root@centos:/usr/src/lxc#
```

To ensure LXC was configured correctly during installation, run the following:

```
root@centos:/usr/src/lxc# lxc-checkconfig
Kernel configuration found at /boot/config-
3.10.0-327.28.2.el7.x86_64
--- Namespaces ---
Namespaces: enabled
Utsname namespace: enabled
Ipc namespace: enabled
Pid namespace: enabled
User namespace: enabled
Network namespace: enabled
Multiple /dev/pts instances: enabled
--- Control groups ---
Cgroup: enabled
Cgroup clone_children flag: enabled
Cgroup device: enabled
Cgroup sched: enabled
Cgroup cpu account: enabled
Cgroup memory controller: enabled
Cgroup cpuset: enabled
--- Misc ---
Veth pair device: enabled
Macvlan: enabled
Vlan: enabled
Bridges: enabled
Advanced netfilter: enabled
CONFIG_NF_NAT_IPV4: enabled
CONFIG_NF_NAT_IPV6: enabled
CONFIG_IP_NF_TARGET_MASQUERADE: enabled
CONFIG_IP6_NF_TARGET_MASQUERADE: enabled
CONFIG_NETFILTER_XT_TARGET_CHECKSUM: enabled
--- Checkpoint/Restore ---
checkpoint restore: enabled
CONFIG_FHANDLE: enabled
CONFIG_EVENTFD: enabled
CONFIG_EPOLL: enabled
CONFIG_UNIX_DIAG: enabled
CONFIG_INET_DIAG: enabled
CONFIG_PACKET_DIAG: enabled
CONFIG_NETLINK_DIAG: enabled
```

```
File capabilities: enabled
Note : Before booting a new kernel, you can check its
configuration:
usage : CONFIG=/path/to/config /usr/bin/lxc-checkconfig
root@centos:/usr/src/lxc#
```

LXC directory installation layout

The following table shows the directory layout of LXC that is created after package and source installation. The directories vary depending on the distribution and installation method:

Ubuntu package	CentOS package	Source installation	Description
/usr/share/lxc	/usr/share/ lxc	/usr/local/share/ lxc	LXC base directory
/usr/share/lxc/ config	/usr/share/lxc/ config	/usr/local/share/lxc/ config	Collection of distribution-based LXC configuration files
/usr/share/lxc/ templates	/usr/share/lxc/ templates	/usr/local/share/lxc/ templates	Collection of container template scripts
/usr/bin	/usr/bin	/usr/local/bin	Location for most LXC binaries
/usr/lib/x86_64-linux-gnu	/usr/lib64	/usr/local/lib	Location of liblxc libraries
/etc/lxc	/etc/lxc	/usr/local/etc/ lxc	Location of default LXC config files
/var/lib/ lxc/	/var/lib/ lxc/	/usr/local/var/ lib/lxc/	Location of the root filesystem and config for created containers
/var/log/lxc	/var/log/lxc	/usr/local/var/ log/lxc	LXC log files

We will explore most of the directories while building, starting, and terminating LXC containers.

> You can change the default installation path when building LXC from source by passing arguments to the configuration script such as `configure --prefix`.

Building and manipulating LXC containers

Managing the container life cycle with the provided userspace tools is quite convenient compared to manually creating namespaces and applying resource limits with cgroups. In essence, this is exactly what the LXC tools do: creation and manipulation of the namespaces and cgroups we saw in Chapter 1, *Introduction to Linux Containers*. The LXC tooling implements functions defined in the liblxc API, as we'll see in Chapter 4, *LXC Code Integration with Python*.

LXC comes packaged with various templates for building root filesystems for different Linux distributions. We can use them to create a variety of container flavors. For example, running a Debian container on a CentOS host. We also have the option of building our own root filesystem with tools such as debootstrap and yum, which we will explore shortly.

Building our first container

We can create our first container using a template. The lxc-download file, like the rest of the templates in the templates directory, is a script written in bash:

```
root@ubuntu:~# ls -la /usr/share/lxc/templates/
drwxr-xr-x 2 root root  4096 Aug 29 20:03 .
drwxr-xr-x 6 root root  4096 Aug 29 19:58 ..
-rwxr-xr-x 1 root root 10557 Nov 18  2015 lxc-alpine
-rwxr-xr-x 1 root root 13534 Nov 18  2015 lxc-altlinux
-rwxr-xr-x 1 root root 10556 Nov 18  2015 lxc-archlinux
-rwxr-xr-x 1 root root  9878 Nov 18  2015 lxc-busybox
-rwxr-xr-x 1 root root 29149 Nov 18  2015 lxc-centos
-rwxr-xr-x 1 root root 10486 Nov 18  2015 lxc-cirros
-rwxr-xr-x 1 root root 17354 Nov 18  2015 lxc-debian
-rwxr-xr-x 1 root root 17757 Nov 18  2015 lxc-download
-rwxr-xr-x 1 root root 49319 Nov 18  2015 lxc-fedora
-rwxr-xr-x 1 root root 28253 Nov 18  2015 lxc-gentoo
-rwxr-xr-x 1 root root 13962 Nov 18  2015 lxc-openmandriva
-rwxr-xr-x 1 root root 14046 Nov 18  2015 lxc-opensuse
```

```
-rwxr-xr-x 1 root root 35540 Nov 18  2015 lxc-oracle
-rwxr-xr-x 1 root root 11868 Nov 18  2015 lxc-plamo
-rwxr-xr-x 1 root root  6851 Nov 18  2015 lxc-sshd
-rwxr-xr-x 1 root root 23494 Nov 18  2015 lxc-ubuntu
-rwxr-xr-x 1 root root 11349 Nov 18  2015 lxc-ubuntu-cloud
root@ubuntu:~#
```

If you examine the scripts closely, you'll notice that most of them create the `chroot` environments, where packages and various configuration files are then installed to create the root filesystem for the selected distribution.

Let's start by building a container using the `lxc-download` template, which will ask for the distribution, release, and architecture, then use the appropriate template to create the filesystem and configuration for us:

```
root@ubuntu:~# lxc-create -t download -n c1
Setting up the GPG keyring
Downloading the image index
---
DIST        RELEASE     ARCH        VARIANT     BUILD
---
centos      6           amd64       default     20160831_02:16
centos      6           i386        default     20160831_02:16
centos      7           amd64       default     20160831_02:16
debian      jessie      amd64       default     20160830_22:42
debian      jessie      arm64       default     20160824_22:42
debian      jessie      armel       default     20160830_22:42

...
ubuntu      trusty      amd64       default     20160831_03:49
ubuntu      trusty      arm64       default     20160831_07:50
ubuntu      yakkety     s390x       default     20160831_03:49
---
Distribution: ubuntu
Release: trusty
Architecture: amd64
Unpacking the rootfs
---
You just created an Ubuntu container (release=trusty, arch=amd64,
variant=default)
To enable sshd, run: apt-get install openssh-server
For security reason, container images ship without user accounts and
without a root password.
Use lxc-attach or chroot directly into the rootfs to set a root password or
create user accounts.
root@ubuntu:~#
```

Let's list all containers:

```
root@ubuntu:~# lxc-ls -f
NAME               STATE      IPV4   IPV6   AUTOSTART
-----------------------------------------------------
c1                 STOPPED    -      -      NO
root@nova-perf:~#
```

Depending on the version of LXC, some of the command options might be different. Read the manual page for each of the tools if you encounter errors.

Our container is currently not running; let's start it in the background and increase the log level to DEBUG:

```
root@ubuntu:~# lxc-start -n c1 -d -l DEBUG
```

On some distributions, LXC does not create the host bridge when building the first container, which results in an error. If this happens, you can create it by running the brctl addbr virbr0 command.

Execute the following command to list all containers:

```
root@ubuntu:~# lxc-ls -f
NAME               STATE      IPV4         IPV6   AUTOSTART
-----------------------------------------------------------
c1                 RUNNING    10.0.3.190   -      NO
root@ubuntu:~#
```

To obtain more information about the container run the following:

```
root@ubuntu:~# lxc-info -n c1
Name:          c1
State:         RUNNING
PID:           29364
IP:            10.0.3.190
CPU use:       1.46 seconds
BlkIO use:     112.00 KiB
Memory use:    6.34 MiB
KMem use:      0 bytes
Link:          vethVRD8T2
 TX bytes:     4.28 KiB
 RX bytes:     4.43 KiB
 Total bytes:  8.70 KiB
root@ubuntu:~#
```

The new container is now connected to the host bridge `lxcbr0`:

```
root@ubuntu:~# brctl show
bridge name          bridge id          STP enabled          interfaces
lxcbr0          8000.fea50feb48ac          no          vethVRD8T2

root@ubuntu:~# ip a s lxcbr0
4: lxcbr0: <BROADCAST,MULTICAST,UP,LOWER_UP> mtu 1500 qdisc noqueue state
UP group default
    link/ether fe:a5:0f:eb:48:ac brd ff:ff:ff:ff:ff:ff
inet 10.0.3.1/24 brd 10.0.3.255 scope global lxcbr0
valid_lft forever preferred_lft forever
inet6 fe80::465:64ff:fe49:5fb5/64 scope link
valid_lft forever preferred_lft forever

root@ubuntu:~# ip a s vethVRD8T2
8: vethVRD8T2: <BROADCAST,MULTICAST,UP,LOWER_UP> mtu 1500 qdisc pfifo_fast
master lxcbr0 state UP group default qlen 1000
    link/ether fe:a5:0f:eb:48:ac brd ff:ff:ff:ff:ff:ff
inet6 fe80::fca5:fff:feeb:48ac/64 scope link
valid_lft forever preferred_lft forever
root@ubuntu:~#
```

Using the download template and not specifying any network settings, the container obtains its IP address from a `dnsmasq` server that runs on a private network, `10.0.3.0/24` in this case. The host allows the container to connect to the rest of the network and the Internet using NAT rules in `iptables`:

```
root@ubuntu:~# iptables -L -n -t nat
Chain PREROUTING (policy ACCEPT)
target     prot opt source               destination
Chain INPUT (policy ACCEPT)
target     prot opt source               destination
Chain OUTPUT (policy ACCEPT)
target     prot opt source               destination
Chain POSTROUTING (policy ACCEPT)
target     prot opt source               destination
MASQUERADE  all  --  10.0.3.0/24          !10.0.3.0/24
root@ubuntu:~#
```

Other containers connected to the bridge will have access to each other and to the host, as long as they are all connected to the same bridge and are not tagged with different VLAN IDs.

Let's see what the process tree looks like after starting the container:

```
root@ubuntu:~# ps axfww
...
1552 ?           S         0:00 dnsmasq -u lxc-dnsmasq --strict-order --bind-
interfaces --pid-file=/run/lxc/dnsmasq.pid --conf-file= --listen-address
10.0.3.1 --dhcp-range 10.0.3.2,10.0.3.254 --dhcp-lease-max=253 --dhcp-no-
override --except-interface=lo --interface=lxcbr0 --dhcp-
leasefile=/var/lib/misc/dnsmasq.lxcbr0.leases --dhcp-authoritative
29356 ?          Ss        0:00 lxc-start -n c1 -d -1 DEBUG
29364 ?          Ss        0:00  \_ /sbin/init
29588 ?          S         0:00     \_ upstart-udev-bridge --daemon
29597 ?          Ss        0:00     \_ /lib/systemd/systemd-udevd --daemon
29667 ?          Ssl       0:00     \_ rsyslogd
29688 ?          S         0:00     \_ upstart-file-bridge --daemon
29690 ?          S         0:00     \_ upstart-socket-bridge --daemon
29705 ?          Ss        0:00     \_ dhclient -1 -v -pf
/run/dhclient.eth0.pid -1f /var/lib/dhcp/dhclient.eth0.leases eth0
29775 pts/6      Ss+       0:00     \_ /sbin/getty -8 38400 tty4
29777 pts/1      Ss+       0:00     \_ /sbin/getty -8 38400 tty2
29778 pts/5      Ss+       0:00     \_ /sbin/getty -8 38400 tty3
29787 ?          Ss        0:00     \_ cron
29827 pts/7      Ss+       0:00     \_ /sbin/getty -8 38400 console
29829 pts/0      Ss+       0:00     \_ /sbin/getty -8 38400 tty1
root@ubuntu:~#
```

Notice the new `init` child process that was cloned from the lxc-start command. This is PID 1 in the actual container.

Next, let's run `attach` with the container, list all processes, and network interfaces, and check connectivity:

```
root@ubuntu:~# lxc-attach -n c1
root@c1:~# ps axfw
PID TTY         STAT    TIME COMMAND
1 ?             Ss      0:00 /sbin/init
176 ?           S       0:00 upstart-udev-bridge --daemon
185 ?           Ss      0:00 /lib/systemd/systemd-udevd --daemon
255 ?           Ssl     0:00 rsyslogd
276 ?           S       0:00 upstart-file-bridge --daemon
278 ?           S       0:00 upstart-socket-bridge --daemon
293 ?           Ss      0:00 dhclient -1 -v -pf /run/dhclient.eth0.pid -1f
/var/lib/dhcp/dhclient.eth0.leases eth0
363 lxc/tty4 Ss+        0:00 /sbin/getty -8 38400 tty4
365 lxc/tty2 Ss+        0:00 /sbin/getty -8 38400 tty2
366 lxc/tty3 Ss+        0:00 /sbin/getty -8 38400 tty3
375 ?           Ss      0:00 cron
415 lxc/console Ss+     0:00 /sbin/getty -8 38400 console
```

```
417 lxc/tty1 Ss+    0:00 /sbin/getty -8 38400 tty1
458 ?       S       0:00 /bin/bash
468 ?       R+      0:00 ps ax

root@c1:~# ip a s
1: lo: <LOOPBACK,UP,LOWER_UP> mtu 65536 qdisc noqueue state UNKNOWN group
default
link/loopback 00:00:00:00:00:00 brd 00:00:00:00:00:00
inet 127.0.0.1/8 scope host lo
valid_lft forever preferred_lft forever
inet6 ::1/128 scope host
valid_lft forever preferred_lft forever
7: eth0: <BROADCAST,MULTICAST,UP,LOWER_UP> mtu 1500 qdisc pfifo_fast state
UP group default qlen 1000
link/ether 00:16:3e:b2:34:8a brd ff:ff:ff:ff:ff:ff
inet 10.0.3.190/24 brd 10.0.3.255 scope global eth0
valid_lft forever preferred_lft forever
inet6 fe80::216:3eff:feb2:348a/64 scope link
valid_lft forever preferred_lft forever

root@c1:~# ping -c 3 google.com
PING google.com (216.58.192.238) 56(84) bytes of data.
64 bytes from ord30s26-in-f14.1e100.net (216.58.192.238): icmp_seq=1 ttl=52
time=1.77 ms
64 bytes from ord30s26-in-f14.1e100.net (216.58.192.238): icmp_seq=2 ttl=52
time=1.58 ms
64 bytes from ord30s26-in-f14.1e100.net (216.58.192.238): icmp_seq=3 ttl=52
time=1.75 ms
--- google.com ping statistics ---
3 packets transmitted, 3 received, 0% packet loss, time 2003ms
rtt min/avg/max/mdev = 1.584/1.705/1.779/0.092 ms

root@c1:~# exit
exit
root@ubuntu:~#
```

On some distributions such as CentOS, or if installed from source, the dnsmasq server is not configured and started by default. You can either install it and configure it manually, or configure the container with an IP address and a default gateway instead, as I'll demonstrate later in this chapter.

Notice how the hostname changed on the terminal once we attached to the container. This is an example of how LXC uses the UTS namespaces, as we saw in Chapter 1, *Introduction to Linux Containers*.

Let's examine the directory that was created after building the c1 container:

```
root@ubuntu:~# ls -la /var/lib/lxc/c1/
total 16
drwxrwx---  3 root root 4096 Aug 31 20:40 .
drwx------  3 root root 4096 Aug 31 21:01 ..
-rw-r--r--  1 root root  516 Aug 31 20:40 config
drwxr-xr-x 21 root root 4096 Aug 31 21:00 rootfs
root@ubuntu:~#
```

The rootfs directory looks like a regular Linux filesystem. You can manipulate the container directly by making changes to the files there, or using chroot.

To demonstrate this, let's change the root password of the c1 container not by attaching to it, but by *chrooting* to its rootfs:

```
root@ubuntu:~# cd /var/lib/lxc/c1/
root@ubuntu:/var/lib/lxc/c1# chroot rootfs
root@ubuntu:/# ls -al
total 84
drwxr-xr-x 21 root root 4096 Aug 31 21:00 .
drwxr-xr-x 21 root root 4096 Aug 31 21:00 ..
drwxr-xr-x  2 root root 4096 Aug 29 07:33 bin
drwxr-xr-x  2 root root 4096 Apr 10  2014 boot
drwxr-xr-x  4 root root 4096 Aug 31 21:00 dev
drwxr-xr-x 68 root root 4096 Aug 31 22:12 etc
drwxr-xr-x  3 root root 4096 Aug 29 07:33 home
drwxr-xr-x 12 root root 4096 Aug 29 07:33 lib
drwxr-xr-x  2 root root 4096 Aug 29 07:32 lib64
drwxr-xr-x  2 root root 4096 Aug 29 07:31 media
drwxr-xr-x  2 root root 4096 Apr 10  2014 mnt
drwxr-xr-x  2 root root 4096 Aug 29 07:31 opt
drwxr-xr-x  2 root root 4096 Apr 10  2014 proc
drwx------  2 root root 4096 Aug 31 22:12 root
drwxr-xr-x  8 root root 4096 Aug 31 20:54 run
drwxr-xr-x  2 root root 4096 Aug 29 07:33 sbin
drwxr-xr-x  2 root root 4096 Aug 29 07:31 srv
drwxr-xr-x  2 root root 4096 Mar 13  2014 sys
drwxrwxrwt  2 root root 4096 Aug 31 22:12 tmp
drwxr-xr-x 10 root root 4096 Aug 29 07:31 usr
drwxr-xr-x 11 root root 4096 Aug 29 07:31 var
root@ubuntu:/# passwd
Enter new UNIX password:
```

```
Retype new UNIX password:
passwd: password updated successfully

root@ubuntu:/# exit
exit
root@ubuntu:/var/lib/lxc/c1#
```

Notice how the path changed on the console when we used `chroot` and after exiting the jailed environment.

To test the root password, let's install **Secure Shell (SSH)** server in the container by first attaching to it and then using `ssh` to connect:

```
root@ubuntu:~# lxc-attach -n c1
root@c1:~# apt-get update&&apt-get install -y openssh-server
root@c1:~# sed -i 's/without-password/yes/g' /etc/ssh/sshd_config
root@c1:~#service ssh restart
root@c1:/# exit
exit

root@ubuntu:/var/lib/lxc/c1# ssh 10.0.3.190
root@10.0.3.190's password:
Welcome to Ubuntu 14.04.5 LTS (GNU/Linux 3.13.0-91-generic x86_64)
* Documentation:  https://help.ubuntu.com/
Last login: Wed Aug 31 22:25:39 2016 from 10.0.3.1
root@c1:~# exit
logout
Connection to 10.0.3.190 closed.
root@ubuntu:/var/lib/lxc/c1#
```

We were able to `ssh` to the container and use the root password that was manually set earlier.

Making custom containers with debootstrap on Ubuntu

Using the provided distribution template scripts and config files is the fastest way to provision LXC. However, having full control of how the root filesystem is laid out – what packages, block devices, and network settings should be present – requires a more manual approach.

For this, we can use the debootstrap utility to create the rootfs of the container, and then manually create the config file that will describe the properties of the containers. This works on Ubuntu and RHEL/CentOS distributions and it provides a way to run Debian and Ubuntu containers on both RHEL/CentOS and Debian/Ubuntu systems.

Let's start by installing debootstrap, if not already installed. On Ubuntu, run the following command:

```
root@ubuntu:~# apt-get install -y debootstrap
```

Similarly, on CentOS, run the following command:

```
root@centos:~# yum install -y debootstrap
```

To create a filesystem for the stable Debian release, we can provide the following arguments:

```
root@ubuntu:~# debootstrap --arch=amd64 --include="openssh-server vim"
stable ~/container http://httpredir.debian.org/debian/
W: Cannot check Release signature; keyring file not available
/usr/share/keyrings/debian-archive-keyring.gpg
I: Retrieving Release
I: Retrieving Packages
I: Validating Packages
...
I: Configuring libc-bin...
I: Configuring systemd...
I: Base system installed successfully.
root@ubuntu:~#
```

We specified the architecture, what packages to be installed, the release of the OS, and the location where the rootfs will be created, in this example, in ~/container.

Next, we'll need a config file for the container. There are many available options for specifying various LXC attributes. Let's start with a somewhat simple configuration:

```
root@ubuntu:~# vim ~/config
lxc.devttydir = lxc
lxc.pts = 1024
lxc.tty = 4
lxc.pivotdir = lxc_putold
lxc.cgroup.devices.deny = a
lxc.cgroup.devices.allow = c *:* m
lxc.cgroup.devices.allow = b *:* m
lxc.cgroup.devices.allow = c 1:3 rwm
lxc.cgroup.devices.allow = c 1:5 rwm
lxc.cgroup.devices.allow = c 1:7 rwm
```

```
lxc.cgroup.devices.allow = c 5:0 rwm
lxc.cgroup.devices.allow = c 5:1 rwm
lxc.cgroup.devices.allow = c 5:2 rwm
lxc.cgroup.devices.allow = c 1:8 rwm
lxc.cgroup.devices.allow = c 1:9 rwm
lxc.cgroup.devices.allow = c 136:* rwm
lxc.cgroup.devices.allow = c 10:229 rwm
lxc.cgroup.devices.allow = c 254:0 rm
lxc.cgroup.devices.allow = c 10:200 rwm
lxc.mount.auto = cgroup:mixed proc:mixed sys:mixed
lxc.mount.entry = /sys/fs/fuse/connections sys/fs/fuse/connections none
bind,optional 0 0
lxc.mount.entry = /sys/kernel/debug sys/kernel/debug none bind,optional 0 0
lxc.mount.entry = /sys/kernel/security sys/kernel/security none
bind,optional 0 0
lxc.mount.entry = /sys/fs/pstore sys/fs/pstore none bind,optional 0 0
lxc.mount.entry = mqueue dev/mqueue mqueue rw,relatime,create=dir,optional
0 0
# Container specific configuration
lxc.arch = x86_64
lxc.rootfs = /root/container
lxc.rootfs.backend = dir
lxc.utsname = manual_container
# Network configuration
lxc.network.type = veth
lxc.network.link = lxcbr0
lxc.network.flags = up
lxc.network.hwaddr = 00:16:3e:e4:68:91
lxc.network.ipv4 = 10.0.3.151/24 10.0.3.255
lxc.network.ipv4.gateway = 10.0.3.1
# Limit the container memory to 512MB
lxc.cgroup.memory.limit_in_bytes = 536870912
```

The preceding configuration was tested on LXC 2.0 and might be incompatible with versions on the 1.0 branch.

The following table provides a brief summary of the most important options we are using:

Option	Description
lxc.devttydir	The console devices location in /dev/
lxc.tty	The number of TTY to make available to the container
lxc.cgroup.devices.allow	The list of devices to allow in the container

`lxc.mount`	The devices to be mounted
`lxc.arch`	The architecture of the container
`lxc.rootfs`	The location of the root filesystem
`lxc.rootfs.backend`	The type of the backend store
`lxc.utsname`	The hostname of the container
`lxc.network.type`	The type of network virtualization
`lxc.network.link`	The name of the host bridge the container will connect to
`lxc.network.flags`	To bring the network interface up
`lxc.network.hwaddr`	The MAC address of the network interface
`lxc.network.ipv4`	The IP address of the network interface if not using DHCP
`lxc.network.ipv4.gateway`	The default gateway inside the container
`lxc.cgroup`	Set cgroup parameters, such as `memory`, `cpu`, and `blkio`

For more information about all of the available configuration options refer to the `lxc.container.conf` man page.

With the configuration set, let's create the container:

```
root@ubuntu:~# lxc-create --name manual_container -t none -B dir --dir
~/container -f ~/config
```

Notice that we did not specify the template this time and provided the `rootfs` that was created previously with `debootstrap`.

Let's start the container by setting the log to DEBUG and redirect it to a file in case we need to troubleshoot errors:

```
root@ubuntu:~# lxc-start -n manual_container -l DEBUG -o container.log
root@ubuntu:~# lxc-ls -f
NAME               STATE   AUTOSTART GROUPS IPV4       IPV6
manual_container RUNNING 0            -       10.0.3.151 -

root@ubuntu:~# lxc-info -n manual_container
Name:         manual_container
State:        RUNNING
PID:          4283
IP:           10.0.3.151
```

```
CPU use:          0.21 seconds
BlkIO use:        0 bytes
Memory use:       11.75 MiB
KMem use:         0 bytes
Link:             vethU29DXE
TX bytes:         690 bytes
RX bytes:         840 bytes
Total bytes:      1.49 KiB
root@ubuntu:~#
```

To test, let's run `attach` with it:

```
root@ubuntu:~# lxc-attach -n manual_container
[root@manual_container ~]# exit
exit
root@ubuntu:~#
```

Making custom containers with yum on CentOS

On CentOS 7, we can use the `debootstrap` utility to create Debian-based and Ubuntu-based root filesystems and build containers in the same way as described in the previous section.

However, to build RHEL, Fedora, or CentOS containers, we'll need to use tools such as `rpm`, `yumdownloader`, and `yum`. Let's look at a slightly more complicated example that builds a CentOS `rootfs` that the new container will use:

1. First, create the directory that will contain the root filesystem:

   ```
   root@centos:~# mkdir container
   ```

2. After making the `container` directory, we need to create and initialize the `rpm` package database:

   ```
   root@centos:~# rpm --root /root/container –initdb
   root@centos:~# ls –la container/var/lib/rpm/
   total 108
   drwxr-xr-x. 2 root root  4096 Sep  1 19:13 .
   drwxr-xr-x. 3 root root    16 Sep  1 19:13 ..
   -rw-r--r--. 1 root root  8192 Sep  1 19:13 Basenames
   -rw-r--r--. 1 root root  8192 Sep  1 19:13 Conflictname
   -rw-r--r--. 1 root root     0 Sep  1 19:13 .dbenv.lock
   -rw-r--r--. 1 root root  8192 Sep  1 19:13 Dirnames
   -rw-r--r--. 1 root root  8192 Sep  1 19:13 Group
   -rw-r--r--. 1 root root  8192 Sep  1 19:13 Installtid
   ```

```
-rw-r--r--. 1 root root  8192 Sep  1 19:13 Name
-rw-r--r--. 1 root root  8192 Sep  1 19:13 Obsoletename
-rw-r--r--. 1 root root 12288 Sep  1 19:13 Packages
-rw-r--r--. 1 root root  8192 Sep  1 19:13 Providename
-rw-r--r--. 1 root root  8192 Sep  1 19:13 Requirename
-rw-r--r--. 1 root root     0 Sep  1 19:13 .rpm.lock
-rw-r--r--. 1 root root  8192 Sep  1 19:13 Sha1header
-rw-r--r--. 1 root root  8192 Sep  1 19:13 Sigmd5
-rw-r--r--. 1 root root  8192 Sep  1 19:13 Triggername
root@centos:~#
```

3. Now that the database is initialized, we can download the release files for the CentOS distribution. If you'd rather build a Fedora container, you can replace the `centos-release` with `fedora-release` on the command line. The release files contain the `yum` repositories and other important files that `yum` and `rpm` use:

```
root@centos:~# yumdownloader --destdir=/tmp centos-release
Loaded plugins: fastestmirror
Loading mirror speeds from cached hostfile
 * base: mirrors.evowise.com
 * extras: mirror.netdepot.com
 * updates: mirror.symnds.com
centos-release-7-2.1511.el7.centos.2.10.x86_64.rpm
| 23 kB  00:00:00
root@centos:~# ls -la /tmp/centos-release
-7-2.1511.el7.centos.2.10.x86_64.rpm
-rw-r--r--. 1 root root 23516 Dec  9  2015 /tmp/centos-release-
7-2.1511.el7.centos.2.10.x86_64.rpm
root@centos:~#
```

4. Next, install the release files from the `rpm` package in the `root` directory of the `container`:

```
root@centos:~# rpm --root /root/container -ivh --nodeps
/tmp/centos-release-7-2.1511.el7.centos.2.10.x86_64.rpm
warning: /tmp/centos-release-7-2.1511.el7.centos.2.10.x86_64.rpm:
Header V3
RSA/SHA256 Signature, key ID f4a80eb5: NOKEY
Preparing...
############################### [100%]
Updating / installing...
   1:centos-release-7-
2.1511.el7.cento###############################[100%]
root@centos:~# ls -la container/
total 8
drwxr-xr-x. 5 root root   36 Sep  1 19:19 .
dr-xr-x---. 4 root root 4096 Sep  1 19:13 ..
```

```
drwxr-xr-x. 6 root root 4096 Sep  1 19:19 etc
drwxr-xr-x. 4 root root   28 Sep  1 19:19 usr
drwxr-xr-x. 3 root root   16 Sep  1 19:13 var
root@centos:~#
```

From the preceding output, we can see that the `container` filesystem is starting to shape up. It currently contains all the necessary files to use the package manager and install the rest of the system files.

5. Now, it's time to install a minimal CentOS distribution in `rootfs`; this is similar to what `debootstrap` does for Debian and Ubuntu:

```
root@centos:~# yum --installroot=/root/container -y group install
"Minimal install"
Loaded plugins: fastestmirror
There is no installed groups file.
Maybe run: yum groups mark convert (see man yum)
Determining fastest mirrors
 * base: centos.aol.com
 * extras: mirror.lug.udel.edu
 * updates: mirror.symnds.com
Resolving Dependencies
--> Running transaction check
---> Package NetworkManager.x86_64 1:1.0.6-30.el7_2 will be installed
--> Processing Dependency: ppp = 2.4.5 for package: 1:NetworkManager-
1.0.6-30.el7_2.x86_64
--> Processing Dependency: NetworkManager-libnm(x86-64) =
1:1.0.6-30.el7_2 for
package: 1:NetworkManager-1.0.6-30.el7_2.x86_64
--> Processing Dependency: wpa_supplicant >= 1:1.1 for
package: 1:NetworkManager-
1.0.6-30.el7_2.x86_64
--> Processing Dependency: libnl3 >= 3.2.21-7 for
package: 1:NetworkManager-
1.0.6-30.el7_2.x86_64
--> Processing Dependency: glib2 >= 2.32.0 for
package: 1:NetworkManager-
1.0.6-30.el7_2.x86_64
. . .
Complete!
root@centos:~#
```

6. Now the `~/container` directory contains the complete root filesystem for CentOS 7 distribution:

```
root@centos:~# ls -la container/
total 32
```

```
dr-xr-xr-x. 17 root root 4096 Sep  1 19:20 .
dr-xr-x---.  4 root root 4096 Sep  1 19:13 ..
lrwxrwxrwx.  1 root root    7 Sep  1 19:20 bin -> usr/bin
dr-xr-xr-x.  3 root root   43 Sep  1 19:21 boot
drwxr-xr-x.  2 root root   17 Sep  1 19:21 dev
drwxr-xr-x. 74 root root 8192 Sep  1 19:21 etc
drwxr-xr-x.  2 root root    6 Aug 12  2015 home
lrwxrwxrwx.  1 root root    7 Sep  1 19:20 lib -> usr/lib
lrwxrwxrwx.  1 root root    9 Sep  1 19:20 lib64 -> usr/lib64
drwxr-xr-x.  2 root root    6 Aug 12  2015 media
drwxr-xr-x.  2 root root    6 Aug 12  2015 mnt
drwxr-xr-x.  2 root root    6 Aug 12  2015 opt
dr-xr-xr-x.  2 root root    6 Aug 12  2015 proc
dr-xr-x---.  2 root root   86 Sep  1 19:21 root
drwxr-xr-x. 16 root root 4096 Sep  1 19:21 run
lrwxrwxrwx.  1 root root    8 Sep  1 19:20 sbin -> usr/sbin
drwxr-xr-x.  2 root root    6 Aug 12  2015 srv
dr-xr-xr-x.  2 root root    6 Aug 12  2015 sys
drwxrwxrwt.  7 root root   88 Sep  1 19:21 tmp
drwxr-xr-x. 13 root root 4096 Sep  1 19:20 usr
drwxr-xr-x. 19 root root 4096 Sep  1 19:21 var
root@centos:~#
```

If you'd like to install more packages or make changes before the container is built, you can `chroot` to `~/containers` and perform the work as usual.

7. Next, make the bridge, if it does not already exist, and write the container configuration file:

```
root@centos:~# brct addbr lxcbr0
root@centos:~# brct show
bridge name     bridge id               STP enabled          interfaces
lxcbr0          8000.000000000000          no

root@centos:~# vim config
lxc.devttydir = lxc
lxc.pts = 1024
lxc.tty = 4
lxc.pivotdir = lxc_putold
lxc.cgroup.devices.deny = a
lxc.cgroup.devices.allow = c *:* m
lxc.cgroup.devices.allow = b *:* m
lxc.cgroup.devices.allow = c 1:3 rwm
lxc.cgroup.devices.allow = c 1:5 rwm
lxc.cgroup.devices.allow = c 1:7 rwm
lxc.cgroup.devices.allow = c 5:0 rwm
lxc.cgroup.devices.allow = c 5:1 rwm
lxc.cgroup.devices.allow = c 5:2 rwm
```

```
lxc.cgroup.devices.allow = c 1:8 rwm
lxc.cgroup.devices.allow = c 1:9 rwm
lxc.cgroup.devices.allow = c 136:* rwm
lxc.cgroup.devices.allow = c 10:229 rwm
lxc.cgroup.devices.allow = c 254:0 rm
lxc.cgroup.devices.allow = c 10:200 rwm
lxc.mount.auto = cgroup:mixed proc:mixed sys:mixed
lxc.mount.entry = /sys/fs/fuse/connections sys/fs/fuse/connections
none bind,optional 0 0
lxc.mount.entry = /sys/kernel/debug sys/kernel/debug none
bind,optional 0 0
lxc.mount.entry = /sys/kernel/security sys/kernel/security none
bind,optional 0 0
lxc.mount.entry = /sys/fs/pstore sys/fs/pstore none bind,optional 0 0
lxc.mount.entry = mqueue dev/mqueue mqueue
rw,relatime,create=dir,optional 0 0
# Container specific configuration
lxc.arch = x86_64
lxc.rootfs = /root/container
lxc.rootfs.backend = dir
lxc.utsname = c1
# Network configuration
lxc.network.type = veth
lxc.network.link = lxcbr0
lxc.network.flags = up
lxc.network.hwaddr = 00:16:3e:e4:68:92
lxc.network.ipv4 = 10.0.3.152/24 10.0.3.255
lxc.network.ipv4.gateway = 10.0.3.1
```

8. With `rootfs` and `config` in place, let's create and start the container:

```
root@centos:~# lxc-create --name c1 -t none -B dir --dir
~/container -f ~/config
root@centos:~# lxc-ls -f
NAME STATE   AUTOSTART GROUPS IPV4         IPV6
c1   RUNNING 0         -      10.0.3.151 -
root@centos:~#
```

9. Finally, we can run `attach` with it, as usual:

```
root@centos:~# lxc-attach -n c1
[root@c1 ~]# exit
exit
root@centos:~#
```

Summary

LXC provides a toolset that makes it quite easy and convenient to build, start, and manipulate containers. Using the included templates and configuration files further simplifies this process. In this chapter, we saw practical examples on how to install, configure, and start LXC on Ubuntu and CentOS distributions. You learned how to create container root filesystems and how to write simple configuration files.

In the next chapter, we'll have a look at how to configure system resources in LXC and explore alternative ways of working with LXC, by utilizing the `libvrit` toolkit and libraries.

3
Command-Line Operations Using Native and Libvirt Tools

LXC supports a variety of backing stores for its root filesystem. In Chapter 2, *Installing and Running LXC on Linux Systems* we used the default `dir` type, which creates a directory under `/var/lib/lxc/containername/rootfs`. Using the default store might be sufficient in some cases, however, to take advantage of more advanced features, such as container snapshots and backups, other types such as the LVM, Btrfs, and ZFS are available.

In addition to container snapshots, LXC provides tools for controlling resource usage through cgroups, the ability to execute programs before, during, and after the container starts, and to freeze/suspend the state of a running LXC instance.

As an alternative to the LXC tools, we will also look at a different set of userspace tools and libraries for creating and managing containers, particularly the one provided by libvirt.

In this chapter, we'll cover the following topics:

- Building containers using the LVM as the backing store
- LXC on Btrfs
- Using the ZFS backing store
- Autostarting containers
- Adding container hooks
- Accessing files from the host and exploring the running filesystem of an instance
- Freezing running containers
- Limiting container resource usage
- Building containers using the libvirt library and tools

Using the LVM backing store

The **Logical Volume Manager** (**LVM**) uses the device mapper framework in the Linux kernel that allows for mapping physical block devices onto more abstract virtual block devices. This abstraction allows for aggregating various block devices into logical volumes for better resource control. With the LVM, one can extend the size of a filesystem by adding more block devices to a pool of resources called **Physical Volumes** (**PVs**). The PVs contain block devices. From the PVs one can then carve out **Volume Groups** (**VGs**). The VGs can then be split, merged, or moved between PVs and can be resized online if enough blocks are available from the PVs. The VGs can have one or more **Logical Volumes** (**LVs**). The LVs can span across multiple disks, and hold the filesystem. If more disk space is to be added, one can just add a new block device to the PVs, then extend the VG and the LV.

The LVM allows for creating snapshots, a feature that LXC takes advantage of, which creates an LV to act as a clone of the original LV. Using this feature, we can clone containers pretty quickly as, we'll see next.

The following diagram shows the LVM layout and the userspace tools that are used to manage the volumes:

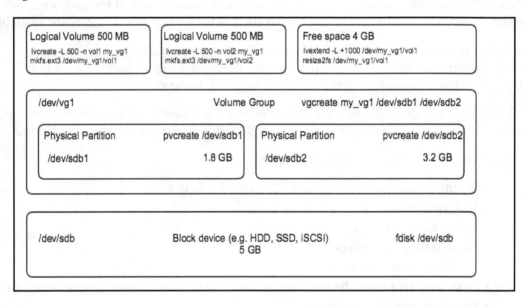

Let's start by first installing the LVM package. On Ubuntu, this can be done with the following:

```
root@ubuntu:~# apt-get install lvm2
```

On CentOS similarly run:

```
[root@centos ~]# yum install lvm2
```

Next, let's examine the block device we are going to use, in this example, xvdb:

```
root@ubuntu:~# fdisk -l /dev/xvdb

Disk /dev/xvdb: 80.5 GB, 80530636800 bytes
255 heads, 63 sectors/track, 9790 cylinders, total 157286400 sectors
Units = sectors of 1 * 512 = 512 bytes
Sector size (logical/physical): 512 bytes / 512 bytes
I/O size (minimum/optimal): 512 bytes / 512 bytes
Disk identifier: 0x00000000
Disk /dev/xvdb doesn't contain a valid partition table
root@ubuntu:~#
```

To create a partition of type LVM, we will use the fdisk utility, following the steps outlined here:

1. Press n for creating a new partition.
2. Then choose p for primary partition.
3. Next, choose the partition number 1.
4. Use the default value by just pressing the *Enter* key two times.
5. Next, press p to print the defined partition.
6. Press L to list all available types.
7. Type t to choose the partitions.
8. Choose 8e for the Linux LVM and press *Enter* to apply.
9. Again use p to print the changes.
10. Finally, use w to save the changes:

    ```
    root@ubuntu:~# fdisk /dev/xvdb
    Device contains neither a valid DOS partition table, nor
    Sun, SGI or OSF disklabel
    Building a new DOS disklabel with disk identifier
    0x115573cb.
    Changes will remain in memory only, until you decide to
    write them.
    After that, of course, the previous content won't be
    recoverable.
    Warning: invalid flag 0x0000 of partition table 4 will be
    corrected by w(rite)
    Command (m for help): p
    Disk /dev/xvdb: 80.5 GB, 80530636800 bytes
    ```

```
255 heads, 63 sectors/track, 9790 cylinders, total
157286400 sectors
Units = sectors of 1 * 512 = 512 bytes
Sector size (logical/physical): 512 bytes / 512 bytes
I/O size (minimum/optimal): 512 bytes / 512 bytes
Disk identifier: 0x115573cb
Device Boot Start End Blocks Id System
Command (m for help): n
Partition type:
  p primary (0 primary, 0 extended, 4 free)
  e extended
Select (default p): p
Partition number (1-4, default 1): 1
First sector (2048-157286399, default 2048):
Using default value 2048
Last sector, +sectors or +size{K,M,G} (2048-157286399,
default 157286399):
Using default value 157286399
Command (m for help): t
Selected partition 1
Hex code (type L to list codes): 8e
Changed system type of partition 1 to 8e (Linux LVM)
Command (m for help): p
Disk /dev/xvdb: 80.5 GB, 80530636800 bytes
255 heads, 63 sectors/track, 9790 cylinders, total
157286400 sectors
Units = sectors of 1 * 512 = 512 bytes
Sector size (logical/physical): 512 bytes / 512 bytes
I/O size (minimum/optimal): 512 bytes / 512 bytes
Disk identifier: 0x115573cb
Device Boot Start  End       Blocks    Id  System
/dev/xvdb1 2048  157286399 78642176  8e  Linux LVM
Command (m for help): w
The partition table has been altered!
Calling ioctl() to re-read partition table.
Syncing disks.
root@ubuntu:~#
```

With the LVM partition defined, let's create the PV:

```
root@ubuntu:~# pvcreate /dev/xvdb1
Physical volume "/dev/xvdb1" successfully created
root@ubuntu:~#
```

With this, the xvdb1 partition is now part of the LVM. It's time to create the VG; we'll name it lxc as this is the default VG that LXC uses:

```
root@ubuntu:~# vgcreate lxc /dev/xvdb1
```

```
Volume group "lxc" successfully created
root@ubuntu:~#
```

Creating LXC containers using the LVM backing store

To create a container using the LVM backing store, we need to specify it on the command line, along with the desired root filesystem size:

```
root@ubuntu:~# lxc-create --bdev lvm --fssize 10G --name lvm_container --
template ubuntu
Logical volume "lvm_container" created
Checking cache download in /var/cache/lxc/trusty/rootfs-amd64 ...
Installing packages in template: apt-transport-https,ssh,vim,language-pack-
en
Downloading ubuntu trusty minimal ...
...
[root@centos ~]# lxc-create --bdev lvm --fssize 3G --name lvm_container --
template centos
...
```

As you can see from the preceding truncated output, the lxc-create command made a new LV named lvm_container and built the container filesystem on it.

Let's list the container and the LVM volumes that were created with the pvs, vgs, and lvs commands:

```
root@ubuntu:~# lxc-ls -f
NAME STATE AUTOSTART GROUPS IPV4 IPV6
lvm_container STOPPED 0 - - -

root@ubuntu:~# pvs
PV VG Fmt Attr PSize PFree
/dev/xvdb1 lxc lvm2 a-- 75.00g 65.00g

root@ubuntu:~# vgs
VG #PV #LV #SN Attr VSize VFree
lxc 1 1 0 wz--n- 75.00g 65.00g

root@ubuntu:~# lvs
LV VG Attr LSize Pool Origin Data% Move Log Copy% Convert
lvm_container lxc -wi-a---- 10.00g
root@ubuntu:~#
```

As expected, we can see the PV and the VG that we created earlier, along with the LV that LXC added.

Let's start the container and make sure it is running:

```
root@ubuntu:~# lxc-start -n lvm_container
root@ubuntu:~# lxc-ls -f
NAME            STATE   AUTOSTART GROUPS IPV4 IPV6
lvm_container RUNNING 0 - - -
root@ubuntu:~#
```

Upon examination of the container configuration file we can see that the backend store for the root filesystem is set to lvm:

```
root@ubuntu:~# cat /var/lib/lxc/lvm_container/config | grep -vi ^# | grep
lxc
lxc.include = /usr/share/lxc/config/ubuntu.common.conf
lxc.rootfs = /dev/lxc/lvm_container
lxc.rootfs.backend = lvm
lxc.utsname = lvm_container
lxc.arch = amd64
lxc.network.type = veth
lxc.network.link = lxcbr0
lxc.network.flags = up
lxc.network.hwaddr = 00:16:3e:60:96:a2
root@ubuntu:~#
```

Have a look at the new block devices that the device mapper has created in /dev/lxc and /dev/mapper, which are links to /dev/dm-0:

```
root@ubuntu:~# ls -la /dev/lxc/
total 0
drwxr-xr-x 2 root root 60 Sep 13 18:14 .
drwxr-xr-x 15 root root 4020 Sep 13 18:25 ..
lrwxrwxrwx 1 root root 7 Sep 13 18:14 lvm_container -> ../dm-0
root@ubuntu:~# ls -la /dev/mapper/
total 0
drwxr-xr-x 2 root root 100 Sep 13 18:35 .
drwxr-xr-x 15 root root 4040 Sep 13 18:35 ..
crw------- 1 root root 10, 236 Aug 30 15:17 control
lrwxrwxrwx 1 root root 7 Sep 13 18:14 lxc-lvm_container -> ../dm-0
root@ubuntu:~# ls -la /dev/mapper/lxc-lvm_container
lrwxrwxrwx 1 root root 7 Sep 13 18:14 /dev/mapper/lxc-lvm_container ->
../dm-0
root@ubuntu:~#
```

Let's create a second, smaller container and observe the effect of the device mapper again:

```
root@ubuntu:~# lxc-create --bdev lvm --fssize 5G --name lvm_container_2 --
template debian
Logical volume "lvm_container_2" created
debootstrap is /usr/sbin/debootstrap
Checking cache download in /var/cache/lxc/debian/rootfs-jessie-amd64 ...
...
root@ubuntu:~# lvs
LV VG Attr LSize Pool Origin Data% Move Log Copy% Convert
lvm_container lxc -wi-ao--- 10.00g
lvm_container_2 lxc -wi-a---- 5.00g
root@ubuntu:~#
root@ubuntu:~# ls -la /dev/lxc/
total 0
drwxr-xr-x 2 root root 80 Sep 13 18:35 .
drwxr-xr-x 15 root root 4040 Sep 13 18:35 ..
lrwxrwxrwx 1 root root 7 Sep 13 18:14 lvm_container -> ../dm-0
lrwxrwxrwx 1 root root 7 Sep 13 18:35 lvm_container_2 -> ../dm-1
root@ubuntu:~# ls -la /dev/mapper/
total 0
drwxr-xr-x 2 root root 100 Sep 13 18:35 .
drwxr-xr-x 15 root root 4040 Sep 13 18:35 ..
crw------- 1 root root 10, 236 Aug 30 15:17 control
lrwxrwxrwx 1 root root 7 Sep 13 18:14 lxc-lvm_container -> ../dm-0
lrwxrwxrwx 1 root root 7 Sep 13 18:35 lxc-lvm_container_2 -> ../dm-1
root@ubuntu:~#
```

Notice how this time the container build was much faster because the root filesystem was cached on disk from the earlier build and the presence of two block devices dm-0 and dm-1.

Let's get more information about the LV the LXC created for the two containers:

```
root@ubuntu:~# lvdisplay
--- Logical volume ---
LV Path                /dev/lxc/lvm_container
LV Name                lvm_container
VG Name                lxc
LV UUID                oBiCEC-mHE7-FHGY-ikUI-tg10-rouD-NBWHVt
LV Write Access        read/write
LV Creation host, time ubuntu, 2016-09-13 18:14:42 +0000
LV Status              available
# open                 1
LV Size                10.00 GiB
Current LE             2560
Segments               1
Allocation             inherit
Read ahead sectors     auto
```

```
- currently set to    256
Block device          252:0
--- Logical volume ---
LV Path               /dev/lxc/lvm_container_2
LV Name               lvm_container_2
VG Name               lxc
LV UUID               ED06VK-xzWv-1GPL-Myff-gN3P-AD21-8zTRko
LV Write Access       read/write
LV Creation host, time ubuntu, 2016-09-13 18:35:52 +0000
LV Status             available
# open                0
LV Size               5.00 GiB
Current LE            1280
Segments              1
Allocation            inherit
Read ahead sectors    auto
- currently set to    256
Block device          252:1
root@ubuntu:~#
```

Notice the presence of two LVs and their respective properties.

Creating container snapshots on the LVM backing store

Now that we have containers on a backing store that supports snapshots, let's experiment with the `lxc-copy` utility. The `lxc-copy` utility creates copies of existing containers that can be either complete clones of the original container, meaning the entire root filesystem is copied to the new container, or snapshots, using **Copy-on-write** (**COW**).

Let's start by creating a snapshot of the second container and observe the effect on the LVs:

```
root@ubuntu:~# lxc-copy --snapshot --name lvm_container_2 --newname
container_2_copy
Logical volume "container_2_copy" created

root@ubuntu:~# lxc-ls -f
NAME               STATE AUTOSTART GROUPS IPV4 IPV6
container_2_copy   STOPPED 0 - - -
lvm_container      RUNNING 0 - 10.0.3.129 -
lvm_container_2    STOPPED 0 - - -

root@ubuntu:~# lvs
LV                 VG Attr LSize Pool Origin Data% Move Log Copy% Convert
container_2_copy lxc swi-a-s-- 5.00g lvm_container_2 0.00
```

```
lvm_container     lxc -wi-ao--- 10.00g
lvm_container_2   lxc owi-a-s-- 5.00g
root@ubuntu:~#
```

Notice from the preceding output the presence of the s attribute, indicating that this container is a snapshot, and the Origin column listing lvm_container_2, from which we cloned. COW is a great way for quickly creating snapshots of containers that will use less disk space, recording only the new changes that occur after the snapshot.

In contrast, we can create a full copy of the original container filesystem, if we don't specify the --snapshot attribute to lxc-copy:

```
root@ubuntu:~# lxc-copy --name lvm_container_2 --newname container_2_hard
Logical volume "container_2_hard" created

root@ubuntu:~# lvs
LV                VG  Attr LSize Pool Origin Data% Move Log Copy% Convert
container_2_copy lxc swi-a-s-- 5.00g lvm_container_2 0.11
container_2_hard lxc -wi-a---- 5.00g
lvm_container    lxc -wi-ao--- 10.00g
lvm_container_2  lxc owi-a-s-- 5.00g
root@ubuntu:~#
```

Observe how the new clone does not have the s attribute and the Origin column is now blank, indicating a full copy instead of a snapshot.

Creating block devices using truncate, dd, and losetup

For the examples in this chapter, it's best to use a cloud provider such as Rackspace or Amazon, because of their free tiers and the ability to add or block devices on demand. However, if you are unable to use block devices for testing, you can create logical block devices with the help of a few tools and use that instead. It goes without saying that this is just for testing and should not be implemented in production due to the inherited overhead of such abstractions.

Let's demonstrate how we can make a block device and create a PV on it for use with the LVM:

1. First, let's create a file that we'll use as a base for the new software block device, using either the `truncate` or `dd` commands, and specify a size of 5 GB:

```
root@ubuntu:~# truncate --size 5G xvdz.img
root@ubuntu:~#
```

The preceding command created a regular 5 GB file on disk:

```
root@ubuntu:~# ls -la xvdz.img
-rw-r--r-- 1 root root 5368709120 Sep 13 19:01 xvdz.img
root@ubuntu:~#
```

2. Next, we'll use the `loop` kernel module and the `losetup` tool to create a new block device by associating the loop device with the regular file we created earlier.

Let's load the kernel module first:

```
root@ubuntu:~# modprobe loop
```

3. Then find the first available loop device that is not in use:

```
root@ubuntu:~# losetup --find
/dev/loop0
root@ubuntu:~#
```

4. Associate the loop device with the image file:

```
root@ubuntu:~# losetup /dev/loop0 xvdz.img
root@ubuntu:~# losetup --all
/dev/loop0: [ca01]:30352 (/root/xvdz.img)
root@ubuntu:~#
```

5. Now, we can use `/dev/loop0` as a regular block device. Let's create the LVM PV on it:

```
root@ubuntu:~# pvcreate /dev/loop0
Physical volume "/dev/loop0" successfully created
root@ubuntu:~#
```

6. Alternatively, we can use the dd command:

```
root@ubuntu:~# dd if=/dev/zero of=/block_device bs=1k
count=500000
500000+0 records in
500000+0 records out
512000000 bytes (512 MB) copied, 2.33792 s, 219 MB/s
root@ubuntu:~# losetup --find
/dev/loop1
root@ubuntu:~#
```

Notice how loop1 is now the next available loop device to use:

```
root@ubuntu:~# losetup /dev/loop1 /block_device
root@ubuntu:~# pvcreate /dev/loop1
Physical volume "/dev/loop1" successfully created
root@ubuntu:~#
```

7. Listing the loop devices now, show two of them associated with the regular files we created with truncate and dd:

```
root@ubuntu:~# losetup --all
/dev/loop0: [ca01]:30352 (/root/xvdz.img)
/dev/loop1: [ca01]:38291 (/block_device)
root@ubuntu:~#
```

8. Finally, to remove the loop devices, run the following:

```
root@ubuntu:~# losetup -d /dev/loop1
root@ubuntu:~# losetup -d /dev/loop0
root@ubuntu:~# losetup --all
root@ubuntu:~#
```

Using the Btrfs backing store

The **B-tree filesystem (Btrfs)** is a COW filesystem that provides modern features such as dynamic inode allocation, compression, and online filesystem defragmentation – and most importantly for the purposes of this book, writable and read-only snapshots.

Without going into much detail about the design of Btrfs, the following diagram shows the main components of the filesystem:

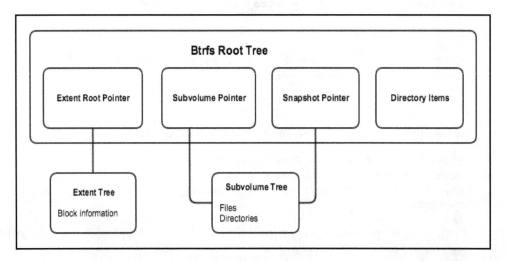

Each Btrfs filesystem consists of a **Btrfs Root Tree**, which records the root block for the **Extent Tree** and **Subvolume Tree**. The root block pointers are updated with each transaction, to point to the new roots created by the transaction. The **Extent Tree** shown in the preceding diagram manages disk space and contains information about the blocks on the device. The **Subvolume Tree** record snapshots, which are subvolumes.

Note that subvolumes are different than the LVs in the LVM, in the sense that the Btrfs subvolume is not an actual block device.

Let's look at a few examples on how to use the Btrfs backing store with LXC:

1. First, let's install the Btrfs support tools.

   On Ubuntu, run the following:

   ```
   root@ubuntu:~# apt-get -y install btrfs-tools
   ```

   On CentOS, install using:

   ```
   [root@centos ~]# yum install -y btrfs-progs
   ```

2. Load the kernel module if not already loaded:

   ```
   root@ubuntu:~# modprobe btrfs
   root@ubuntu:~# lsmod | grep btrfs
   btrfs        840205  0
   ```

```
raid6_pq      97812    1      btrfs
xor           21411    1      btrfs
libcrc32c     12644    2      xfs,btrfs
root@ubuntu:~#
```

3. With Btrfs, we don't need to have a partition on the block device, so let's go ahead and create the filesystem:

```
root@ubuntu:~# mkfs -t btrfs /dev/xvdd
fs created label (null) on /dev/xvdd
nodesize 16384 leafsize 16384 sectorsize 4096 size 75.00GiB
Btrfs v3.12
root@ubuntu:~#
```

Notice the filesystem type on the xvdd block device:

```
root@ubuntu:~# file -s /dev/xvdd
/dev/xvdd: BTRFS Filesystem sectorsize 4096, nodesize 16384,
leafsize 16384,
UUID=58ef810a-c009-4302-9579-a2a9ed7f7ced, 114688/80530636800
bytes used,
1 devices
root@ubuntu:~#
```

4. To get more information about the filesystem we can use the btrfs tool:

```
root@ubuntu:~# btrfs filesystem show
Label: none uuid: 9c84a092-4791-4031-ad16-2cb8488c5633
Total devices 1 FS bytes used 331.25MiB
devid 1 size 75.00GiB used 3.04GiB path /dev/xvdb
Btrfs v3.12
root@ubuntu:~#
```

5. Let's mount the block device so we can actually use it:

```
root@ubuntu:~# mkdir btrfs_c1
root@ubuntu:~# mount /dev/xvdd btrfs_c1
root@ubuntu:~# cat /proc/mounts | grep btrfs
/dev/xvdd /root/btrfs_c1 btrfs rw,relatime,ssd,space_cache 0 0
root@ubuntu:~#
```

6. With the device mounted, let's show the subvolumes and disk space utilization:

```
root@ubuntu:~# btrfs subvolume show /root/btrfs_c1/
/root/btrfs_c1 is btrfs root
root@ubuntu:~#
root@ubuntu:~# btrfs filesystem df /root/btrfs_c1
Data, single: total=1.01GiB, used=309.14MiB
```

```
System, DUP: total=8.00MiB, used=16.00KiB
System, single: total=4.00MiB, used=0.00
Metadata, DUP: total=1.00GiB, used=22.09MiB
Metadata, single: total=8.00MiB, used=0.00
root@ubuntu:~#
```

Creating LXC containers using the Btrfs backing store

Now that we have the backing store ready, let's create a new LXC container by specifying the Btrfs backing store and the location for the root filesystem:

```
root@ubuntu:~# lxc-create --bdev btrfs --lxcpath=btrfs_c1 --name
btrfs_container --template ubuntu
Checking cache download in /var/cache/lxc/trusty/rootfs-amd64 ...
Copy /var/cache/lxc/trusty/rootfs-amd64 to btrfs_c1/btrfs_container/rootfs
...
Copying rootfs to btrfs_c1/btrfs_container/rootfs ...
...
root@ubuntu:~# lxc-ls --lxcpath=/root/btrfs_c1 -f
NAME STATE AUTOSTART GROUPS IPV4 IPV6
btrfs_container STOPPED 0 - - -
root@ubuntu:~#
```

Note that we are using a different path for the root filesystem of the container than the default one in /var/lib/lxc. We specified it with the --lxcpath parameter to point to the Btrfs volume. We need to pass the same path each time we run LXC commands, or we can update the default path for the container with the lxc-config command:

```
root@ubuntu:~# lxc-config lxc.lxcpath
/var/lib/lxc
root@ubuntu:~# echo "lxc.lxcpath = /root/btrfs_c1" >> /etc/lxc/lxc.conf
root@ubuntu:~# lxc-config lxc.lxcpath
/root/btrfs_c1
root@ubuntu:~#
```

Now we can list all running Btrfs containers without explicitly specifying the path:

```
root@ubuntu:~# lxc-ls -f
NAME STATE AUTOSTART GROUPS IPV4 IPV6
btrfs_container STOPPED 0 - - -
root@ubuntu:~#
```

The container root filesystem and configuration file reside on the Btrfs volume:

```
root@ubuntu:~# ls -la btrfs_c1/btrfs_container/
total 20
drwxrwx--- 1 root root 24 Sep 13 20:08 .
drwxr-xr-x 1 root root 30 Sep 13 20:07 ..
-rw-r--r-- 1 root root 714 Sep 13 20:08 config
drwxr-xr-x 1 root root 132 Sep 13 18:18 rootfs
root@ubuntu:~#
```

To make sure that the container's root resides on the Btrfs filesystem, let's list all subvolumes:

```
root@ubuntu:~# btrfs subvolume list /root/btrfs_c1/
ID 257 gen 9 top level 5 path btrfs_container/rootfs
root@ubuntu:~#
```

Creating container snapshots on the Btrfs backing store

Creating a COW snapshot with Btrfs is similar to that of the LVM: we specify the backend store, the location of the container's root filesystem, and the name for the new container:

```
root@ubuntu:~# lxc-copy --lxcpath=/root/btrfs_c1 -s -n btrfs_container -N
btrfs_cow_clone
root@ubuntu:~# lxc-ls --lxcpath=/root/btrfs_c1 -f
NAME              STATE AUTOSTART GROUPS IPV4 IPV6
btrfs_container STOPPED 0 - - -
btrfs_cow_clone STOPPED 0 - - -
root@ubuntu:~#
```

Let's see what the effect on the Brtfs filesystem is after the cloning:

```
root@ubuntu:~# btrfs subvolume list /root/btrfs_c1/
ID 257 gen 12 top level 5 path btrfs_container/rootfs
ID 259 gen 12 top level 5 path btrfs_cow_clone/rootfs
root@ubuntu:~# ls -la btrfs_c1/
total 20
drwxr-xr-x 1 root root 60 Sep 13 20:23 .
drwx------ 6 root root 4096 Sep 13 19:58 ..
drwxrwx--- 1 root root 24 Sep 13 20:08 btrfs_container
drwxrwx--- 1 root root 24 Sep 13 20:23 btrfs_cow_clone
root@ubuntu:~#
```

As we can see from the preceding output, we now have two subvolumes and directories on the Btrfs filesystem.

Before we can start the containers, make sure that the `lxc.rootfs` config option points to the correct root filesystem:

```
root@ubuntu:~# cat btrfs_c1/btrfs_container/config | grep -vi ^# | grep lxc
lxc.include = /usr/share/lxc/config/ubuntu.common.conf
lxc.rootfs = /root/btrfs_c1/btrfs_container/rootfs
lxc.rootfs.backend = btrfs
lxc.utsname = btrfs_container
lxc.arch = amd64
lxc.network.type = veth
lxc.network.link = lxcbr0
lxc.network.flags = up
lxc.network.hwaddr = 00:16:3e:f2:a9:04
root@ubuntu:~#
```

On some Linux distributions and LXC versions, the `lxc.rootfs` might not point to the correct location of the container's filesystem, resulting in failure during the start. If this is the case, change the path and start the container again.

If all looks good, let's start the containers and make sure they are running:

```
root@ubuntu:~# lxc-start --lxcpath=/root/btrfs_c1 -n btrfs_cow_clone
root@ubuntu:~# lxc-start --lxcpath=/root/btrfs_c1 -n btrfs_container
root@ubuntu:~# lxc-ls -f
NAME             STATE AUTOSTART GROUPS IPV4 IPV6
btrfs_container RUNNING 0 - 10.0.3.137 -
btrfs_cow_clone RUNNING 0 - 10.0.3.136 -
root@ubuntu:~#
```

To cleanup, let's first stop the containers, unmount the Btrfs block device, and restore the LXC default path:

```
root@ubuntu:~# lxc-stop --lxcpath=/root/btrfs_c1 -n btrfs_cow_clone
root@ubuntu:~# lxc-stop --lxcpath=/root/btrfs_c1 -n btrfs_container
root@ubuntu:~# umount /root/btrfs_c1
root@ubuntu:~# echo "lxc.lxcpath = /var/lib/lxc" > /etc/lxc/lxc.conf
root@ubuntu:~# lxc-config lxc.lxcpath
/var/lib/lxc
root@ubuntu:~#
```

Using the ZFS backing store

ZFS is both a filesystem and LVM. It consists of a storage pool that manages multiple block devices and provides a virtual storage interface to the filesystem that can then easily be extended on the go. The following diagram shows the general structure of ZFS and its components:

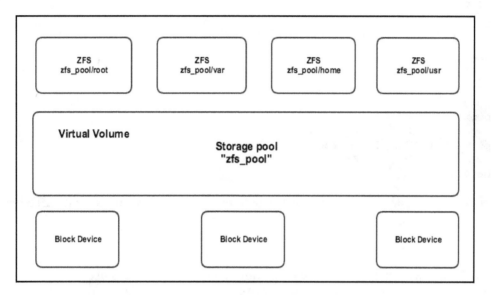

Similar to the LVM, multiple block devices can be aggregated into a **Storage pool**, from which different directories can be carved.

The main features ZFS provides are data reliability due to the implementation of transparent checksums, automatic compression and deduplication of data, parallel constant time directory operations and, most importantly in the context of LXC, COW snapshots and clones.

Let's install the userspace tools on Ubuntu:

```
root@ubuntu:~# apt-add-repository ppa:zfs-native/daily
root@ubuntu:~# apt-get update
root@ubuntu:~# apt-get install ubuntu-zfs
```

The package names are different on CentOS:

```
[root@centos ~]# yum update
[root@centos ~]# reboot
[root@centos ~]# yum localinstall --nogpgcheck
http://archive.zfsonlinux.org/epel/zfs-release.el7.noarch.rpm
[root@centos ~]# yum install kernel-devel
[root@centos ~]# yum install zfs
```

Next, load the kernel module and ensure it's being used:

```
root@ubuntu:~# modprobe zfs
root@ubuntu:~# lsmod | grep zfs
zfs         3089200 0
zunicode 331170   1 zfs
zcommon   66797    1 zfs
znvpair   89131    2 zfs,zcommon
spl        106271   3 zfs,zcommon,znvpair
zavl       15236    1 zfs
root@ubuntu:~#
```

Let's create a pool named `lxc` as this is the default name that LXC uses for the ZFS backend when creating the container root filesystem:

```
root@ubuntu:~# zpool create -f lxc xvdb
```

Substitute `xvdb` with the name of the block device you would like to use.

Let's list the newly created pool and check its status:

```
root@ubuntu:~# zpool list
NAME SIZE ALLOC FREE EXPANDSZ FRAG CAP DEDUP HEALTH ALTROOT
lxc 74.5G 51.5K 74.5G - 0% 0% 1.00x ONLINE -
root@ubuntu:~# zpool status
pool: lxc
state: ONLINE
scan: none requested
config:
NAME STATE READ WRITE CKSUM
lxc ONLINE 0 0 0
xvdb ONLINE 0 0 0
errors: No known data errors
root@ubuntu:~#
```

Everything looks good; let's see the mount point:

```
root@ubuntu:~# zfs list
NAME USED AVAIL REFER MOUNTPOINT
lxc 56.5K 72.2G 19K /lxc
root@ubuntu:~#
root@ubuntu:~# df -h | grep -w lxc
lxc 73G 0 73G 0% /lxc
root@ubuntu:~#
```

With this, we are ready to use ZFS as a backing store for LXC.

Creating LXC containers using the ZFS backing store

Let's create a new LXC container by specifying the backing store and the root filesystem path in the same way we did with the LVM and Btrfs:

```
root@ubuntu:~# lxc-create --bdev zfs --lxcpath=/lxc --name zfs_container --
template ubuntu
Checking cache download in /var/cache/lxc/trusty/rootfs-amd64 ...
Installing packages in template: apt-transport-https,ssh,vim,language-pack-
en
Downloading ubuntu trusty minimal ...
...

root@ubuntu:~# lxc-ls --lxcpath=/lxc -f
NAME            STATE AUTOSTART GROUPS IPV4 IPV6
zfs_container STOPPED 0 - - -
root@ubuntu:~#
```

 Note that since we are using a custom path for the root filesystem of the container, each LXC command will need to be passed the --lxcpath parameter. This can be avoided by specifying the new path with the lxc.lxcpath variable in the system wide LXC config file, as we saw in the Btrfs section earlier in this chapter.

Note that the root filesystem resides on the ZFS volume:

```
root@ubuntu:~# ls -la /lxc/
total 5
drwxr-xr-x 3 root root 3 Sep 14 13:57
drwxr-xr-x 23 root root 4096 Sep 14 13:54 ..
drwxrwx--- 3 root root 4 Sep 14 14:02 zfs_container
root@ubuntu:~#
```

Creating container snapshots on the ZFS backing store

Let's make a snapshot based on the container we just built. Make sure the original container is stopped and the location of the root filesystem is specified:

```
root@ubuntu:~# lxc-copy --lxcpath=/lxc -s -n zfs_container -N zfs_cow_clone
root@ubuntu:~# lxc-ls --lxcpath=/lxc -f
NAME STATE AUTOSTART GROUPS IPV4 IPV6
zfs_container STOPPED 0 - - -
zfs_cow_clone STOPPED 0 - - -
root@ubuntu:~#
```

1. The clone directory resides on the ZFS filesystem:

   ```
   root@ubuntu:~# ls -la /lxc
   total 6
   drwxr-xr-x 4 root root 4 Sep 14 14:03 .
   drwxr-xr-x 23 root root 4096 Sep 14 13:54 ..
   drwxrwx--- 3 root root 4 Sep 14 14:02 zfs_container
   drwxrwx--- 3 root root 4 Sep 14 14:03 zfs_cow_clone
   root@ubuntu:~#
   ```

2. Next, start both containers and ensure they are in a running state:

   ```
   root@ubuntu:~# lxc-start --lxcpath=/lxc --name zfs_container
   root@ubuntu:~# lxc-start --lxcpath=/lxc --name zfs_cow_clone
   root@ubuntu:~# lxc-ls --lxcpath=/lxc -f
   NAME STATE AUTOSTART GROUPS IPV4 IPV6
   zfs_container RUNNING 0 - 10.0.3.238 -
   zfs_cow_clone RUNNING 0 - 10.0.3.152 -
   root@ubuntu:~#
   ```

3. Finally let's clean up. First, stop the containers:

   ```
   root@ubuntu:~# lxc-stop --lxcpath=/lxc --name zfs_cow_clone
   root@ubuntu:~# lxc-stop --lxcpath=/lxc --name zfs_container
   root@ubuntu:~#
   ```

4. Next, try to destroy both the containers:

   ```
   root@ubuntu:~# lxc-destroy --lxcpath=/lxc --name zfs_cow_clone
   Destroyed container zfs_cow_clone
   root@ubuntu:~# lxc-destroy --lxcpath=/lxc --name zfs_container
   cannot destroy 'lxc/zfs_container': filesystem has children
   use '-r' to destroy the following datasets:
   ```

```
lxc/zfs_container@zfs_cow_clone
lxc-destroy: lxccontainer.c: container_destroy: 2376 Error destroying
rootfs for
zfs_container
Destroying zfs_container failed
root@ubuntu:~#
```

5. The clone got destroyed but the original container failed. This is because we first
   need to clean up the child ZFS dataset that was created when snapshotting the
   original container:

```
root@ubuntu:~# zfs destroy lxc/zfs_container@zfs_cow_clone
root@ubuntu:~# lxc-destroy --lxcpath=/lxc --name zfs_container
Destroyed container zfs_container
root@ubuntu:~# lxc-ls --lxcpath=/lxc -f
root@ubuntu:~#
```

6. Finally, delete the ZFS pool:

```
root@ubuntu:~# zpool destroy lxc
root@ubuntu:~# zpool status
no pools available
root@ubuntu:~# zfs list
no datasets available
root@ubuntu:~#
```

With this, ZFS does not contain any datasets or pools.

Autostarting LXC containers

By default, LXC containers do not start after a server reboot. To change that, we can use the
`lxc-autostart` tool and the containers configuration file:

1. To demonstrate this, let's create a new container first:

```
root@ubuntu:~# lxc-create --name autostart_container --template
ubuntu
root@ubuntu:~# lxc-ls -f
NAME STATE AUTOSTART GROUPS IPV4 IPV6
autostart_container STOPPED 0 - - -
root@ubuntu:~#
```

2. Next, add the `lxc.start.auto` stanza to its config file:

```
root@ubuntu:~# echo "lxc.start.auto = 1" >>
/var/lib/lxc/autostart_container/config
root@ubuntu:~#
```

3. List all containers that are configured to start automatically:

```
root@ubuntu:~# lxc-autostart --list
autostart_container
root@ubuntu:~#
```

4. Now we can use the `lxc-autostart` command again to start all containers configured to autostart, in this case just one:

```
root@ubuntu:~# lxc-autostart --all
root@ubuntu:~# lxc-ls -f
NAME                STATE AUTOSTART GROUPS IPV4 IPV6
autostart_container RUNNING 1 - 10.0.3.98 -
root@ubuntu:~#
```

5. Two other useful autostart configuration parameters are adding a delay to the start, and defining a group in which multiple containers can start as a single unit. Stop the container and add the following to configuration options:

```
root@ubuntu:~# lxc-stop --name autostart_container
root@ubuntu:~# echo "lxc.start.delay = 5" >>
/var/lib/lxc/autostart_container/config

root@ubuntu:~# echo "lxc.group = high_priority" >>
/var/lib/lxc/autostart_container/config
root@ubuntu:~#
```

6. Next, let's list the containers configured to autostart again:

```
root@ubuntu:~# lxc-autostart --list
root@ubuntu:~#
```

Notice that no containers showed from the preceding output. This is because our container now belongs to an autostart group. Let's specify it:

```
root@ubuntu:~# lxc-autostart --list --group high_priority
autostart_container 5
root@ubuntu:~#
```

7. Similarly, start all containers belonging to a given autostart group:

```
root@ubuntu:~# lxc-autostart --group high_priority
root@ubuntu:~# lxc-ls -f
NAME                 STATE AUTOSTART GROUPS IPV4 IPV6
autostart_container RUNNING 1 high_priority 10.0.3.98 -
root@ubuntu:~#
```

For `lxc-autostart` to automatically start containers after a server reboot, it first needs to be started. This can be achieved by either adding the preceding command in `crontab`, or creating an init script.

8. Finally, in order to clean up, run the following:

```
root@ubuntu:~# lxc-destroy --name autostart_container
Destroyed container autostart_container
root@ubuntu:~# lxc-ls -f
root@ubuntu:~#
```

LXC container hooks

LXC provides a convenient way to execute programs during the life cycle of containers. The following table summarizes the various configuration options available to allow this feature:

Option	Description
`lxc.hook.pre-start`	A hook to be run in the host namespace before the container ttys, consoles, or mounts are loaded
`lxc.hook.pre-mount`	A hook to be run in the container's filesystem namespace, but before the `rootfs` has been set up
`lxc.hook.mount`	A hook to be run in the container after mounting has been done, but before the `pivot_root`
`lxc.hook.autodev`	A hook to be run in the container after mounting has been done and after any mount hooks have run, but before the `pivot_root`
`lxc.hook.start`	A hook to be run in the container right before executing the container's init
`lxc.hook.stop`	A hook to be run in the host's namespace after the container has been shut down

`lxc.hook.post-stop`	A hook to be run in the host's namespace after the container has been shut down
`lxc.hook.clone`	A hook to be run when the container is cloned
`lxc.hook.destroy`	A hook to be run when the container is destroyed

To demonstrate this, let's create a new container and write a simple script that will output the values of four LXC variables to a file, when the container starts:

1. First, create the container and add the `lxc.hook.pre-start` option to its configuration file:

```
root@ubuntu:~# lxc-create --name hooks_container --template
ubuntu
root@ubuntu:~# echo "lxc.hook.pre-start =
/var/lib/lxc/hooks_container/pre_start.sh" >> /var/lib
/lxc/hooks_container/config
root@ubuntu:~#
```

2. Next, create a simple bash script and make it executable:

```
root@ubuntu:~# vi /var/lib/lxc/hooks_container/pre_start.sh
#!/bin/bash
LOG_FILE=/tmp/container.log
echo "Container name: $LXC_NAME" | tee -a $LOG_FILE
echo "Container mounted rootfs: $LXC_ROOTFS_MOUNT" | tee -a
$LOG_FILE
echo "Container config file $LXC_CONFIG_FILE" | tee -a $LOG_FILE
echo "Container rootfs: $LXC_ROOTFS_PATH" | tee -a $LOG_FILE
root@ubuntu:~#

root@ubuntu:~# chmod u+x /var/lib/lxc/hooks_container
/pre_start.sh
root@ubuntu:~#
```

3. Start the container and check the contents of the file that the bash script should have written to, ensuring the script got triggered:

```
root@ubuntu:~# lxc-start --name hooks_container
root@ubuntu:~# lxc-ls -f
NAME            STATE AUTOSTART GROUPS IPV4 IPV6
hooks_container RUNNING 0 - 10.0.3.237 -
root@ubuntu:~# cat /tmp/container.log
Container name: hooks_container
Container mounted rootfs: /usr/lib/x86_64-linux-gnu/lxc
```

```
Container config file /var/lib/lxc/hooks_container/config
Container rootfs: /var/lib/lxc/hooks_container/rootfs
root@ubuntu:~#
```

From the preceding output, we can see that the script got triggered when we started the container, and the value of the LXC variables got written to the temp file.

Attaching directories from the host OS and exploring the running filesystem of a container

The root filesystem of LXC containers is visible from the host OS as a regular directory tree. We can directly manipulate files in a running container by just making changes in that directory. LXC also allows for attaching directories from the host OS inside the container using bind mount. A bind mount is a different view of the directory tree. It achieves this by replicating the existing directory tree under a different mount point.

1. To demonstrate this, let's create a new container, directory, and a file on the host:

```
root@ubuntu:~# mkdir /tmp/export_to_container
root@ubuntu:~# hostname -f > /tmp/export_to_container/file
root@ubuntu:~# lxc-create --name mount_container --template
ubuntu
root@ubuntu:~#
```

2. Next, we are going to use the lxc.mount.entry option in the configuration file of the container, telling LXC what directory to bind mount from the host, and the mount point inside the container to bind to:

```
root@ubuntu:~# echo "lxc.mount.entry = /tmp/export_to_container/
/var/lib/lxc/mount_container/rootfs/mnt none ro,bind 0 0" >>
/var/lib/lxc/mount_container/config
root@ubuntu:~#
```

3. Once the container is started, we can see that the /mnt inside it now contains the file that we created in the /tmp/export_to_container directory on the host OS earlier:

```
root@ubuntu:~# lxc-start --name mount_container
root@ubuntu:~# lxc-attach --name mount_container
root@mount_container:~# cat /mnt/file
ubuntu
```

```
root@mount_containerr:~# exit
exit
root@ubuntu:~#
```

4. When an LXC container is in a running state, some files are only visible from
    /proc on the host OS. To examine the running directory of a container, first grab
    its PID:

```
root@ubuntu:~# lxc-info --name mount_container
Name:         mount_container
State:        RUNNING
PID:          8594
IP:           10.0.3.237
CPU use:      1.96 seconds
BlkIO use:    212.00 KiB
Memory use:   8.50 MiB
KMem use:     0 bytes
Link:         vethBXR2HO
TX bytes:     4.74 KiB
RX bytes:     4.73 KiB
Total bytes: 9.46 KiB
root@ubuntu:~#
```

With the PID in hand, we can examine the running directory of the container:

```
root@ubuntu:~# ls -la /proc/8594/root/run/
total 44
drwxr-xr-x 10 root root 420 Sep 14 23:28 .
drwxr-xr-x 21 root root 4096 Sep 14 23:28 ..
-rw-r--r-- 1 root root 4 Sep 14 23:28 container_type
-rw-r--r-- 1 root root 5 Sep 14 23:28 crond.pid
---------- 1 root root 0 Sep 14 23:28 crond.reboot
-rw-r--r-- 1 root root 5 Sep 14 23:28 dhclient.eth0.pid
drwxrwxrwt 2 root root 40 Sep 14 23:28 lock
-rw-r--r-- 1 root root 112 Sep 14 23:28 motd.dynamic
drwxr-xr-x 3 root root 180 Sep 14 23:28 network
drwxr-xr-x 3 root root 100 Sep 14 23:28 resolvconf
-rw-r--r-- 1 root root 5 Sep 14 23:28 rsyslogd.pid
drwxr-xr-x 2 root root 40 Sep 14 23:28 sendsigs.omit.d
drwxrwxrwt 2 root root 40 Sep 14 23:28 shm
drwxr-xr-x 2 root root 40 Sep 14 23:28 sshd
-rw-r--r-- 1 root root 5 Sep 14 23:28 sshd.pid
  drwxr-xr-x 2 root root 80 Sep 14 23:28 udev
-rw-r--r-- 1 root root 5 Sep 14 23:28 upstart-file-bridge.pid
-rw-r--r-- 1 root root 4 Sep 14 23:28 upstart-socket-bridge.pid
-rw-r--r-- 1 root root 5 Sep 14 23:28 upstart-udev-bridge.pid
drwxr-xr-x 2 root root 40 Sep 14 23:28 user
-rw-rw-r-- 1 root utmp 2688 Sep 14 23:28 utmp
```

```
root@ubuntu:~#
```

Make sure you replace the PID with the output of `lxc-info` from your host, as it will differ from the preceding example.

In order to make persistent changes in the root filesystem of a container, modify the files in `/var/lib/lxc/mount_container/rootfs/` instead.

Freezing a running container

LXC takes advantage of the `freezer` cgroup to freeze all the processes running inside a container. The processes will be in a blocked state until thawed. Freezing a container can be useful in cases where the system load is high and you want to free some resources without actually stopping the container and preserving its running state.

Ensure you have a running container and check its state from the `freezer` cgroup:

```
root@ubuntu:~# lxc-ls -f
NAME              STATE AUTOSTART GROUPS IPV4 IPV6
hooks_container RUNNING 0 - 10.0.3
root@ubuntu:~# cat /sys/fs/cgroup/freezer/lxc/hooks_container/freezer.state
THAWED
root@ubuntu:~#
```

Notice how a currently running container shows as thawed. Let's freeze it:

```
root@ubuntu:~# lxc-freeze -n hooks_container
root@ubuntu:~# lxc-ls -f
NAME              STATE AUTOSTART GROUPS IPV4 IPV6
hooks_container FROZEN 0 - 10.0.3.237 -
root@ubuntu:~#
```

The container state shows as frozen, let's check the cgroup file:

```
root@ubuntu:~# cat /sys/fs/cgroup/freezer/lxc/hooks_container/freezer.state
FROZEN
root@ubuntu:~#
```

To unfreeze it, run the following command:

```
root@ubuntu:~# lxc-unfreeze --name hooks_container
root@ubuntu:~# lxc-ls -f
NAME              STATE AUTOSTART GROUPS IPV4 IPV6
```

```
hooks_container RUNNING 0 - 10.0.3.237 -
root@ubuntu:~# cat /sys/fs/cgroup/freezer/lxc/hooks_container/freezer.state
THAWED
root@ubuntu:~#
```

We can monitor the state change by running the `lxc-monitor` command on a separate console while freezing and unfreezing a container. The change of the container's state will show as the following:

```
root@ubuntu:~# lxc-monitor --name hooks_container
'hooks_container' changed state to [FREEZING]
'hooks_container' changed state to [FROZEN]
'hooks_container' changed state to [THAWED]
```

Limiting container resource usage

In `Chapter 1`, *Introduction to Linux Containers* we saw how easy it is to limit process resources by either directly manipulating files in the cgroup hierarchy or using the userspace tools.

Similarly, LXC comes with tools that are just as straightforward and easy to use.

Let's start by setting up the available memory for a container to 512 MB:

```
root@ubuntu:~# lxc-cgroup -n hooks_container memory.limit_in_bytes
536870912
root@ubuntu:~#
```

We can verify that the new setting has been applied by directly inspecting the `memory` cgroup for the container:

```
root@ubuntu:~# cat
/sys/fs/cgroup/memory/lxc/hooks_container/memory.limit_in_bytes
536870912
root@ubuntu:~#
```

Changing the value only requires running the same command again. Let's change the available memory to 256 MB and inspect the container by attaching to it and running the free utility:

```
root@ubuntu:~# lxc-cgroup -n hooks_container memory.limit_in_bytes
268435456

root@ubuntu:~# cat
/sys/fs/cgroup/memory/lxc/hooks_container/memory.limit_in_bytes
```

```
268435456
root@ubuntu:~# lxc-attach --name hooks_container
root@hooks_container:~# free -m
     total used free shared buffers cached
Mem: 256   63   192  0      0       54
-/+ buffers/cache: 9 246
Swap: 0 0 0
root@hooks_container:~# exit
root@ubuntu:~#
```

As the preceding output shows, the container only has a total available memory of 256 MB.

We can also pin a CPU core to a container. In the next example, our test server has two cores. Let's allow the container to only run on core 0:

```
root@ubuntu:~# cat /proc/cpuinfo | grep processor
processor : 0
processor : 1
root@ubuntu:~#
root@ubuntu:~# lxc-cgroup -n hooks_container cpuset.cpus 0
root@ubuntu:~# cat /sys/fs/cgroup/cpuset/lxc/hooks_container/cpuset.cpus
0
root@ubuntu:~# lxc-attach --name hooks_container
root@hooks_container:~# cat /proc/cpuinfo | grep processor
processor : 0
root@hooks_container:~# exit
exit
root@ubuntu:~#
```

By attaching to the container and checking the available CPUs, we see that only one is presented, as expected.

To make changes to persist server reboots, we need to add them to the configuration file of the container:

```
root@ubuntu:~# echo "lxc.cgroup.memory.limit_in_bytes = 536870912" >>
/var/lib/lxc/hooks_container/config
root@ubuntu:~#
```

Setting various other cgroup parameters is done in a similar way. For example, let's see the cpu shares and the block IO on a container:

```
root@ubuntu:~# lxc-cgroup -n hooks_container cpu.shares 512
root@ubuntu:~# lxc-cgroup -n hooks_container blkio.weight 500
root@ubuntu:~# lxc-cgroup -n hooks_container blkio.weight
500
root@ubuntu:~#
```

For a full list of all available cgroup options refer to `Chapter 1`, *Introduction to Linux Containers,* or explore the mounted cgroup hierarchy.

Building and running LXC containers with libvirt

Libvirt is a set of libraries and language bindings used to interact with various virtualization technologies in a standard and uniform way. These include KVM, XEN, QEMU, OpenVZ, and of course LXC. Libvirt uses XML files to define virtualized entities such as LXC containers, and describe their properties, such as available memory, block devices, networking, the init system, and other metadata. It supports multiple storage drivers such as the LVM, local and network filesystems, iSCSI, and others.

Libvirt provides a completely independent way of working with Linux containers from the mainstream LXC project and the toolset we've seen and used so far. It implements the kernel feature set that constitutes LXC, and exposes its own tools and libraries to work with containers without the need to install other packages. In `Chapter 4`, *LXC Code Integration with Python,* we'll see how to write Python programs using the libvirt API, but for now let's explore the toolkit that it provides.

Installing libvirt from packages on Debian and CentOS

Both Ubuntu and CentOS package libvirt, though the versions are lagging behind from the upstream trunk. For the latest version, we'll compile it from source in the next section.

 To get the most out of the examples in this chapter and avoid conflicts and errors, I recommend that you use a fresh VM or a new cloud instance.

To install the packages on Ubuntu run the following:

```
root@ubuntu:~# apt-get update && apt-get -y install libvirt-bin python-
libvirt virtinst cgmanager cgroup-lite
root@ubuntu:~#
```

Once installed, make sure the libvirt daemon is running:

```
root@ubuntu:~# /etc/init.d/libvirt-bin status
libvirt-bin start/running, process 15987
root@ubuntu:~#
```

On CentOS, the package name is different:

```
[root@centos ~]# yum install libvirt
[root@centos ~]#
```

Once package install is complete, start the libvirt service and ensure it's running:

```
[root@centos ~]# service libvirtd start
Redirecting to /bin/systemctl start libvirtd.service
[root@centos ~]# systemctl status libvirtd
  libvirtd.service - Virtualization daemon
Loaded: loaded (/usr/lib/systemd/system/libvirtd.service; enabled; vendor
preset: enabled)
Active: active (running) since Thu 2016-09-15 19:42:50 UTC; 59s ago
Docs: man:libvirtd(8)
http://libvirt.org
Main PID: 10578 (libvirtd)
CGroup: /system.slice/libvirtd.service
|-10578 /usr/sbin/libvirtd
|-10641 /sbin/dnsmasq --conf-file=/var/lib/libvirt/dnsmasq/default.conf --
leasefile-ro --dhcp-script=/usr/libexec/libvi...
|-10642 /sbin/dnsmasq --conf-file=/var/lib/libvirt/dnsmasq/default.conf --
leasefile-ro --dhcp-script=/usr/libexec/libvi...
Sep 15 19:42:50 centos systemd[1]: Started Virtualization daemon.
Sep 15 19:42:51 centos dnsmasq[10641]: started, version 2.66 cachesize 150
Sep 15 19:42:51 centos dnsmasq[10641]: compile time options: IPv6 GNU-
getopt DBus no-i18n IDN DHCP DHCPv6 no-Lua TFTP no-co...et auth
Sep 15 19:42:51 centos dnsmasq-dhcp[10641]: DHCP, IP range 192.168.122.2 --
192.168.122.254, lease time 1h
Sep 15 19:42:51 centos dnsmasq[10641]: reading /etc/resolv.conf
Sep 15 19:42:51 centos dnsmasq[10641]: using nameserver 173.203.4.8#53
Sep 15 19:42:51 centos dnsmasq[10641]: using nameserver 173.203.4.9#53
Sep 15 19:42:51 centos dnsmasq[10641]: read /etc/hosts - 5 addresses
Sep 15 19:42:51 centos dnsmasq[10641]: read
/var/lib/libvirt/dnsmasq/default.addnhosts - 0 addresses
Sep 15 19:42:51 centos dnsmasq-dhcp[10641]: read
/var/lib/libvirt/dnsmasq/default.hostsfile
Hint: Some lines were ellipsized, use -l to show in full.
[root@centos ~]#
```

For the rest of the examples in this chapter we'll be using the latest version of libvirt compiled from source on Ubuntu.

Installing libvirt from source

On Ubuntu, make sure your system is up to date:

```
root@ubuntu:~# apt-get update && apt-get upgrade && reboot
```

Next, install the prerequisite packages that will enable us to obtain the source from `git` and build it:

```
root@ubuntu:~# apt-get install build-essential automake pkg-config git
bridge-utils libcap-dev libcgmanager-dev cgmanager git cgmanager cgroup-
lite

root@ubuntu:~# apt-get install libtool libxml2 libxml2-dev libxml2-utils
autopoint xsltproc libyajl-dev libpciaccess-dev libdevmapper-dev libnl-dev
gettext libgettextpo-dev ebtables dnsmasq dnsmasq-utils
```

With all the packages installed, let's clone the source from the master `git` branch:

```
root@ubuntu:~# cd /usr/src/
root@ubuntu:/usr/src# git clone git://libvirt.org/libvirt.git
root@ubuntu:/usr/src# cd libvirt/
root@ubuntu:/usr/src/libvirt#
```

Generate the config file, compile and install the binaries:

```
root@ubuntu:/usr/src/libvirt# ./autogen.sh
root@ubuntu:/usr/src/libvirt# make
root@ubuntu:/usr/src/libvirt# make install
root@ubuntu:/usr/src/libvirt#
```

Update the necessary links and cache to the most recent shared libraries:

```
root@ubuntu:/usr/src/libvirt# ldconfig
root@ubuntu:/usr/src/libvirt#
```

Start the libvirt daemon and check its version:

```
root@ubuntu:~# libvirtd -d
root@ubuntu:~# libvirtd --version
libvirtd (libvirt) 2.3.0
root@ubuntu:~#
```

Defining LXC containers with libvirt

To build a container, we need to define its properties in an XML file that Libvirt will use. Once defined, libvirt starts a helper process called `libvirt_lxc`, responsible for creating the actual container, spawning the first process and handling I/O. Depending on the installation type, version, and distribution, its location may differ, so let's find it.

On Ubuntu, run:

```
root@ubuntu:~# find / -name libvirt_lxc
/usr/lib/libvirt/libvirt_lxc
root@ubuntu:~#
```

On CentOS, the location will be different:

```
[root@centos ~]# find / -name libvirt_lxc
/usr/libexec/libvirt_lxc
[root@centos ~]#
```

As pointed out earlier, libvirt supports many different hypervisors and to accommodate working with all of them it uses hypervisor canonical URIs. The URI points to the hypervisor that libvirt will communicate with. To list the currently configured URI, run the following command:

```
root@ubuntu:~# virsh uri
qemu:///system
root@ubuntu:~#
```

From the preceding output, we can see that the default URI is QEMU. To work with LXC we'll need to change it. To do that, run the following command:

```
root@ubuntu:~# export LIBVIRT_DEFAULT_URI=lxc:///
root@ubuntu:~# virsh uri
lxc:///
root@ubuntu:~#
```

For the life of your session, the default hypervisor will now be LXC. You can explicitly tell libvirt what to use by passing it as a command-line option. For example, to list all LXC containers you can run the following command:

```
root@ubuntu:~# virsh --connect lxc:/// list --all
 Id Name State
----------------------------------------------------
root@ubuntu:~#
```

Before we can define and build a container, we'll need a root filesystem for it. Let's build one using `debootstrap`:

```
root@ubuntu:~# apt-get install debootstrap
root@ubuntu:~# debootstrap --arch=amd64 --include="openssh-server vim"
stable /root/container http://httpredir.debian.org/debian/
I: Retrieving Release
I: Retrieving Packages
I: Validating Packages
...
I: Configuring systemd...
I: Base system installed successfully.
root@ubuntu:~#
```

With the root filesystem in place, let's define the container properties:

```
root@ubuntu:~# vim libvirt_container1.xml
<domain type='lxc'>
  <name>libvirt_container1</name>
  <uuid>902b56ed-969c-458e-8b55-58daf5ae97b3</uuid>
  <memory unit='KiB'>524288</memory>
  <currentMemory unit='KiB'>524288</currentMemory>
  <vcpu placement='static'>1</vcpu>
  <os>
    <type arch='x86_64'>exe</type>
    <init>/sbin/init</init>
  </os>
  <features>
    <capabilities policy='allow'>
    </capabilities>
  </features>
  <clock offset='utc'/>
  <on_poweroff>destroy</on_poweroff>
  <on_reboot>restart</on_reboot>
  <on_crash>destroy</on_crash>
  <devices>
    <emulator>/usr/local/libexec/libvirt_lxc</emulator>
    <filesystem type='mount' accessmode='passthrough'>
      <source dir='/root/container'/>
      <target dir='/'/>
    </filesystem>
    <interface type='bridge'>
      <mac address='00:17:4e:9f:36:f8'/>
      <source bridge='lxcbr0'/>
      <link state='up'/>
    </interface>
    <console type='pty' />
  </devices>
```

```
</domain>
```

The file is mostly self-explanatory and well documented. We define the domain type to be lxc, memory and CPU properties, the location of the root filesystem, and most importantly, the location of the libvirt_lxc helper process. In the networking section, we define a MAC address and the name of the host bridge. Not all options need to be specified, and if omitted, libvirt will create sane defaults. Later in this chapter, I'll demonstrate how we can generate this file from an LXC container that was built with the LXC tools instead.

With the file in place let's define the container:

```
root@ubuntu:~# virsh define libvirt_container1.xml
Domain libvirt_container1 defined from libvirt_container1.xml
root@ubuntu:~# virsh list --all
Id Name State
-------------------------------------------------------
- libvirt_container1 shut off
root@ubuntu:~#
```

We see that the container is now defined but in a shut-off state.

Starting and connecting to LXC containers with libvirt

The container we defined earlier specifies the lxcbr0 bridge. We need to create it before we can start the container:

```
root@ubuntu:~# brctl addbr lxcbr0 && ifconfig lxcbr0 up
```

Now that we have a defined container and a bridge to connect it to, let's go ahead and start it:

```
root@ubuntu:~# virsh start libvirt_container1
Domain libvirt_container1 started
root@ubuntu:~# virsh list --all
Id Name State
-------------------------------------------------------
2618 libvirt_container1 running
root@ubuntu:~#
```

Before we can connect to the container's console, we need to add it to the allowed terminals. To do this, we can `chroot` to the filesystem of the container and edit the `securetty` file:

```
root@ubuntu:~# chroot container
root@ubuntu:/# echo "pts/0" >> /etc/securetty
root@ubuntu:/# exit
exit
root@ubuntu:~#
```

Let's connect to the console:

```
root@ubuntu:~# virsh console libvirt_container1
Connected to domain libvirt_container1
Escape character is ^]
systemd 215 running in system mode. (+PAM +AUDIT +SELINUX +IMA +SYSVINIT
+LIBCRYPTSETUP +GCRYPT +ACL +XZ -SECCOMP -APPARMOR)
Detected virtualization 'lxc-libvirt'.
Detected architecture 'x86-64'.
Welcome to Debian GNU/Linux 8 (jessie)!
...
[ OK ] Reached target Graphical Interface.
Starting Update UTMP about System Runlevel Changes...
[ OK ] Started Update UTMP about System Runlevel Changes.
Debian GNU/Linux 8 server-33 console
ubuntu login:
```

Attaching block devices to running containers with libvirt

Libvirt provides a convenient way of attaching block devices to an already running container. To demonstrate this, let's create a block device from a regular file, as demonstrated earlier in this chapter using the `truncate` and `losetup` commands:

```
root@ubuntu:~# truncate --size 5G xvdz.img
root@ubuntu:~# modprobe loop
root@ubuntu:~# losetup --find
/dev/loop0
root@ubuntu:~# losetup /dev/loop0 xvdz.img
root@ubuntu:~# losetup --all
/dev/loop0: [ca01]:1457 (/root/xvdz.img)
root@ubuntu:~#
```

Our new block device is now /dev/loop0. Let's create a filesystem on it, mount it, and create a test file:

```
root@ubuntu:~# mkfs.ext4 /dev/loop0
root@ubuntu:~# mount /dev/loop0 /mnt/
root@ubuntu:~# echo test > /mnt/file
root@ubuntu:~# umount /mnt
```

Time to define the block device:

```
root@ubuntu:~# vim new_disk.xml
<disk type='block' device='disk'>
  <driver name='lxc' cache='none'/>
  <source dev='/dev/loop0'/>
  <target dev='vdb' bus='virtio'/>
</disk>
```

In the preceding config file, we define the driver to be lxc, the path to the block device we just created, and the name of the device that will be presented inside the container, in this case vdb. It's time to attach the device:

```
root@ubuntu:~# virsh attach-device libvirt_container1 new_disk.xml
Device attached successfully
root@ubuntu:~#
```

Let's connect to the container and make sure the block device is there:

```
root@ubuntu:~# virsh console libvirt_container1
Connected to domain libvirt_container1
Escape character is ^]
root@ubuntu:~# ls -la /dev/vdb
brwx------ 1 root root 7, 0 Sep 22 15:13 /dev/vdb
root@ubuntu:~# mount /dev/vdb /mnt
root@ubuntu:~# cat /mnt/file
test
root@ubuntu:~# exit
exit
root@ubuntu:~#
```

To detach the block device we can similarly run the following:

```
root@ubuntu:~# virsh detach-device libvirt_container1 new_disk.xml --live
Device detached successfully
root@ubuntu:~#
```

Networking with libvirt LXC

Libvirt comes with a default network that uses dnsmasq and is configured to start automatically. To list all networks, run the following command:

```
root@ubuntu:~# virsh net-list --all
Name State Autostart Persistent
---------------------------------------------------------------
default active yes yes
root@ubuntu:~#
```

To examine the configuration of the default network let's dump it to XML:

```
root@ubuntu:~# virsh net-dumpxml default
<network>
  <name>default</name>
  <uuid>9995bf85-a6d8-4eb9-887d-656b7d44de6d</uuid>
  <forward mode='nat'>
    <nat>
      <port start='1024' end='65535'/>
    </nat>
  </forward>
  <bridge name='virbr0' stp='on' delay='0'/>
  <mac address='52:54:00:9b:72:83'/>
  <ip address='192.168.122.1' netmask='255.255.255.0'>
    <dhcp>
      <range start='192.168.122.2' end='192.168.122.254'/>
    </dhcp>
  </ip>
</network>
root@ubuntu:~#
```

From the output, it's apparent that the default networks will create a bridge named virbr0, and what the network ranges configured in dnsmasq are. If we'd rather use our own network, we can describe its properties in a new XML file:

```
root@ubuntu:~# vim lxc_net.xml
<network>
  <name>lxc</name>
  <bridge name="br0"/>
  <forward/>
  <ip address="192.168.0.1" netmask="255.255.255.0">
    <dhcp>
      <range start="192.168.0.2" end="192.168.0.254"/>
    </dhcp>
  </ip>
</network>
```

```
root@ubuntu:~#
```

In this example, the name of the bridge will be `br0` and it will use a different subnet. Let's define it and list the networks:

```
root@ubuntu:~# virsh net-define lxc_net.xml
Network lxc defined from lxc_net.xml:
root@ubuntu:~# virsh net-list --all
Name State Autostart Persistent
--------------------------------------------------------
default active yes yes
lxc active no no
root@ubuntu:~#
```

We can confirm that the two networks created the bridges by running the following:

```
root@ubuntu:~# brctl show
bridge name bridge id STP enabled interfaces
br0 8000.525400628c5e yes br0-nic
lxcbr0 8000.76ccc8474468 no vnet0
virbr0 8000.5254009b7283 yes virbr0-nic
root@ubuntu:~#
```

Notice that the `lxcbr0` is the one we created manually earlier. Each network will start a `dnsmasq` process:

```
root@ubuntu:~# pgrep -lfa dnsmasq
22521 /sbin/dnsmasq --conf-
file=/usr/local/var/lib/libvirt/dnsmasq/default.conf --leasefile-ro --dhcp-
script=/usr/local/libexec/libvirt_leaseshelper
22522 /sbin/dnsmasq --conf-
file=/usr/local/var/lib/libvirt/dnsmasq/default.conf --leasefile-ro --dhcp-
script=/usr/local/libexec/libvirt_leaseshelper
22654 /sbin/dnsmasq --conf-file=/usr/local/var/lib/libvirt/dnsmasq/lxc.conf
--leasefile-ro --dhcp-script=/usr/local/libexec/libvirt_leaseshelper
22655 /sbin/dnsmasq --conf-file=/usr/local/var/lib/libvirt/dnsmasq/lxc.conf
--leasefile-ro --dhcp-script=/usr/local/libexec/libvirt_leaseshelper
root@ubuntu:~#
```

To build a container that will be part of one of the defined networks, we need to change the name of the bridge in the XML file, log in the container, and configure the network interface.

Generating config from an existing LXC container with libvirt

Libvirt provides a way to convert the config file of an existing LXC container that was built with the LXC tools we used in the beginning of this chapter to a format that libvirt can use.

To demonstrate this, let's create a new LXC container with `lxc-create`:

```
root@ubuntu:~# apt-get install -y lxc=2.0.3-0ubuntu1~ubuntu14.04.1
lxc1=2.0.3-0ubuntu1~ubuntu14.04.1 liblxc1=2.0.3-0ubuntu1~ubuntu14.04.1
python3-lxc=2.0.3-0ubuntu1~ubuntu14.04.1 cgroup-lite=1.11~ubuntu14.04.2
lxc-templates=2.0.3-0ubuntu1~ubuntu14.04.1 bridge-utils debootstrap
root@ubuntu:~# lxc-create --name lxc-container --template ubuntu
root@ubuntu:~# lxc-ls -f
NAME STATE AUTOSTART GROUPS IPV4 IPV6
lxc-container STOPPED 0 - - -
root@ubuntu:~#
```

With the new container ready, let's convert its configuration file to the XML specification that libvirt supports:

```
root@ubuntu:~# virsh domxml-from-native lxc-tools /var/lib/lxc/lxc-
container/config | tee -a lxc-container.xml
<domain type='lxc'>
  <name>lxc-container</name>
  <uuid>1ec0c47d-0399-4f8c-b2a4-924834e369e7</uuid>
  <memory unit='KiB'>65536</memory>
  <currentMemory unit='KiB'>65536</currentMemory>
  <vcpu placement='static'>1</vcpu>
  <os>
    <type arch='x86_64'>exe</type>
    <init>/sbin/init</init>
  </os>
  <features>
    <capabilities policy='allow'>
    </capabilities>
  </features>
  <clock offset='utc'/>
  <on_poweroff>destroy</on_poweroff>
  <on_reboot>restart</on_reboot>
  <on_crash>destroy</on_crash>
  <devices>
    <emulator>/usr/local/libexec/libvirt_lxc</emulator>
    <filesystem type='mount' accessmode='passthrough'>
      <source dir='/var/lib/lxc/lxc-container/rootfs'/>
      <target dir='/'/>
    </filesystem>
```

```
    <interface type='bridge'>
      <mac address='00:16:3e:0f:dc:ed'/>
      <source bridge='lxcbr0'/>
      <link state='up'/>
    </interface>
  </devices>
</domain>
root@ubuntu:~#
```

The output of the command is the new configuration file for the container in XML format saved in the lxc-container.xml file. We can use this file to start the container with virsh instead of lxc-start. Before we can do this, we need to specify a console type first:

```
root@ubuntu:~# sed -i "/<\/devices>/i <console type='pty' \/>" lxc-
container.xml
root@ubuntu:~#
```

Define the new container:

```
root@ubuntu:~# virsh define lxc-container.xml
Domain lxc-container defined from lxc-container.xml
root@ubuntu:~#
```

And start it:

```
root@ubuntu:~# virsh start lxc-container
Domain lxc-container started
root@ubuntu:~# virsh list --all
Id Name State
--------------------------------------------------------
18062 lxc-container running
22958 libvirt_container1 running
24893 libvirt_container2 running
root@ubuntu:~#
```

Stopping and removing LXC containers with libvirt

Let's stop all the running libvirt containers:

```
root@ubuntu:~# virsh destroy lxc-container
Domain lxc-container destroyed
root@ubuntu:~# virsh destroy libvirt_container1
Domain libvirt_container1 destroyed
root@ubuntu:~# virsh destroy libvirt_container2
Domain libvirt_container2 destroyed
```

```
root@ubuntu:~# virsh list --all
Id Name State
----------------------------------------------------------
- libvirt_container1 shut off
- libvirt_container2 shut off
- lxc-container shut off
root@ubuntu:~#
```

To completely remove the containers, we need to undefine them:

```
root@ubuntu:~# virsh undefine lxc-container
Domain lxc-container has been undefined
root@ubuntu:~# virsh undefine libvirt_container1
Domain libvirt_container1 has been undefined
root@ubuntu:~# virsh undefine libvirt_container2
Domain libvirt_container2 has been undefined
root@ubuntu:~# virsh list --all
Id Name State
----------------------------------------------------------
root@ubuntu:~#
```

Summary

LXC supports various backing stores for its filesystem. In this chapter, we explored how to use the LVM, Btrfs, and ZFS backing stores to create COW snapshots. We also looked into how to create block devices from regular files for testing purposes.

We demonstrated how to autostart containers, create hooks that will execute programs during the life cycle of the instance, and how to expose directories and files from the host OS to LXC.

LXC uses the cgroup mechanism for controlling and allocating resources to containers. Changes to these resources are stored in the config file and can be persisted if the need arises. We explored ways of doing that with the provided toolset.

Finally, we introduced a different way of creating and managing LXC with libvirt and the `virsh` command.

In the next chapter, you'll have a look at how to create and manage containers using the LXC APIs and libvirt bindings for Python.

4

LXC Code Integration with Python

This chapter will introduce you to the Python bindings provided by both the LXC and libvirt APIs. We'll explore which container functionalities are possible and which are not, using the upstream `lxc-dev` and `python-libvirt` packages on Ubuntu and the `lxc-devel` and `libvirt-python` packages on CentOS.

To gain the most out of this chapter, some knowledge of Python is required. If you are a developer, this chapter is probably the most important one for you.

In this chapter, we'll cover the following topics in this order:

- Building and managing containers using the `lxc` Python bindings
- Creating and orchestrating containers using the libvirt Python bindings
- Using LXC as a backend for development and testing with Vagrant
- Developing a simple frontend RESTful API to LXC, using the Bottle micro framework and the `lxc` libraries

LXC Python bindings

LXC comes with stable C API and Python bindings for both Python 2.x and 3.x versions. Let's explore some of the functionalities that are available to us using Python 2.7.6, by writing a code that will cover most of the features provided by the userspace tools we saw in earlier chapters.

Installing the LXC Python bindings and preparing the development environment on Ubuntu and CentOS

Let's start by installing all the necessary packages that will allow us to write a functioning Python code. This includes the LXC API libraries and a Python development environment with `ipython` and `virtualenv`.

1. To prepare an Ubuntu host, run the following commands:

   ```
   root@ubuntu:~# apt-get update && apt-get upgrade && reboot
   root@ubuntu:~# apt-get install python-pip python-dev ipython
   root@ubuntu:~# apt-get install lxc-dev=2.0.3-0ubuntu1~ubuntu14.04.1
   liblxc1=2.0.3-0ubuntu1~ubuntu14.04.1 cgroup-lite=1.11~ubuntu14.04.2

   root@ubuntu:~# apt-get install
   lxc-templates=2.0.3-0ubuntu1~ubuntu14.04.1
   lxc1=2.0.3-0ubuntu1~ubuntu14.04.1
   python3-lxc=2.0.3-0ubuntu1~ubuntu14.04.1
   ```

   The preceding commands will ensure we are running the latest Ubuntu packages, along with tools such as `pip`, to install and manage Python packages, and the `ipython` tool for interactive programming in Python. On CentOS, install the following packages to provide the same functionality:

   ```
   [root@centos ~]# yum update && reboot
   [root@centos ~]# yum install python-devel python-pip lxc
   lxc-devel lxc-templates libcgroup-devel ipython
   ```

2. At this point, let's create a Linux bridge for the containers to connect to later on:

   ```
   [root@centos ~]# brctl addbr virbr0
   ```

   For the examples in this chapter, we are going to use a separate Python virtual environment to keep the dependency requirements for our project separate. We can do this by utilizing the `virtualenv` package.

3. Let's install it first with `pip`:

```
root@ubuntu:~# pip install virtualenv
```

4. Next, let's create a working directory for our project and activate the virtual environment:

```
root@ubuntu:~# mkdirlxc_python
root@ubuntu:~# virtualenv lxc_python
New python executable in /root/lxc_python/bin/python
Installing setuptools, pip, wheel...done.
root@ubuntu:~#

root@ubuntu:~# source lxc_python/bin/activate
(lxc_python) root@ubuntu:~# cd lxc_python
(lxc_python) root@ubuntu:~/lxc_python#
```

5. With the virtual environment activated, let's install the Python LXC API bindings package and list what is present in our development environment using `pip`:

```
(lxc_python) root@ubuntu:~/lxc_python# pip install lxc-python2
(lxc_python) root@ubuntu:~/lxc_python# pip freeze
lxc-python2==0.1
(lxc_python) root@ubuntu:~/lxc_python#
```

With this, we have all the required packages, libraries, and tools for creating and using LXC containers with Python. Let's have some fun writing Python code!

Building our first container with Python

Let's start the `ipython` tool and import the LXC library we installed earlier:

```
(lxc_python) root@ubuntu:~/lxc_python# ipython
In [1]: import lxc
```

Next, we need to create the `container` object using the `Container` class and by specifying a name:

```
In [2]: container = def build():Container("python_container")
In [3]: type(container)
Out[3]: lxc.Container
```

Now that we have a `container` object, we can use the `create` method to build our first container.

The `container.create()` method definition along with the explanation for each parameter is as follows:

Definition: `container.create(self, template=None, flags=0, args=())`, creates a new `rootfs` for the container. The Following is a description of the parameters:

- `template`: This parameter must be a valid template name in order to be passed.
- `flags`: This is optional. It is an integer representing the optional create flags to be passed.
- `args`: This is optional. It is a tuple of arguments to pass to the template. It can also be provided as a dictionary.

Creating an Ubuntu container is as easy as running the following code:

```
In [4]: container.create("ubuntu")

Checking cache download in /var/cache/lxc/trusty/rootfs-amd64 ...
Copy /var/cache/lxc/trusty/rootfs-amd64 to
/var/lib/lxc/python_container/rootfs ...
Copying rootfs to /var/lib/lxc/python_container/rootfs ...
Generating locales...
en_US.UTF-8... up-to-date
Generation complete.
Creating SSH2 RSA key; this may take some time ...
Creating SSH2 DSA key; this may take some time ...
Creating SSH2 ECDSA key; this may take some time ...
Creating SSH2 ED25519 key; this may take some time ...
update-rc.d: warning: default stop runlevel arguments (0 1 6) do not match
ssh Default-Stop values (none)
invoke-rc.d: policy-rc.d denied execution of start.

Current default time zone: 'Etc/UTC'
Local time is now: Tue Sep 20 16:30:31 UTC 2016.
Universal Time is now: Tue Sep 20 16:30:31 UTC 2016.

##
# The default user is 'ubuntu' with password 'ubuntu'!
# Use the 'sudo' command to run tasks as root in the container.
##

Out[4]: True
```

An output of `True` indicates that the operation was successful in defining the container.

Gathering container information with Python

Now that we've built our first LXC container, let's examine a few of its properties.

First, let's check the container's name:

```
In [5]: container.name
Out[5]: u'python_container'
```

Also check its state:

```
In [6]: container.state
Out[6]: u'STOPPED'
```

Let's list all containers currently present on the host OS:

```
In [7]: lxc.list_containers()
Out[7]: (u'python_container')
```

The preceding `containers()` method returns a tuple containing the container names. In this case, just the single container we've just built.

By default, when we build LXC containers with the userspace tools such as `lxc-create`, the root filesystem and the configuration file are located in `/var/lib/lxc/containername/`. Let's see where the root filesystem for the container we built is, by calling the `get_config_path()` and `get_config_item()` methods on the `container` object:

```
In [8]: container.get_config_path()
Out[8]: u'/var/lib/lxc'
In [9]: container.get_config_item('lxc.rootfs')
Out[9]: u'/var/lib/lxc/python_container/rootfs'
```

From the output of the `get_config_path()` method, we can observe that the default LXC config location is the same as the one if the `lxc-create` command was used to build the container.

In the preceding code example, we also passed the `lxc.rootfs` configuration option to the `get_config_item()` method to obtain the root filesystem location, which is also in line with the default, if using the command line tools.

We can pass various configuration parameters to the `get_config_item()` method to obtain the container's current settings. Let's query for the `memory.limit_in_bytes` option:

```
In [10]:
container.get_config_item('lxc.cgroup.memory.limit_in_bytes')
Out[10]: u''
```

 To list all available methods and variables on the `container` object we created, in `ipython`, type `container` and press the *Tab* key once. To get more information about a method, function, or variable, type its name followed by question mark, for example, `container.get_ips?`.

You can experiment further by opening the container's configuration file as shown from the preceding output and pass it as a parameter to the `get_config_item()` method.

To obtain the IP configuration of our container, we can call the `get_ips()` method with no arguments, as the following:

```
In [11]: container.get_ips()
Out[11]: ()
```

Since the container is not running and no memory limits have been applied, the output is an empty string and an empty tuple, respectively. Working with a stopped container is not very interesting; let's explore what we can do in Python with a running container.

Starting containers, applying changes, and listing configuration options with Python

Let's check if the container is running by printing the value of the running Boolean on the `container` object:

```
In [12]: container.running
Out[12]: False
```

To start the container, we can use the `start()` method. The docstring for that method reads as follows:

```
start(useinit = False, daemonize=True, close_fds=False, cmd = (,))
->boolean
```

Start the container and return `True` on success. When set, `useinit` will make LXC use `lxc-init` to start the container. The container can be started in the foreground with `daemonize=False`. All `fds` may also be closed by passing `close_fds=True`. Looks easy enough. Let's start our container by daemonizing it and not using the `lxc-init` manager, but the Python interpreter instead:

```
In [13]: container.start(useinit = False, daemonize = True)
Out[13]: True
```

Just as earlier, an output of `True` indicates that the operation was executed successfully. Let's use the `wait()` method to wait for the container to reach the `RUNNING` state, or to timeout in 5 seconds:

```
In [14]: container.wait("RUNNING", 5)
Out[14]: True
```

The output indicates that the container is now running. Let's double-check by printing the values of the running and state variables:

```
In [15]: container.running
Out[15]: True
In [16]: container.state
Out[16]: u'RUNNING'
```

In a separate terminal, let's use the LXC userspace tools to examine the container we built with the Python library:

```
root@ubuntu:~# lxc-ls -f
NAME             STATE    AUTOSTART GROUPS IPV4       IPV6
python_container RUNNING 0          -       10.0.3.29 -
root@ubuntu:~#
```

The output of the `lxc-ls` command confirms what the `container.state` variable returned.

Let's obtain the PID of the container in our Python shell:

```
In [17]: container.init_pid
Out[17]: 4688L
```

The PID in this case is `4688`; we can confirm if it matches what's currently running on the host system by executing the following command:

```
root@ubuntu:~# psaxfw
...
4683 ?Ss      0:00 /usr/bin/python /usr/bin/ipython
4688 ?Ss      0:00  \_ /sbin/init
5405 ?      S      0:00       \_ upstart-socket-bridge --daemon
6224 ?      S      0:00       \_ upstart-udev-bridge --daemon
6235 ?Ss     0:00       \_ /lib/systemd/systemd-udevd --daemon
6278 ?      S      0:00       \_ upstart-file-bridge --daemon
6280 ?Ss1    0:00       \_ rsyslogd
6375 ?Ss     0:00       \_ dhclient -1 -v -pf /run/dhclient.eth0.pid -lf
/var/lib/dhcp/dhclient.eth0.leases eth0
6447 pts/3   Ss+    0:00       \_ /sbin/getty -8 38400 tty4
6450 pts/1   Ss+    0:00       \_ /sbin/getty -8 38400 tty2
6451 pts/2   Ss+    0:00       \_ /sbin/getty -8 38400 tty3
6462 ?Ss     0:00       \_ /usr/sbin/sshd -D
6468 ?Ss     0:00       \_ cron
6498 pts/4   Ss+    0:00       \_ /sbin/getty -8 38400 console
6501 pts/0   Ss+    0:00       \_ /sbin/getty -8 38400 tty1
root@ubuntu:~#
```

No real surprises here. Notice how the main process that started the container's `init` system is `python` and not `lxc-init`, because that is what we passed as an argument to the `start()` method earlier.

Now that our container is running, we can get some more information from it. Let's start by obtaining its IP address:

```
In [18]: container.get_ips()
Out[18]: (u'10.0.3.29',)
```

The result is a tuple, containing the IP addresses of all interfaces for the container, in this case just one IP.

We can programmatically attach to the container and run commands just like we saw in the Chapter 3, *Command-line Operations Using Native and Libvirt Tools*, with the `lxc-attach` command, by invoking the `attach_wait()` method, as follows:

```
In [19]: container.attach_wait(lxc.attach_run_command, ["ifconfig",
"eth0"])
eth0      Link encap:EthernetHWaddr 00:16:3e:ea:1c:38
inet addr:10.0.3.29  Bcast:10.0.3.255  Mask:255.255.255.0
inet6addr: fe80::216:3eff:feea:1c38/64 Scope:Link
          UP BROADCAST RUNNING MULTICAST  MTU:1500  Metric:1
          RX packets:53 errors:0 dropped:0 overruns:0 frame:0
```

```
        TX packets:52 errors:0 dropped:0 overruns:0 carrier:0
        collisions:0 txqueuelen:1000
        RX bytes:5072 (5.0 KB)  TX bytes:4892 (4.8 KB)
Out[19]: 0L
```

The `attach_wait()` method takes a function as its argument, in the preceding example, the built-in `lxc.attach_run_command`, but it can be any other function in Python that you wrote. We also specified a list consisting of the command we want to execute and its arguments.

We can also specify the namespace context the command should run in. For example, to list all files in the container's mount namespace designated by the CLONE_NEWNS flag, we can pass the `namespaces` parameter:

```
In [20]: container.attach_wait(lxc.attach_run_command, ["ls", "-la"],
namespaces=(lxc.CLONE_NEWNS))
total 68
drwxr-xr-x  21 root root 4096 Sep 20 18:51 .
drwxr-xr-x  21 root root 4096 Sep 20 18:51 ..
drwxr-xr-x   2 root root 4096 Sep 14 15:20 bin
drwxr-xr-x   2 root root 4096 Apr 10  2014 boot
drwxr-xr-x   7 root root 1140 Sep 20 18:51 dev
drwxr-xr-x  65 root root 4096 Sep 20 18:51 etc
drwxr-xr-x   3 root root 4096 Sep 20 16:30 home
drwxr-xr-x  12 root root 4096 Sep 14 15:19 lib
drwxr-xr-x   2 root root 4096 Sep 14 15:19 lib64
drwxr-xr-x   2 root root 4096 Sep 14 15:18 media
drwxr-xr-x   2 root root 4096 Apr 10  2014 mnt
drwxr-xr-x   2 root root 4096 Sep 14 15:18 opt
dr-xr-xr-x 143 root root    0 Sep 20 18:51 proc
drwx------   2 root root 4096 Sep 14 15:18 root
drwxr-xr-x  10 root root  420 Sep 20 18:51 run
drwxr-xr-x   2 root root 4096 Sep 14 15:20 sbin
drwxr-xr-x   2 root root 4096 Sep 14 15:18 srv
dr-xr-xr-x  13 root root    0 Sep 20 18:51 sys
drwxrwxrwt   2 root root 4096 Sep 20 19:17 tmp
drwxr-xr-x  10 root root 4096 Sep 14 15:18 usr
drwxr-xr-x  11 root root 4096 Sep 14 15:18 var
Out[20]: 0L
```

We can run commands by specifying multiple `namespaces` flags. In the next example, we list all processes in the container by explicitly specifying the mount and process namespaces with the `CLONE_NEWNS` and `CLONE_NEWPID` flags, respectively:

```
In [21]: container.attach_wait(lxc.attach_run_command, ["ps", "axfw"],
namespaces=(lxc.CLONE_NEWNS + lxc.CLONE_NEWPID))
  PID TTY        STAT    TIME COMMAND
 1751 pts/0      R+      0:00psaxfw
1 ?Ss       0:00 /sbin/init
670 ?          S       0:00 upstart-socket-bridge --daemon
1487 ?         S       0:00 upstart-udev-bridge --daemon
1498 ?Ss       0:00 /lib/systemd/systemd-udevd --daemon
1541 ?         S       0:00 upstart-file-bridge --daemon
1543 ?Ssl      0:00 rsyslogd
1582 ?Ss       0:00 dhclient -1 -v -pf /run/dhclient.eth0.pid -lf
/var/lib/dhcp/dhclient.eth0.leases eth0
 1654 lxc/tty4 Ss+     0:00 /sbin/getty -8 38400 tty4
 1657 lxc/tty2 Ss+     0:00 /sbin/getty -8 38400 tty2
 1658 lxc/tty3 Ss+     0:00 /sbin/getty -8 38400 tty3
1669 ?Ss       0:00 /usr/sbin/sshd -D
1675 ?Ss       0:00 cron
 1705 lxc/console Ss+   0:00 /sbin/getty -8 38400 console
 1708 lxc/tty1 Ss+     0:00 /sbin/getty -8 38400 tty1
Out[21]: 0L
```

Using the `set_config_item()` and `get_config_item()` methods, we can apply configuration changes and query them on a running container. To demonstrate this, let's specify a memory limit for the container and then obtain the newly set value:

```
In [22]: container.set_config_item("lxc.cgroup.memory.limit_in_bytes",
"536870912")
Out[22]: True
In [23]: container.get_config_item('lxc.cgroup.memory.limit_in_bytes')
Out[23]: [u'536870912']
```

The preceding changes will not persist when a container restarts; to make the changes permanent, we can write them in the configuration file using the `append_config_item()` and `save_config()` methods:

```
In [24]: container.append_config_item("lxc.cgroup.memory.limit_in_bytes",
"536870912")
Out[24]: True
In [25]: container.save_config()
Out[25]: True
```

To verify this, the `lxc.cgroup.memory.limit_in_bytes` parameter was saved in the configuration file; let's examine it:

```
root@ubuntu:~# cat /var/lib/lxc/python_container/config
lxc.include = /usr/share/lxc/config/ubuntu.common.conf
# Container specific configuration
lxc.rootfs = /var/lib/lxc/python_container/rootfs
lxc.rootfs.backend = dir
lxc.utsname = python_container
lxc.arch = amd64
# Network configuration
lxc.network.type = veth
lxc.network.link = lxcbr0
lxc.network.flags = up
lxc.network.hwaddr = 00:16:3e:ea:1c:38
lxc.cgroup.memory.limit_in_bytes = 536870912
root@ubuntu:~#
```

> The last line in the configuration file is the one we appended with the two Python calls.

In addition to the `set_config_item()` method, the Python bindings also provide the `set_cgroup_item()` and `get_cgroup_item()` methods for specifically manipulating the cgroup parameters. Let's set and get the same `memory.limit_in_bytes` option using those two calls:

```
In [26]: container.get_cgroup_item("memory.limit_in_bytes")
Out[26]: u'536870912'
In [27]: container.set_cgroup_item("memory.limit_in_bytes", "268435456")
Out[27]: True
In [28]: container.get_cgroup_item("memory.limit_in_bytes")
Out[28]: u'268435456'
```

Changing container state with Python

In Chapter 3, *Command-Line Operations Using Native and Libvirt Tools*, we saw how to freeze and unfreeze LXC containers to preserve their state using the `lxc-freeze` and `lxc-unfreeze` commands. We can do the same with the `freeze()` and `unfreeze()` methods. To freeze the container, execute the following:

```
In [29]: container.freeze()
Out[29]: u'FROZEN'
```

Check the status as follows:

```
In [30]: container.state
Out[30]: u'FROZEN'
```

We can examine the cgroup file as well, to confirm the change took place:

```
root@ubuntu:~# cat
/sys/fs/cgroup/freezer/lxc/python_container/freezer.state
FROZEN
root@ubuntu:~#
```

To unfreeze the container and check the new state, call the unfreeze() method:

```
In [31]: container.unfreeze()
Out[31]: True
In [32]: container.state
Out[32]: u'RUNNING'
root@ubuntu:~# cat
/sys/fs/cgroup/freezer/lxc/python_container/freezer.state
THAWED
root@ubuntu:~#
```

Stopping containers with Python

The Python bindings provide a convenient way of stopping containers with the stop() method. Let's stop our container and check its state:

```
In [33]: container.stop()
Out[33]: True
In [34]: container.state
Out[34]: u'STOPPED'
```

Finally, list all the containers on the host:

```
root@ubuntu:~# lxc-ls -f
NAME             STATE    AUTOSTART  GROUPS  IPV4  IPV6
python_container STOPPED  0          -       -     -
root@ubuntu:~#
```

Cloning containers with Python

With the container in a STOPPED state, let's run the clone() method and create a copy:

```
In [35]: cloned_container = container.clone("cloned_container")
In [35]: True
```

Listing the available containers with the list_containers() method on the lxc object, we get a tuple:

```
In [36]: lxc.list_containers()
Out[36]: (u'cloned_container', u'python_container')
```

To confirm on the host OS, execute the following:

```
root@ubuntu:~# lxc-ls -f
NAME              STATE    AUTOSTART  GROUPS  IPV4  IPV6
cloned_container  STOPPED  0          -       -     -
python_container  STOPPED  0          -       -     -
root@ubuntu:~#
```

To find where the root filesystem for the cloned container is, we can call the get_config_item() method on the new container object:

```
In [37]: cloned_container.get_config_item('lxc.rootfs')
Out[37]: u'/var/lib/lxc/cloned_container/rootfs'
```

Two directories now exist in the default container path:

```
root@ubuntu:~# ls -la /var/lib/lxc
total 20
drwx------   5 root root 4096 Sep 20 19:51 .
drwxr-xr-x  47 root root 4096 Sep 16 13:40 ..
drwxrwx---   3 root root 4096 Sep 20 19:51 cloned_container
drwxrwx---   3 root root 4096 Sep 20 16:30 python_container
root@ubuntu:~#
```

Finally, let's start the cloned container and ensure it's running:

```
In [38]: cloned_container.start()
Out[38]: True
In [39]: cloned_container.state
Out[39]: u'RUNNING'
```

Destroying containers with Python and cleaning up the virtual environment

Before we can remove or destroy containers in Python, just like with the command line tools, we need to stop them first:

```
In [40]: cloned_container.stop()
Out[40]: True
In [41]: container.stop()
Out[41]: True
```

Invoke the `destroy()` method on the `container` object to delete the root filesystem and free all resources used by it:

```
In [42]: cloned_container.destroy()
Out[42]: True
In [43]: container.destroy()
Out[43]: True
```

List the containers through the `list_containers()` method to now return an empty tuple:

```
In [44]: lxc.list_containers()
Out[44]: ()
```

Lastly, let's deactivate the Python virtual environment we created earlier – note that the files will still be present on the disk:

```
(lxc_python) root@ubuntu:~/lxc_python# deactivate
root@ubuntu:~/lxc_python# cd ..
root@ubuntu:~#
```

Libvirt Python bindings

In Chapter 3, *Command-Line Operations Using Native and Libvirt Tools*, we explored an alternative way of working with LXC through the use of the libvirt userspace tools. Libvirt provides Python bindings that we can use to write applications, with the main benefit of uniformity with other virtualization technologies. It's quite convenient to write Python applications for KVM, XEN, and LXC using just one common library.

In this section, we are going to explore some of the Python methods provided by the libvirt library to create and control LXC containers.

Installing the libvirt Python development packages

Let's start by installing the required packages and starting the service.

On Ubuntu, run the following:

```
root@ubuntu:~# apt-get install python-libvirt debootstrap
root@ubuntu:~# service libvirt-bin start
```

On CentOS, the library and the service are named differently:

```
[root@centos ~]# yum install libvirt libvirt-python debootstrap
[root@centos ~]# service libvirtd start
```

Since libvirt does not provide templates to work with, we need to create our own root filesystem:

```
root@ubuntu:~# debootstrap --arch=amd64 --include="openssh-server vim"
stable ~/container http://httpredir.debian.org/debian/
...
root@ubuntu:~#
```

Activate the Python virtual environment and start the interpreter:

```
root@ubuntu:~# source lxc_python/bin/activate
(lxc_python) root@ubuntu:~# ipython
In [1]:
```

Building LXC containers with libvirt Python

It's time to import the library and call the open() method to create a connection to the LXC driver. The argument that we pass to the open() method should look familiar – we used it in Chapter 3, *Command-Line Operations Using Native and Libvirt Tools*, when exporting the LIBVIRT_DEFAULT_URI environment variable, telling libvirt that LXC is going to be the default virtualization driver:

```
In [1]: import libvirt
In [2]: lxc_conn = libvirt.open('lxc:///')
```

After specifying the default virtualization driver and URI, we can use the next two methods to return the name and path of the driver we set:

```
In [3]: lxc_conn.getType()
Out[3]: 'LXC'
In [4]: lxc_conn.getURI()
Out[4]: 'lxc:///'
```

To get a list of the available methods and variables on the lxc_conn object we created earlier, type lxc_conn. and press the *Tab* key. To get more information about a method, function, or variable, type its name followed by a question mark, for example, lxc_conn.getURI?.

We can use the getInfo() method to extract hardware information about the host node:

```
In [5]: lxc_conn.getInfo()
Out[5]: ['x86_64', 1996L, 2, 3000, 1, 2, 1, 1]
```

The result is a list with the following values:

Member	Description
list[0]	String indicating the CPU model
list[1]	Memory size in megabytes
list[2]	The number of active CPUs
list[3]	Expected CPU frequency in MHz
list[4]	The number of NUMA nodes, 1 for uniform memory access
list[5]	Number of CPU sockets per node
list[6]	Number of cores per socket
list[7]	Number of threads per core

To build a container, we need to define it first in a XML file. Let's use the following example and assign it to the domain_xml string variable:

```
In [6]: domain_xml = '''
<domain type='lxc'>
  <name>libvirt_python</name>
  <memory unit='KiB'>524288</memory>
  <currentMemory unit='KiB'>524288</currentMemory>
  <vcpu placement='static'>1</vcpu>
```

```
    <os>
      <type arch='x86_64'>exe</type>
      <init>/sbin/init</init>
    </os>
    <clock offset='utc'/>
    <on_poweroff>destroy</on_poweroff>
    <on_reboot>restart</on_reboot>
    <on_crash>destroy</on_crash>
    <devices>
      <emulator>/usr/lib/libvirt/libvirt_lxc</emulator>
      <filesystem type='mount' accessmode='passthrough'>
        <sourcedir='/root/container/'/>
        <targetdir='/'/>
      </filesystem>
      <interface type='bridge'>
        <mac address='00:17:3e:9f:33:f7'/>
        <source bridge='lxcbr0'/>
        <link state='up'/>
      </interface>
      <console type='pty' />
    </devices>
  </domain>
  '''
```

With the preceding XML configuration assigned to a variable, we can use the `defineXML()` method to define the container. This method takes the XML definition as an argument and defines the container, but does not start it:

```
In [7]: container = lxc_conn.defineXML(domain_xml)
```

Let's verify the container was successfully defined on the host:

```
root@ubuntu:~# virsh --connect lxc:/// list --all
Id    Name                         State
----------------------------------------------------
-       libvirt_python             shut off
root@ubuntu:~#
```

We can use the `listDefinedDomains()` method to list all the defined but not the running domains, which returns a list:

```
In [8]: lxc_conn.listDefinedDomains()
Out[8]: ['libvirt_python']
```

Starting containers and running basic operations with libvirt Python

To start the previously defined container, we need to call the `create()` method:

```
In [9]: container.create()
Out[9]: 07
```

To verify the container is running on the host, after calling the `create()` method, we'll execute the following:

```
root@ubuntu:~# virsh --connect lxc:/// list --all
Id    Name                          State
-----------------------------------------------------------
23749 libvirt_python                running
root@ubuntu:~#
```

There are quite a few methods for obtaining information about the container. We can fetch the XML definition by calling the `XMLDesc()` method on the `container` object:

```
In [10]: container.XMLDesc()
Out[10]: "<domain type='lxc' id='25535'>\n  <name>libvirt_python</name>\n
<uuid>6a46bd23-f0df-461b-85e7-19fd36be90df</uuid>\n  <memory
unit='KiB'>524288</memory>\n  <currentMemory
unit='KiB'>524288</currentMemory>\n  <vcpu placement='static'>1</vcpu>\n
<resource>\n    <partition>/machine</partition>\n  </resource>\n  <os>\n
<type arch='x86_64'>exe</type>\n    <init>/sbin/init</init>\n  </os>\n
<clock offset='utc'/>\n  <on_poweroff>destroy</on_poweroff>\n
<on_reboot>restart</on_reboot>\n  <on_crash>destroy</on_crash>\n
<devices>\n    <emulator>/usr/lib/libvirt/libvirt_lxc</emulator>\n
<filesystem type='mount' accessmode='passthrough'>\n        <source
dir='/root/container/'/>\n        <target dir='/'/>\n      </filesystem>\n
<interface type='bridge'>\n        <mac address='00:17:3e:9f:33:f7'/>\n
<source bridge='lxcbr0'/>\n        <target dev='vnet0'/>\n        <link
state='up'/>\n      </interface>\n      <console type='pty' tty='/dev/pts/1'>\n
<source path='/dev/pts/1'/>\n        <target type='lxc' port='0'/>\n
<alias name='console0'/>\n      </console>\n  </devices>\n  <seclabel
type='none'/>\n</domain>\n"
```

Let's verify that the container is running by calling the `isAlive()` function that returns a Boolean:

```
In [11]: lxc_conn.isAlive()
Out[11]: 1
```

We can obtain the container ID that should match the ID we received back by running the preceding `virsh` command:

```
In [12]: lxc_conn.listDomainsID()
Out[12]: [23749]
```

No surprise here, the ID is the same.

The next code snippet iterates over a list of defined containers and returns a list of domain objects from which we print their name, by calling the `listAllDomains()` method:

```
In [13]: domains = lxc_conn.listAllDomains(0)
In [13]: for domain in domains:
    ....:     print('  '+domain.name())
    ....:
libvirt_python
```

The API provides two methods to lookup a container, by name and by ID, and assigns it to an object variable:

```
In [14]: container = lxc_conn.lookupByName("libvirt_python")
In [15]: container = lxc_conn.lookupByID(23749)
```

This is useful when we want to work with containers that already exist. The `container` object can now be used as usual, by calling its methods.

Collecting container information with libvirt Python

Let's collect information about the memory of the container. The `maxMemory()` method returns the maximum memory configured on the container:

```
In [16]: container.maxMemory()
Out[16]: 524288L
```

Collecting memory statistics is done with the `memoryStats()` method, which returns a dictionary object:

```
In [17]: container.memoryStats()
Out[17]: {'actual': 524288L, 'rss': 1388L, 'swap_in': 1388L}
```

When we defined our container earlier in the XML file, we specified the OS type of the domain to be `exe`, meaning the container will execute the specified binary. To obtain that on a running container, call the `OSType()` method:

```
In [18]: container.OSType()
Out[18]: 'exe'
```

Finally, to get more information on the container, we can call the `info()` function:

```
In [19]: container.info()
Out[19]: [1, 524288L, 1352L, 1, 8080449759L]
```

The result is a list with the following values:

Member	Description
`list[0]`	String indicating the state of the container
`list[1]`	Max container memory
`list[2]`	Current memory utilization
`list[3]`	Number of CPUs
`list[4]`	CPU time

With the container running, let's look at how we can stop it and clean up the environment next.

Stopping and deleting LXC containers with libvirt Python

Before we can destroy the container, let's verify its state and name.

```
In [20]: container.isActive()
Out[20]: 1
In [21]: container.name()
Out[21]: 'libvirt_python'
```

To stop it, call the `destroy()` method on the `container` object:

```
In [22]: container.destroy()
Out[22]: 0
```

Let's verify the container is not running on the host before we can delete it:

```
root@ubuntu:~# virsh --connect lxc:/// list --all
Id    Name                        State
--------------------------------------------------------
-       libvirt_python              shut off
root@ubuntu:~#
```

To delete the container, we invoke the `undefine()` method:

```
In [23]: container.undefine()
Out[23]: 0
root@ubuntu:~# virsh --connect lxc:/// list --all
Id    Name                        State
--------------------------------------------------------
root@ubuntu:~#
```

It's important to note that not all methods, functions, and variables are available to the libvirt LXC driver, even though they can be listed in the ipython interpreter after importing the libvirt library. This is due to the libvirt support for multiple hypervisors such as KVM and XEN. Keep this in mind when exploring the rest of the API calls.

Vagrant and LXC

Vagrant is a great open source project that provides a way for building isolated development environments, utilizing various virtualization technologies such as KVM and LXC, through the use of plugins.

In this section, we are going to briefly touch on how to set up a Vagrant development environment using LXC for isolation.

Let's start by downloading and installing Vagrant on Ubuntu:

```
root@ubuntu:~# cd /usr/src/
root@ubuntu:/usr/src# wget
https://releases.hashicorp.com/vagrant/1.8.5/vagrant_1.8.5_x86_64.deb
--2016-09-26 21:11:56--
https://releases.hashicorp.com/vagrant/1.8.5/vagrant_1.8.5_x86_64.deb
Resolving releases.hashicorp.com (releases.hashicorp.com)... 151.101.44.69
Connecting to releases.hashicorp.com
(releases.hashicorp.com)|151.101.44.69|:443... connected.
HTTP request sent, awaiting response... 200 OK
Length: 76325224 (73M) [application/x-debian-package]
Saving to: 'vagrant_1.8.5_x86_64.deb'
```

```
100%[================================================================
================================>] 76,325,224   104MB/s   in 0.7s
2016-09-26 21:11:57 (104 MB/s) - 'vagrant_1.8.5_x86_64.deb' saved
[76325224/76325224]
root@ubuntu:/usr/src#
```

Installing the package is trivial:

```
root@ubuntu:/usr/src# dpkg --install vagrant_1.8.5_x86_64.deb
Selecting previously unselected package vagrant.
(Reading database ... 60326 files and directories currently installed.)
Preparing to unpack vagrant_1.8.5_x86_64.deb ...
Unpacking vagrant (1:1.8.5) ...
Setting up vagrant (1:1.8.5) ...
root@ubuntu:/usr/src#
```

On CentOS, the steps are as follows:

1. Run the following command for downloading and installing Vagrant:

```
[root@centos ~]# cd /usr/src/
[root@centossrc]# wget
https://releases.hashicorp.com/vagrant/1.8.5/
vagrant_1.8.5_x86_64.rpm
--2016-09-26 21:16:06--
https://releases.hashicorp.com/vagrant/1.8.5/
vagrant_1.8.5_x86_64.rpm
Resolving releases.hashicorp.com (releases.hashicorp.com)...
151.101.44.69
Connecting to releases.hashicorp.com
(releases.hashicorp.com)|151.101.44.69|:443... connected.
HTTP request sent, awaiting response... 200 OK
Length: 75955433 (72M) []
Saving to: 'vagrant_1.8.5_x86_64.rpm'
100%
[==========================================================
======================================>]
75,955,433   104MB/s   in 0.7s
2016-09-26 21:16:07 (104 MB/s) - 'vagrant_1.8.5_x86_64.rpm' saved
[75955433/75955433]
[root@centossrc]# rpm --install vagrant_1.8.5_x86_64.rpm
```

2. Next, create a new bridge if it does not already exist, for LXC to attach to:

```
[root@centossrc]# brctladdbr lxcbr0
```

3. It's time to install the LXC plugin:

```
root@ubuntu:/usr/src# vagrant plugin install vagrant-lxc
Installing the 'vagrant-lxc' plugin. This can take a few minutes...
Installed the plugin 'vagrant-lxc (1.2.1)'!
root@ubuntu:/usr/src#
```

4. If all went well, list the installed Vagrant plugins:

```
root@ubuntu:/usr/src# vagrant plugin list
vagrant-lxc (1.2.1)
vagrant-share (1.1.5, system)
root@ubuntu:/usr/src#
```

5. With the LXC plugin installed, create a new project directory:

```
root@ubuntu:/usr/src# mkdirmy_project
root@ubuntu:/usr/src# cd my_project/
```

6. Next, initialize a new Vagrant environment by specifying the type of box, or virtual machine image we are going to use. In the following example, we are going to use the Ubuntu Precise LXC image from the fgremh repository:

```
root@ubuntu:/usr/src/my_project# vagrant init fgrehm/precise64-lxc
A `Vagrantfile` has been placed in this directory. You are now
ready to `vagrant up` your first virtual environment! Please read
the comments in the Vagrantfile as well as documentation on
`vagrantup.com` for more information on using Vagrant.
root@ubuntu:/usr/src/my_project#
```

As the output indicates, a new Vagrantfile was created in the project directory:

```
root@ubuntu:/usr/src/my_project# ls -alh
total 12K
drwxr-xr-x 2 root root 4.0K Sep 26 21:45 .
drwxr-xr-x 5 root root 4.0K Sep 26 21:18 ..
-rw-r--r-- 1 root root 3.0K Sep 26 21:45 Vagrantfile
root@ubuntu:/usr/src/my_project#
```

For a list of Vagrant boxes you can visit: https://atlas.hashicorp.com
/boxes/search.

Let's take a look at `Vagrantfile`:

```
root@ubuntu:/usr/src/my_project# cat Vagrantfile | grep -v "#"
| sed '/^$/d'
Vagrant.configure("2") do |config|
config.vm.box = "fgrehm/precise64-lxc"
end
root@ubuntu:/usr/src/my_project#
```

7. The configuration is very minimal, specifying the image that the Vagrant machine will use. Let's start the container, by explicitly specifying the provider:

```
root@ubuntu:/usr/src/my_project# vagrant up --provider=lxc
Bringing machine 'default' up with 'lxc' provider...
==>default: Importing base box 'fgrehm/precise64-lxc'...
==>default: Checking if box 'fgrehm/precise64-lxc' is up to date...
==>default: Setting up mount entries for shared folders...
default: /vagrant => /usr/src/my_project
==>default: Starting container...
==>default: Waiting for machine to boot. This may take a few
minutes...
default: SSH address: 10.0.3.181:22
default: SSH username: vagrant
default: SSH auth method: private key
default:
default: Vagrant insecure key detected. Vagrant will automatically
replace
default: this with a newly generated keypair for better security.
default:
default: Inserting generated public key within guest...
default: Removing insecure key from the guest if it's present...
default: Key inserted! Disconnecting and reconnecting using new SSH
key...
==>default: Machine booted and ready!
root@ubuntu:/usr/src/my_project#
```

8. To verify that we have a running LXC container, execute the following on the command line:

```
root@ubuntu:/usr/src/my_project# lxc-ls -f
NAME                            STATE   AUTOSTART GROUPS IPV4      IPV6
my_project_default_1474926399170_41712 RUNNING 0              -
10.0.3.80 -
root@ubuntu:/usr/src/my_project#
```

9. Let's check the status of the Vagrant machine:

```
root@ubuntu:/usr/src/my_project# vagrant status
Current machine states:
default                    running (lxc)
...
root@ubuntu:/usr/src/my_project#
```

10. To connect to the LXC container, run the following:

```
root@ubuntu:/usr/src/my_project# vagrant ssh
Welcome to Ubuntu 12.04.5 LTS (GNU/Linux 3.13.0-91-generic x86_64)
 * Documentation:  https://help.ubuntu.com/
vagrant@vagrant-base-precise-amd64:~$ ps ax
  PID TTY        STAT   TIME COMMAND
1 ?Ss       0:00 /sbin/init
194 ?          S       0:00 upstart-socket-bridge --daemon
2630 ?         S       0:00 upstart-udev-bridge --daemon
2653 ?Ss       0:00 /sbin/udevd --daemon
2672 ?Sl       0:00 rsyslogd -c5
2674 ?Ss       0:00 rpcbind -w
2697 ?Ss       0:00 rpc.statd -L
2830 ?Ss       0:00 dhclient3 -e IF_METRIC=100 -pf
/var/run/dhclient.eth0.pid -lf
/var/lib/dhcp/dhclient.eth0.leases -1 eth0
2852 ?Ss       0:00 /usr/sbin/sshd -D
2888 ?Ss       0:00 cron
3259 ?Ss       0:00 /sbin/getty -8 38400 tty4
3260 ?Ss       0:00 /sbin/getty -8 38400 tty2
3261 ?Ss       0:00 /sbin/getty -8 38400 tty3
3262 ?Ss       0:00 /sbin/getty -8 38400 console
3263 ?Ss       0:00 /sbin/getty -8 38400 tty1
3266 ?Ss       0:00 sshd: vagrant [priv]
3278 ?         S       0:00 sshd: vagrant@pts/9
 3279 pts/9     Ss    0:00 -bash
 3305 pts/9     R+    0:00ps ax
vagrant@vagrant-base-precise-amd64:~$ exit
logout
Connection to 10.0.3.181 closed.
root@ubuntu:/usr/src/my_project#
```

Configuring Vagrant LXC

The Vagrantfile is very well documented, but here's a brief example on how to customize the Vagrant machine by specifying the amount of memory available to the LXC container:

1. Stop the running Vagrant machine:

```
root@ubuntu:/usr/src/my_project# vagrant halt
==>default: Attempting graceful shutdown of VM...
root@ubuntu:/usr/src/my_project#
```

2. Edit Vagrantfile and set the cgroup.memory.limit_in_bytes cgroup limit. The new config should looks like this:

```
root@ubuntu:/usr/src/my_project# vim Vagrantfile
Vagrant.configure("2") do |config|
config.vm.box = "fgrehm/trusty64-lxc"
config.vm.provider :lxc do |lxc|
lxc.customize 'cgroup.memory.limit_in_bytes', '1024M'
end
end
root@ubuntu:/usr/src/my_project#
```

3. Save the file and start back the Vagrant machine:

```
root@ubuntu:/usr/src/my_project# vagrant up --provider=lxc
Bringing machine 'default' up with 'lxc' provider...
==>default: Setting up mount entries for shared folders...
default: /vagrant => /usr/src/my_project
==>default: Starting container...
==>default: Waiting for machine to boot. This may take a few
minutes...
default: SSH address: 10.0.3.181:22
default: SSH username: vagrant
default: SSH auth method: private key
==>default: Machine booted and ready!
==>default: Machine already provisioned. Run `vagrant provision` or
use the `--provision`
==>default: flag to force provisioning. Provisioners marked to run
always will still run.
root@ubuntu:/usr/src/my_project#
```

4. Verify that the cgroup limit was applied:

```
root@ubuntu:/usr/src/my_project# cat /sys/fs/cgroup/memory/lxc/
my_project_default_1474926399170_41712/memory.limit_in_bytes
1073741824
root@ubuntu:/usr/src/my_project#
```

5. Finally, let's clean up by deleting all remnants of the Vagrant machine:

```
root@ubuntu:/usr/src/my_project# vagrant destroy
default: Are you sure you want to destroy the 'default' VM? [y/N] y
==>default: Forcing shutdown of container...
==>default: Destroying VM and associated drives...
root@ubuntu:/usr/src/my_project# lxc-ls -f
NAME                      STATE    AUTOSTART GROUPS IPV4 IPV6
root@ubuntu:/usr/src/my_project#
```

Putting it all together – building a simple RESTful API to LXC with Python

With all the knowledge we have in hand by experimenting with the LXC bindings for Python earlier, we can write a simple RESTful API that will build, manage, and destroy LXC containers.

 To keep the code as simple as possible, we are going to skip all error and exception handling and any input validation from the program.

One of the simplest Python web frameworks for building APIs is Bottle. Let's install it first:

```
root@ubuntu:~# source lxc_python/bin/activate
(lxc_python) root@ubuntu:~# pip install bottle
Collecting bottle
  Downloading bottle-0.12.9.tar.gz (69kB)
    100% |███████████████████████████████████| 71kB
7.1MB/s
Building wheels for collected packages: bottle
  Running setup.py bdist_wheel for bottle ... done
  Stored in directory:
/root/.cache/pip/wheels/6e/87/89/f7ddd6721f4a208d44f2dac02f281b2403a314dd73
5d2b0e61
Successfully built bottle
Installing collected packages: bottle
```

```
Successfully installed bottle-0.12.9
(lxc_python) root@ubuntu:~#
```

Make sure you have both the `bottle` and `lxc-python2` libraries installed before continuing:

```
(lxc_python) root@ubuntu:~# pip freeze
bottle==0.12.9
lxc-python2==0.1
(lxc_python) root@ubuntu:~#
```

Let's open the new `lxc_api.py` file and write the following code:

```
import lxc
from bottle import run, request, get, post

@get('/list')
def list():
    container_list = lxc.list_containers()

    return "List of containers: {0}\n".format(container_list)

run(host='localhost', port=8080, debug=True)
```

The `run` class provides the `run()` call, which starts a built-in server. In our example, the server will be listening on localhost, port `8080`. The `get()` decorator links the code from the function below it to an URL path. In the preceding code, the `/list` path is bound to the `list()` function. Of course, you are already familiar with the `list_containers()` method.

To test this simple API frontend, save the file and execute the program:

```
(lxc_python) root@ubuntu:~# python lxc_api.py
Bottle v0.12.9 server starting up (using WSGIRefServer())...
Listening on http://localhost:8080/
Hit Ctrl+C to quit.
```

If you get the `socket.error: [Errno 98] Address already in use` error, there's another process that is bound to port `8080`. To fix this, simply change the port your Python application is listening on in the `run()` method.

In a separate terminal window, execute the following:

```
root@ubuntu:~# curl localhost:8080/list
List of containers: ()
root@ubuntu:~#
```

It's just that simple; we created an API call to list LXC containers!

API calls to build and configure LXC containers

Let's expand the functionality a bit by adding the ability to build containers. Edit the file and add the following function:

```
@post('/build')
def build():
    name = request.headers.get('X-LXC-Name')
    template = str(request.headers.get('X-LXC-Template'))

    container = lxc.Container(name)
    container.create(template)
    return "Building container {0} using the {1} template\n".format(
    name, template)
```

We are going to use the `@post` decorator in this case and the provided `headers.get()` method from the `request` class to get the custom headers that will contain the container and template names.

 For a complete API reference of the Bottle framework refer to `http://bott lepy.org/docs/dev/api.html`.

Save the updated file and restart the program. Let's test the new call in the second terminal:

```
root@ubuntu:~# curl -XPOST --header "X-LXC-Name: api_container" --header "X-LXC-
Template: ubuntu" localhost:8080/build

Building container api_container using the ubuntu template
root@ubuntu:~#
```

We used the `--header` flags to pass the container and template names with `curl` as headers, using the `POST` verb. If you check the terminal where the application is running you can see the logs of the container being built, along with the HTTP route and the error code:

```
Bottle v0.12.9 server starting up (using WSGIRefServer())...
Listening on http://localhost:8080/
Hit Ctrl-C to quit.
Copying rootfs to /var/lib/lxc/api_container/rootfs ...
Generating locales...
```

```
en_US.UTF-8... up-to-date
Generation complete.
Creating SSH2 RSA key; this may take some time ...
Creating SSH2 DSA key; this may take some time ...
Creating SSH2 ECDSA key; this may take some time ...
Creating SSH2 ED25519 key; this may take some time ...
update-rc.d: warning: default stop runlevel arguments (0 1 6) do not match
ssh
Default-Stop values (none)
invoke-rc.d: policy-rc.d denied execution of start.
...
127.0.0.1 - - [06/Oct/2016 21:36:10] "POST /build HTTP/1.1" 200 59
```

Let's use the /list route we defined earlier to list all containers:

```
root@ubuntu:~# curl localhost:8080/list
List of containers: (u'api_container',)
root@ubuntu:~#
```

Great! We can now build and list containers. Let's create a new route that will start LXC. Add the following function to the lxc_api.py file:

```
@post('/container/<name>/start')
def container_start(name):
    container = lxc.Container(name)
    container.start(useinit = False, daemonize = True)

    return "Starting container {0}\n".format(name)
```

We are using the POST decorator again and a dynamic route. The dynamic route consists of a name, in our example called <name>, which will hold whatever string value we pass to the route with the curl command. The method that is bound to the container_start(name) route also accepts a variable with the same name. Save the changes, restart the application, and execute the following:

```
root@ubuntu:~# curl -XPOST localhost:8080/container/api_container/start
Starting container api_container
root@ubuntu:~#
```

We passed api_container in the URL, and the route we defined was able to match it and pass it as a variable to the container_start function.

Our simple API does not yet provide a route to get the status of a container, so let's ensure it's really running:

```
root@ubuntu:~# lxc-ls -f
NAME            STATE    AUTOSTART GROUPS IPV4        IPV6
api_container RUNNING 0           -      10.0.3.198 -
root@ubuntu:~#
```

Let's add a `state` call to our API:

```
@get('/container/<name>/state')
def container_status(name):
    container = lxc.Container(name)
    state = container.state

    return "The state of container {0} is {1}\n".format(name, state)
```

This time we are using the `@get` decorator and calling the `state()` method on the `container` object. Let's test the new route:

```
root@ubuntu:~# curl localhost:8080/container/api_container/state
The state of container api_container is RUNNING
root@ubuntu:~#
```

Now that we have a running container, let's add the functionality to list its IP address:

```
@get('/container/<name>/ips')
def container_status(name):
    container = lxc.Container(name)
    ip_list = container.get_ips()

    return "Container {0} has the following IP's {1}\n".format(
    name, ip_list)
```

There is nothing new to note here, so let's see what we get back:

```
root@ubuntu:~# curl localhost:8080/container/api_container/ips
Container api_container has the following IP's (u'10.0.3.198',)
root@ubuntu:~#
```

We saw how to freeze and unfreeze containers earlier in this chapter; let's now add that functionality to our API:

```
@post('/container/<name>/freeze')
def container_start(name):
    container = lxc.Container(name)
    container.freeze()
```

```
    return "Freezing container {0}\n".format(name)

@post('/container/<name>/unfreeze')
def container_start(name):
    container = lxc.Container(name)
    container.unfreeze()

    return "Unfreezing container {0}\n".format(name)
```

The POST verb makes more sense here, since we are making changes to the state of the container. Let's freeze the container and check its state:

```
root@ubuntu:~# curl -XPOST localhost:8080/container/api_container/freeze
Freezing container api_container
root@ubuntu:~# curl localhost:8080/container/api_container/state
The state of container api_container is FROZEN
root@ubuntu:~# lxc-ls -f
NAME          STATE  AUTOSTART GROUPS IPV4      IPV6
api_container FROZEN 0          -        10.0.3.198 -
root@ubuntu:~#
```

Finally, let's unfreeze it with the new API call we made:

```
root@ubuntu:~# curl -XPOST localhost:8080/container/api_container/unfreeze
Unfreezing container api_container
root@ubuntu:~# curl localhost:8080/container/api_container/state
The state of container api_container is RUNNING
root@ubuntu:~# lxc-ls -f
NAME          STATE   AUTOSTART GROUPS IPV4      IPV6
api_container RUNNING 0          -        10.0.3.198 -
root@ubuntu:~#
```

Next, as a conclusion, let's write two new functions to stop and delete the container:

```
@post('/container/<name>/stop')
def container_start(name):
    container = lxc.Container(name)
    container.stop()

    return "Stopping container {0}\n".format(name)

@post('/container/<name>/destroy')
def container_start(name):
    container = lxc.Container(name)
    container.destroy()

    return "Destroying container {0}\n".format(name)
```

All the methods we've used so far, we've tested earlier in this chapter; feel free to refer back to their description as needed.

Cleaning up using the API calls

It's time to clean up, by calling the `stop` API route:

```
root@ubuntu:~# curl -XPOST localhost:8080/container/api_container/stop
Stopping container api_container

root@ubuntu:~# curl localhost:8080/container/api_container/state
The state of container api_container is STOPPED
root@ubuntu:~#
```

The console with the running application should show something similar to this after making all the preceding API calls:

```
127.0.0.1 - - [06/Oct/2016 22:00:08] "GET /container/api_container/state
HTTP/1.1" 200 48
127.0.0.1 - - [06/Oct/2016 22:02:45] "GET /container/api_container/ips
HTTP/1.1" 200 64
127.0.0.1 - - [06/Oct/2016 22:08:14] "POST /container/api_container/freeze
HTTP/1.1" 200 33
127.0.0.1 - - [06/Oct/2016 22:08:19] "GET /container/api_container/state
HTTP/1.1" 200 47
127.0.0.1 - - [06/Oct/2016 22:08:30] "POST
/container/api_container/unfreeze HTTP/1.1" 200 35
127.0.0.1 - - [06/Oct/2016 22:08:32] "GET /container/api_container/state
HTTP/1.1" 200 48
127.0.0.1 - - [06/Oct/2016 22:18:39] "POST /container/api_container/stop
HTTP/1.1" 200 33
127.0.0.1 - - [06/Oct/2016 22:18:41] "GET /container/api_container/state
HTTP/1.1" 200 48
```

Finally, let's destroy the container:

```
root@ubuntu:~# curl -XPOST localhost:8080/container/api_container/destroy
Destroying container api_container
root@ubuntu:~# lxc-ls -f
root@ubuntu:~#
```

We can easily add all the LXC Python methods we experimented with earlier, by following the same pattern – just remember to catch all exceptions and validate the input.

Here's the entire program:

```python
import lxc
from bottle import run, request, get, post

@post('/build')
def build():
    name = request.headers.get('X-LXC-Name')
    memory = request.headers.get('X-LXC-Memory')
    template = str(request.headers.get('X-LXC-Template'))

    container = lxc.Container(name)
    container.create(template)

    return "Building container {0} using the {1} template\n".format(
    name, template)

@post('/container/<name>/start')
def container_start(name):
    container = lxc.Container(name)
    container.start(useinit=False, daemonize=True)

    return "Starting container {0}\n".format(name)

@post('/container/<name>/stop')
def container_start(name):
    container = lxc.Container(name)
    container.stop()

    return "Stopping container {0}\n".format(name)

@post('/container/<name>/destroy')
def container_start(name):
    container = lxc.Container(name)
    container.destroy()

    return "Destroying container {0}\n".format(name)

@post('/container/<name>/freeze')
def container_start(name):
    container = lxc.Container(name)
    container.freeze()

    return "Freezing container {0}\n".format(name)

@post('/container/<name>/unfreeze')
def container_start(name):
    container = lxc.Container(name)
```

```
    container.unfreeze()

    return "Unfreezing container {0}\n".format(name)

@get('/container/<name>/state')
def container_status(name):
    container = lxc.Container(name)
    state = container.state

    return "The state of container {0} is {1}\n".format(name, state)

@get('/container/<name>/ips')
def container_status(name):
    container = lxc.Container(name)
    ip_list = container.get_ips()

    return "Container {0} has the following IP's {1}\n".format(
    name, ip_list)

@get('/list')
def list():
    container_list = lxc.list_containers()

    return "List of containers: {0}\n".format(container_list)

run(host='localhost', port=8080, debug=True)
```

Summary

The bindings for Python provided by the LXC and libvirt APIs are a great way to programmatically create and manage LXC containers.

In this chapter, we explored both sets of Python bindings, by writing simple code snippets that implement most of the functions provided by the userspace tools. In fact, the best way to learn about those APIs is to look at the source code of the command-line tools, although they are implemented in C.

We had a brief introduction in how to provision LXC with Vagrant for testing your code in isolation. We ended the chapter with a working implementation of a simple RESTful API that uses some of the methods we explored earlier to provision, manage, and destroy LXC. In Chapter 5, *Networking in LXC with the Linux Bridge and Open vSwitch*, we'll explore the networking aspects of LXC, using the Linux bridge, Open vSwitch in NAT, and direct routing modes, and look into examples of how to interconnect containers and the host OS.

5
Networking in LXC with the Linux Bridge and Open vSwitch

To enable network connectivity for a newly built container we need a way to connect the virtual network interfaces from the container's network namespace to the host and provide routing to either other containers or the Internet, if needed. Linux provides a software bridge that allows us to *wire* LXC containers together in a variety of ways, as we'll explore in this chapter.

There are two popular software bridge implementations – the Linux bridge provided by the `bridge-utils` package and the Open vSwitch project. These extend the basic functionality of the Linux bridge even further, by separating the control and management planes of the switch, allowing for the control of the traffic flow and providing for hardware integration among other things.

By default, when we build a container from the provided templates, the template script sets up networking by configuring a software bridge on the host OS using **Network Address Translation (NAT)** rules in `iptables`. In this mode, the container gets its IP address from a `dnsmasq` server that LXC starts. However, we have full control on what bridge, mode, or routing we would like to use, by means of the container's configuration file.

In this chapter, we'll explore the following topics:

- Installing and configuring the Linux bridge
- Installing and creating an Open vSwitch switch
- Configuring networking in LXC using NAT, direct connect, VLAN, and other modes

Software bridging in Linux

Connecting LXC or any other type of virtual machine such as KVM or Xen, the hypervisor layer, or in the case of LXC, the host OS, requires the ability to bridge traffic between the containers/VMs and the outside world. Software bridging in Linux has been supported since the kernel version 2.4. To take advantage of this functionality, bridging needs to be enabled in the kernel by setting **Networking support** | **Networking options** | **802.1d Ethernet Bridging** to yes, or as a kernel module when configuring the kernel.

To check what bridging options are compiled in the kernel, or available as modules, run the following command:

```
root@host:~# cat /boot/config-`uname -r` | grep -ibridge
# PC-card bridges
CONFIG_BRIDGE_NETFILTER=y
CONFIG_NF_TABLES_BRIDGE=m
CONFIG_BRIDGE_NF_EBTABLES=m
CONFIG_BRIDGE_EBT_BROUTE=m
CONFIG_BRIDGE_EBT_T_FILTER=m
CONFIG_BRIDGE_EBT_T_NAT=m
CONFIG_BRIDGE_EBT_802_3=m
CONFIG_BRIDGE_EBT_AMONG=m
CONFIG_BRIDGE_EBT_ARP=m
CONFIG_BRIDGE_EBT_IP=m
CONFIG_BRIDGE_EBT_IP6=m
CONFIG_BRIDGE_EBT_LIMIT=m
CONFIG_BRIDGE_EBT_MARK=m
CONFIG_BRIDGE_EBT_PKTTYPE=m
CONFIG_BRIDGE_EBT_STP=m
CONFIG_BRIDGE_EBT_VLAN=m
CONFIG_BRIDGE_EBT_ARPREPLY=m
CONFIG_BRIDGE_EBT_DNAT=m
CONFIG_BRIDGE_EBT_MARK_T=m
CONFIG_BRIDGE_EBT_REDIRECT=m
CONFIG_BRIDGE_EBT_SNAT=m
CONFIG_BRIDGE_EBT_LOG=m
# CONFIG_BRIDGE_EBT_ULOG is not set
CONFIG_BRIDGE_EBT_NFLOG=m
CONFIG_BRIDGE=m
CONFIG_BRIDGE_IGMP_SNOOPING=y
CONFIG_BRIDGE_VLAN_FILTERING=y
CONFIG_SSB_B43_PCI_BRIDGE=y
CONFIG_DVB_DDBRIDGE=m
CONFIG_EDAC_SBRIDGE=m
# VME Bridge Drivers
root@host:~#
```

On Ubuntu and CentOS systems, the bridging is available as kernel modules. To verify that they are loaded, run the following command:

```
root@ubuntu:~# lsmod | grep bridge
bridge                110925  0
stp                    12976  1 bridge
llc                    14552  2 stp,bridge
root@ubuntu:~#
```

To obtain more information about the `bridge` kernel module, execute the following command:

```
[root@centos ~]# modinfo bridge
filename:
/lib/modules/3.10.0-327.28.3.el7.x86_64/kernel/net/bridge/bridge.ko
alias:          rtnl-link-bridge
version:        2.3
license:        GPL
rhelversion:    7.2
srcversion:     905847C53FF43DEFAA0EB3C
depends:        stp,llc
intree:         Y
vermagic:       3.10.0-327.28.3.el7.x86_64 SMP mod_unloadmodversions
signer:         CentOS Linux kernel signing key
sig_key:        15:64:6F:1E:11:B7:3F:8C:2A:ED:8A:E2:91:65:5D:52:58:05:6E:E9
sig_hashalgo:   sha256
[rootcentos ~]#
```

If you are using a distribution that does not have the bridge compiled in the kernel, or available as a module, or if you would like to experiment with different kernel options, you'll need the kernel source first.

To install it on Ubuntu, you can do this by running the following command:

```
root@ubuntu:~# cd /usr/src/
root@ubuntu:/usr/src# apt-get install linux-source ncurses-dev
root@ubuntu:/usr/src# cd linux-source-3.13.0/
root@ubuntu:/usr/src/linux-source-3.13.0# tar jxfv linux-
source-3.13.0.tar.bz2
root@ubuntu:/usr/src/linux-source-3.13.0# cd linux-source-3.13.0/
```

On CentOS, install the kernel source with `yum`:

```
[root@bridge ~]# yum install kernel-devel ncurses-devel
```

To use the `ncurses` menu for configuring the kernel, run the following command:

```
root@ubuntu:/usr/src/linux-source-3.13.0/linux-source-3.13.0# make
menuconfig
```

Navigate to **Networking support** | **Networking options** | **802.1d Ethernet Bridging** and select either **Y** to compile the bridging functionality in the kernel, or **M** to compile it as a module.

The kernel configuration menu looks like this:

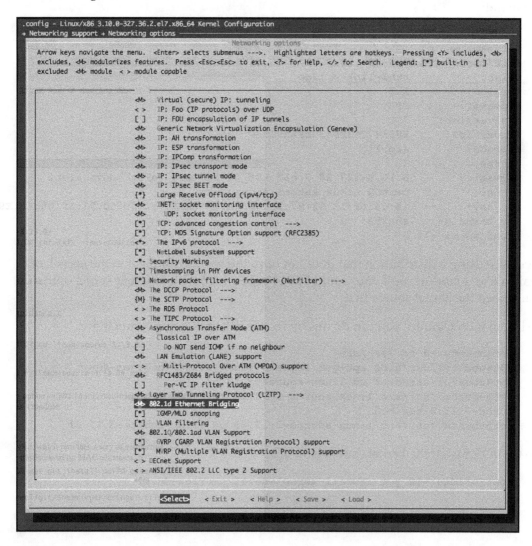

Once you make the selections, build the new kernel package and install it:

```
root@bridge:/usr/src/linux-source-3.13.0/linux-source-3.13.0# make deb-pkg
  CHK     include/config/kernel.release
make KBUILD_SRC=
SYSHDR  arch/x86/syscalls/../include/generated/uapi/asm/unistd_32.h
SYSHDR  arch/x86/syscalls/../include/generated/uapi/asm/unistd_64.h
...
dpkg-deb: building package `linux-firmware-image-3.13.11-ckt39'
in `../linux-firmware-image-3.13.11-ckt39_3.13.11-ckt39-1_amd64.deb'.
dpkg-deb: building package `linux-headers-3.13.11-ckt39'
in `../linux-headers-3.13.11-ckt39_3.13.11-ckt39-1_amd64.deb'.
dpkg-deb: building package `linux-libc-dev'
in `../linux-libc-dev_3.13.11-ckt39-1_amd64.deb'.
dpkg-deb: building package `linux-image-3.13.11-ckt39'
in `../linux-image-3.13.11-ckt39_3.13.11-ckt39-1_amd64.deb'.
dpkg-deb: building package `linux-image-3.13.11-ckt39-dbg'
in `../linux-image-3.13.11-ckt39-dbg_3.13.11-ckt39-1_amd64.deb'.

root@ubuntu:/usr/src/linux-source-3.13.0/linux-source-3.13.0# ls -la
../*.deb
-rw-r--r-- 1 root root    803530 Oct 19 18:04 ../linux-firmware-
image-3.13.11-ckt39_3.13.11-ckt39-1_amd64.deb
-rw-r--r-- 1 root root   6435516 Oct 19 18:04 ../linux-headers-3.13.11-
ckt39_3.13.11-ckt39-1_amd64.deb
-rw-r--r-- 1 root root  39640242 Oct 19 18:07 ../linux-image-3.13.11-
ckt39_3.13.11-ckt39-1_amd64.deb
-rw-r--r-- 1 root root 363727500 Oct 19 18:37 ../linux-image-3.13.11-ckt39-
dbg_3.13.11-ckt39-1_amd64.deb
-rw-r--r-- 1 root root    768606 Oct 19 18:04 ../linux-libc-dev_3.13.11-
ckt39-1_amd64.deb
root@ubuntu:/usr/src/linux-source-3.13.0/linux-source-3.13.0#
```

To use the new kernel, install the packages and reboot.

 For more information on how to compile and install the Linux kernel from source, refer to your distribution's documentation.

The Linux bridge

The built-in Linux bridge is a software layer 2 device. OSI layer 2 devices provide a way of connecting multiple Ethernet segments together and forward traffic based on MAC addresses, effectively creating separate broadcast domains.

Let's start by installing the latest version from source on Ubuntu:

```
root@ubuntu:~# cd /usr/src/
root@ubuntu:/usr/src# apt-get update && apt-get install build-essential
automakepkg-config git
root@ubuntu:/usr/src# git clone
git://git.kernel.org/pub/scm/linux/kernel/git/shemminger/bridge-utils.git
Cloning into 'bridge-utils'...
remote: Counting objects: 654, done.
remote: Total 654 (delta 0), reused 0 (delta 0)
Receiving objects: 100% (654/654), 131.72 KiB | 198.00 KiB/s, done.
Resolving deltas: 100% (425/425), done.
Checking connectivity... done.

root@ubuntu:/usr/src# cd bridge-utils/
root@ubuntu:/usr/src/bridge-utils# autoconf
root@ubuntu:/usr/src/bridge-utils# ./configure && make && make install
root@ubuntu:/usr/src/bridge-utils# brctl --version
bridge-utils, 1.5
root@ubuntu:/usr/src/bridge-utils#
```

From the preceding output, we can see that we first cloned the `git` repository for the `bridge-utils` project and then compiled the source code.

To compile the bridging software on CentOS, the process is similar to what we did in the previous section; first we install the prerequisite packages, then configure and compile, as follows:

```
[root@centos ~]# cd /usr/src/
[root@centossrc]#
[root@centossrc]# yum groupinstall "Development tools"
[root@centossrc]# git clone
git://git.kernel.org/pub/scm/linux/kernel/git/shemminger/bridge-utils.git
Cloning into 'bridge-utils'...
remote: Counting objects: 654, done.
remote: Total 654 (delta 0), reused 0 (delta 0)
Receiving objects: 100% (654/654), 131.72 KiB | 198.00 KiB/s, done.
Resolving deltas: 100% (425/425), done.
Checking connectivity... done.

[root@centossrc]# cd bridge-utils
[root@centos bridge-utils]# autoconf
[root@centos bridge-utils]# ./configure && make && make install
[root@centos bridge-utils]# brctl --version
bridge-utils, 1.5
[root@centos bridge-utils]#
```

Invoking the `brctl` command without any parameters shows what operations are available:

```
root@ubuntu:/usr/src/bridge-utils# brctl
Usage: brctl [commands]
commands:
  addbr     <bridge>        add bridge
  delbr     <bridge>        delete bridge
  addif     <bridge><device>  add interface to bridge
  delif     <bridge><device>  delete interface from bridge
  hairpin        <bridge><port> {on|off}  turn hairpin on/off
  setageing  <bridge><time>     set ageing time
  setbridgeprio  <bridge><prio>    set bridge priority
  setfd     <bridge><time>    set bridge forward delay
  sethello  <bridge><time>    set hello time
  setmaxage  <bridge><time>     set max message age
  setpathcost  <bridge><port><cost>  set path cost
  setportprio  <bridge><port><prio>  set port priority
  show  [ <bridge> ]      show a list of bridges
  showmacs  <bridge>      show a list of mac addrs
  showstp  <bridge>       show bridge stp info
  stp  <bridge> {on|off}  turn stp on/off
root@ubuntu:/usr/src/bridge-utils#
```

The Linux bridge and the LXC package on Ubuntu

Let's install the LXC package and dependencies. To check the latest available package version from the repositories you have configured on your system, run the following command:

```
root@ubuntu:~# apt-cache madison lxc
    lxc | 2.0.4-0ubuntu1~ubuntu14.04.1 |
http://us-east-1.ec2.archive.ubuntu.com/ubuntu/ trusty-backports/main amd64
Packages
    lxc | 1.0.8-0ubuntu0.3 |
http://us-east-1.ec2.archive.ubuntu.com/ubuntu/ trusty-updates/main amd64
Packages
    lxc | 1.0.7-0ubuntu0.7 | http://security.ubuntu.com/ubuntu/ trusty-
security/main amd64 Packages
    lxc | 1.0.3-0ubuntu3 | http://us-east-1.ec2.archive.ubuntu.com/ubuntu/
trusty/main amd64 Packages
    lxc | 1.0.3-0ubuntu3 | http://us-east-1.ec2.archive.ubuntu.com/ubuntu/
trusty/main Sources
    lxc | 1.0.8-0ubuntu0.3 |
http://us-east-1.ec2.archive.ubuntu.com/ubuntu/ trusty-updates/main Sources
    lxc | 2.0.4-0ubuntu1~ubuntu14.04.1 |
```

```
http://us-east-1.ec2.archive.ubuntu.com/ubuntu/ trusty-backports/main
Sources
    lxc | 1.0.7-0ubuntu0.7 | http://security.ubuntu.com/ubuntu/ trusty-
security/main Sources
root@ubuntu:~#
```

The output is from an Amazon EC2 instance, showing that the latest LXC version is
`2.0.4-0ubuntu1~ubuntu14.04.1`. Let's install it and observe the output:

```
root@ubuntu:/usr/src/bridge-utils# apt-get install -y
lxc=2.0.4-0ubuntu1~ubuntu14.04.1 lxc1=2.0.4-0ubuntu1~ubuntu14.04.1
liblxc1=2.0.4-0ubuntu1~ubuntu14.04.1 python3-
lxc=2.0.4-0ubuntu1~ubuntu14.04.1 cgroup-lite=1.11~ubuntu14.04.2 lxc-
templates=2.0.4-0ubuntu1~ubuntu14.04.1
...
Setting up lxc1 (2.0.4-0ubuntu1~ubuntu14.04.1) ...
lxc-net start/running
Setting up lxc dnsmasq configuration.
...
root@ubuntu:/usr/src/bridge-utils#
```

Notice how the package installs and configures the `dnsmasq` service, due to package
dependencies in the `lxc1.postinst` script part of the `lxc` package. This is quite
convenient on Ubuntu, but if the distribution you are running does not support that, or you
are compiling LXC from source, you can always install that manually. You only need to do
this if you prefer `dnsmasq` to assign IP addresses to your containers dynamically. You can
always configure the LXC containers with static IP addresses.

From the preceding output, we can also observe that the package started the `lxc-net`
service. Let's look into that by checking its status:

```
root@ubuntu:/usr/src/bridge-utils# service lxc-net status
lxc-net start/running
root@ubuntu:/usr/src/bridge-utils#
```

Also, take a look at the `init` configuration file:

```
root@ubuntu:/usr/src/bridge-utils# cat /etc/init/lxc-net.conf
description "lxc network"
author "Serge Hallyn<serge.hallyn@canonical.com>"
start on starting lxc
stop on stopped lxc
pre-start exec /usr/lib/x86_64-linux-gnu/lxc/lxc-net start
post-stop exec /usr/lib/x86_64-linux-gnu/lxc/lxc-net stop
root@ubuntu:/usr/src/bridge-utils#
```

We can see that the `init` script starts the `lxc-net` service. Let's see what this provides:

```
root@ubuntu:/usr/src/bridge-utils# head -24 /usr/lib/x86_64-linux-
gnu/lxc/lxc-net
#!/bin/sh -
distrosysconfdir="/etc/default"
varrun="/run/lxc"
varlib="/var/lib"
# These can be overridden in /etc/default/lxc
#   or in /etc/default/lxc-net
USE_LXC_BRIDGE="true"
LXC_BRIDGE="lxcbr0"
LXC_ADDR="10.0.3.1"
LXC_NETMASK="255.255.255.0"
LXC_NETWORK="10.0.3.0/24"
LXC_DHCP_RANGE="10.0.3.2,10.0.3.254"
LXC_DHCP_MAX="253"
LXC_DHCP_CONFILE=""
LXC_DOMAIN=""
LXC_IPV6_ADDR=""
LXC_IPV6_MASK=""
LXC_IPV6_NETWORK=""
LXC_IPV6_NAT="false"
root@bridge:/usr/src/bridge-utils#
```

From the first few lines of the preceding script we can see that it sets up LXC networking defaults, such as the name of the Linux bridge and the subnet that will be assigned by the `dnsmasq` service. It also points us to the default LXC network file that we can use to override those options.

Let's take a look at the default `lxc-net` file:

```
root@ubuntu:/usr/src/bridge-utils# cat /etc/default/lxc-net  | grep -vi ^#
USE_LXC_BRIDGE="true"
LXC_BRIDGE="lxcbr0"
LXC_ADDR="10.0.3.1"
LXC_NETMASK="255.255.255.0"
LXC_NETWORK="10.0.3.0/24"
LXC_DHCP_RANGE="10.0.3.2,10.0.3.254"
LXC_DHCP_MAX="253"
root@ubuntu:/usr/src/bridge-utils#
```

LXC on Ubuntu is packaged in such a way that it also creates the bridge for us:

```
root@ubuntu:/usr/src/bridge-utils# brctl show
bridge name    bridge id              STP enabled   interfaces
lxcbr0         8000.000000000000      no
root@ubuntu:/usr/src/bridge-utils#
```

Notice the name of the bridge—`lxcbr0`—is the one specified in the `/etc/default/lxc-net` file and the `/usr/lib/x86_64-linux-gnu/lxc/lxc-net` script.

The Linux bridge and the LXC package on CentOS

Unfortunately, not all Linux distributions package LXC with the extra functionality of building the bridge, and configuring and starting `dnsmasq`, as we saw in the earlier section with Ubuntu. Building LXC from source, as described in Chapter 2, *Installing and Running LXC on Linux Systems*, or using the CentOS packages, will not automatically create the Linux bridge, or configure and start the `dnsmasq` service.

Let's explore this in more detail on CentOS, by building an LXC container named `bridge`, using the `centos` template:

```
[root@centos ~]# yum install lxc lxc-templates
[root@centos ~]# lxc-create --name bridge -t centos
Host CPE ID from /etc/os-release: cpe:/o:centos:centos:7
Checking cache download in /var/cache/lxc/centos/x86_64/7/rootfs ...
Downloading centos minimal ...
Loaded plugins: fastestmirror, langpacks
...
Container rootfs and config have been created.
Edit the config file to check/enable networking setup.
...
[root@centos ~]#
```

Let's check if a bridge was created after the `lxc` package was installed and the container was built:

```
[root@centos ~]# brctl show
[root@centos ~]#
```

If we try to start the container, we'll get the following errors:

```
[root@centos ~]# lxc-ls -f
bridge

[root@centos ~]# lxc-start --name bridge
lxc-start: conf.c: instantiate_veth: 3105 failed to attach 'veth5TVOEO' to
the bridge 'virbr0': No such device
lxc-start: conf.c: lxc_create_network: 3388 failed to create netdev
lxc-start: start.c: lxc_spawn: 841 failed to create the network
lxc-start: start.c: __lxc_start: 1100 failed to spawn 'bridge'
```

```
lxc-start: lxc_start.c: main: 341 The container failed to start.
lxc-start: lxc_start.c: main: 345 Additional information can be obtained by
setting the --logfile and --logpriority options.
[root@centos ~]#
```

The preceding output shows that the container is trying to connect to a bridge named virbr0, which does not exist. The name is defined in the following file and then assigned to the container's configuration:

```
[root@centos ~]# cat /etc/lxc/default.conf
lxc.network.type = veth
lxc.network.link = virbr0
lxc.network.flags = up

[root@centos ~]# cat /var/lib/lxc/bridge/config  | grep -vi "#" | sed
'/^$/d' | grep network
lxc.network.type = veth
lxc.network.flags = up
lxc.network.link = virbr0
lxc.network.hwaddr = fe:6e:b6:af:24:2b
[root@centos ~]#
```

In order to successfully start the container, we'll have to first create the bridge that LXC expects:

```
[root@centos ~]# brctl addbr virbr0
```

Then start the container again and check the bridge:

```
[root@centos~]# lxc-start --name bridge
[root@centos~]# brctl show
bridge name     bridge id             STP enabled    interfaces
virbr0          8000.fe1af1cb0b2e     no             vethB6CRLW
[root@centos ~]#
```

The vethB6CRLW interface is the virtual interface that the LXC container presents to the host and connects to the virbr0 bridge port:

```
[root@centos ~]# ifconfig vethB6CRLW
vethB6CRLW: flags=4163<UP,BROADCAST,RUNNING,MULTICAST>mtu 1500
inet6 fe80::fc1a:f1ff:fecb:b2e  prefixlen 64  scopeid 0x20<link>
ether fe:1a:f1:cb:0b:2e  txqueuelen 1000   (Ethernet)
        RX packets 14  bytes 2700 (2.6 KiB)
        RX errors 0  dropped 0  overruns 0   frame 0
        TX packets 8  bytes 648 (648.0 B)
        TX errors 0  dropped 0 overruns 0   carrier 0   collisions
        0
[root@centos ~]#
```

The preceding output displays the current configuration for the virtual interface of the `bridge` container we built earlier, as seen by the host OS.

Using dnsmasq service to obtain an IP address in the container

The `dnsmasq` service that was started after installing the `lxc` package on Ubuntu should look similar to the following:

```
root@bridge:/usr/src/bridge-utils# pgrep -lfaww dnsmasq
12779 dnsmasq -u lxc-dnsmasq --strict-order --bind-interfaces
--pid-file=/run/lxc/dnsmasq.pid --listen-address 10.0.3.1
--dhcp-range 10.0.3.2,10.0.3.254 --dhcp-lease-max=253
--dhcp-no-override --except-interface=lo --interface=lxcbr0
--dhcp-leasefile=/var/lib/misc/dnsmasq.lxcbr0.leases
--dhcp-authoritative
root@bridge:/usr/src/bridge-utils#
```

 Note, the `dhcp-range` parameter matches what was defined in the `/etc/default/lxc-net` file.

Let's create a new container and explore its network settings:

```
root@bridge:/usr/src/bridge-utils# lxc-create -t ubuntu --name br1
Checking cache download in /var/cache/lxc/trusty/rootfs-amd64 ...
Installing packages in template: apt-transport-https,ssh,vim,language-pack-
en
Downloading ubuntu trusty minimal ...
...
##
# The default user is 'ubuntu' with password 'ubuntu'!
# Use the 'sudo' command to run tasks as root in the container.
##
root@bridge:/usr/src/bridge-utils# lxc-start --name br1
root@bridge:/usr/src/bridge-utils# lxc-info --name br1
Name:          br1
State:         RUNNING
PID:           1773
IP:            10.0.3.65
CPU use:       1.66 seconds
BlkIO use:     160.00 KiB
Memory use:    7.27 MiB
KMem use:      0 bytes
```

```
Link:           veth366R6F
 TX bytes:      1.85 KiB
 RX bytes:      1.59 KiB
 Total bytes:   3.44 KiB
root@bridge:/usr/src/bridge-utils#
```

Notice the name of the virtual interface that was created on the host OS – `veth366R6F`, from the output of the `lxc-info` command. The interface should have been added as a port to the bridge. Let's confirm this using the `brctl` utility:

```
root@bridge:/usr/src/bridge-utils# brctl show
bridge name   bridge id          STP enabled    interfaces
lxcbr0        8000.fe7a39cee87c  no             veth366R6F
root@bridge:/usr/src/bridge-utils#
```

Listing all interfaces on the host shows the bridge and the virtual interface associated with the container:

```
root@bridge:~# ifconfig
eth0      Link encap:EthernetHWaddr bc:76:4e:10:6a:31
inet addr:10.208.131.214  Bcast:10.208.255.255  Mask:255.255.128.0
inet6addr: fe80::be76:4eff:fe10:6a31/64 Scope:Link
          UP BROADCAST RUNNING MULTICAST  MTU:1500  Metric:1
          RX packets:322 errors:0 dropped:0 overruns:0 frame:0
          TX packets:337 errors:0 dropped:0 overruns:0 carrier:0
          collisions:0 txqueuelen:1000
          RX bytes:14812 (14.8 KB)  TX bytes:14782 (14.7 KB)
lo        Link encap:Local Loopback
inet addr:127.0.0.1  Mask:255.0.0.0
inet6addr: ::1/128 Scope:Host
          UP LOOPBACK RUNNING  MTU:65536  Metric:1
          RX packets:9 errors:0 dropped:0 overruns:0 frame:0
          TX packets:9 errors:0 dropped:0 overruns:0 carrier:0
          collisions:0 txqueuelen:0
          RX bytes:668 (668.0 B)  TX bytes:668 (668.0 B)
lxcbr0    Link encap:EthernetHWaddr fe:7a:39:ce:e8:7c
inet addr:10.0.3.1  Bcast:0.0.0.0  Mask:255.255.255.0
inet6addr: fe80::fc7a:39ff:fece:e87c/64 Scope:Link
          UP BROADCAST RUNNING MULTICAST  MTU:1500  Metric:1
          RX packets:53 errors:0 dropped:0 overruns:0 frame:0
          TX packets:57 errors:0 dropped:0 overruns:0 carrier:0
          collisions:0 txqueuelen:0
          RX bytes:4268 (4.2 KB)  TX bytes:5450 (5.4 KB)
veth366R6F Link encap:EthernetHWaddr fe:7a:39:ce:e8:7c
inet6addr: fe80::fc7a:39ff:fece:e87c/64 Scope:Link
          UP BROADCAST RUNNING MULTICAST  MTU:1500  Metric:1
          RX packets:53 errors:0 dropped:0 overruns:0 frame:0
          TX packets:58 errors:0 dropped:0 overruns:0 carrier:0
```

```
                collisions:0 txqueuelen:1000
                RX bytes:5010 (5.0 KB)  TX bytes:5528 (5.5 KB)
    root@bridge:~#
```

Notice the IP address assigned to the `lxcbr0` interface—it's the same IP address passed as the `listen-address` argument to the `dnsmasq` process. Let's examine the network interface and the routes inside the container by attaching to it first:

```
root@bridge:~# lxc-attach --name br1
root@br1:~# ifconfig
eth0      Link encap:EthernetHWaddr 00:16:3e:39:cf:e9
inet addr:10.0.3.65  Bcast:10.0.3.255  Mask:255.255.255.0
inet6addr: fe80::216:3eff:fe39:cfe9/64 Scope:Link
          UP BROADCAST RUNNING MULTICAST  MTU:1500  Metric:1
          RX packets:58 errors:0 dropped:0 overruns:0 frame:0
          TX packets:53 errors:0 dropped:0 overruns:0 carrier:0
          collisions:0 txqueuelen:1000
          RX bytes:5528 (5.5 KB)  TX bytes:5010 (5.0 KB)
lo        Link encap:Local Loopback
inet addr:127.0.0.1  Mask:255.0.0.0
inet6addr: ::1/128 Scope:Host
          UP LOOPBACK RUNNING  MTU:65536  Metric:1
          RX packets:0 errors:0 dropped:0 overruns:0 frame:0
          TX packets:0 errors:0 dropped:0 overruns:0 carrier:0
          collisions:0 txqueuelen:0
          RX bytes:0 (0.0 B)  TX bytes:0 (0.0 B)

root@br1:~# route -n
Kernel IP routing table
Destination     Gateway         Genmask         Flags Metric Ref    Use
Iface
0.0.0.0         10.0.3.1        0.0.0.0         UG    0      0        0
eth0
10.0.3.0        0.0.0.0         255.255.255.0   U     0      0        0
eth0
root@br1:~#
```

The IP address assigned to the `eth0` interface by `dnsmasq` is part of the `10.0.3.0/24` subnet and the default gateway is the IP of the bridge interface on the host. The reason the container automatically obtained an IP address is its interface configuration file:

```
root@br1:~# cat /etc/network/interfaces
# This file describes the network interfaces available on your system
# and how to activate them. For more information, see interfaces(5).
# The loopback network interface
auto lo
iface lo inet loopback
auto eth0
```

```
iface eth0 inetdhcp
root@br1:~#
```

As the preceding output shows, eth0 is configured to use DHCP. If we would rather use statically assigned addresses, we only have to change that file and specify whatever IP address we would like to use. Using DHCP with dnsmasq is not required for LXC networking, but it can be a convenience.

Let's change the range of IPs that dnsmasq offers, by not assigning the first one hundred IPs in the /etc/default/lxc-net file:

```
root@bridge:/usr/src/bridge-utils# sed -i
's/LXC_DHCP_RANGE="10.0.3.2,10.0.3.254"/LXC_DHCP_RANGE="10.0.3.100,10.0.3.2
54"/g' /etc/default/lxc-net

root@bridge:/usr/src/bridge-utils# grep LXC_DHCP_RANGE /etc/default/lxc-net
LXC_DHCP_RANGE="10.0.3.100,10.0.3.254"
root@bridge:/usr/src/bridge-utils#
```

After restarting dnsmasq, observe the new DHCP range passed as the dhcp-range parameter:

```
root@bridge:/usr/src/bridge-utils# pgrep -lfaww dnsmasq
4215 dnsmasq -u lxc-dnsmasq --strict-order --bind-interfaces
--pid-file=/run/lxc/dnsmasq.pid --listen-address 10.0.3.1
--dhcp-range 10.0.3.100,10.0.3.254 --dhcp-lease-max=253
--dhcp-no-override --except-interface=lo --interface=lxcbr0 --dhcp-
leasefile=/var/lib/misc/dnsmasq.lxcbr0.leases
--dhcp-authoritative
root@bridge:/usr/src/bridge-utils#
```

The next time we build a container using the Ubuntu template, the IP address that will be assigned to the container will start from 100 for the fourth octet. This is handy if we want to use the first 100 IPs for manual assignment, as we'll see next.

Statically assigning IP addresses in the LXC container

Assigning an IP address inside the container is not any different than configuring a regular Linux server. While attached to the container, run the following commands:

```
root@br1:~# ifconfig eth0 10.0.3.10 netmask 255.255.255.0
root@br1:~# route add default gw 10.0.3.1
root@br1:~# ping -c 3 10.0.3.1
```

```
PING 10.0.3.1 (10.0.3.1) 56(84) bytes of data.
64 bytes from 10.0.3.1: icmp_seq=1 ttl=64 time=0.053 ms
64 bytes from 10.0.3.1: icmp_seq=2 ttl=64 time=0.073 ms
64 bytes from 10.0.3.1: icmp_seq=3 ttl=64 time=0.074 ms
--- 10.0.3.1 ping statistics ---
3 packets transmitted, 3 received, 0% packet loss, time 1998ms
rtt min/avg/max/mdev = 0.053/0.066/0.074/0.013 ms
root@br1:~#
```

To make the change persistent, edit the file as follows, then stop and start the container:

```
root@br1:~# cat /etc/network/interfaces
auto lo
iface lo inet loopback
auto eth0
  iface eth0 inet static
  address 10.0.3.10
  netmask 255.255.255.0
  gateway 10.0.3.1
root@br1:~# exit
root@ubuntu:~#lxc-stop --name br1 && lxc-start --name br1
```

Let's use the `brctl` utility to see what MAC addresses the bridge knows about:

```
root@ubuntu:~# brctl showmacs lxcbr0
port no    mac addr          is local?    ageing timer
1          fe:7a:39:ce:e8:7c   yes          0.00
root@ubuntu:~#
```

Notice how this is the MAC of the `veth366R6F` virtual interface and the bridge, as listed by `ifconfig` on the host from the earlier output.

Overview of LXC network configuration options

Let's examine the network configuration for the `br1` container we built earlier:

```
root@ubuntu:~# cat /var/lib/lxc/br1/config | grep -vi "#" | sed  '/^$/d' |
grep -i network
lxc.network.type = veth
lxc.network.link = lxcbr0
lxc.network.flags = up
lxc.network.hwaddr = 00:16:3e:39:cf:e9
root@ubuntu:~#
```

An impoing to note is the `lxc.network.hwaddr` option. It is the MAC of `eth0` inside the container that was dynamically generated for us. All of the configuration options can be changed, before or after the creation of the container.

The following table describes briefly what network configuration options are available to the container:

Option	Description
`lxc.network.type`	The type of network virtualization to be used
`lxc.network.link`	The interface on the host
`lxc.network.flags`	An action to perform on the interface
`lxc.network.hwaddr`	Sets a MAC address on the container's interface
`lxc.network.mtu`	Sets the **Maximum Transfer Unit (MTU)** for the container's interface
`lxc.network.name`	Specifies the interface name
`lxc.network.ipv4`	The IPv4 address to be assigned to the container
`lxc.network.ipv4.gateway`	The IPv4 address to be used as the default gateway
`lxc.network.ipv6`	The IPv6 address to be assigned to the container
`lxc.network.ipv6.gateway`	The IPv6 address to be used as the default gateway
`lxc.network.script.up`	Specifies a script to be executed after creating and configuring the network
`lxc.network.script.down`	Specifies a script to be executed before destroying the network

Table 5.1

We'll explore most of the options from this table in more detail, later in this chapter.

Manually manipulating the Linux bridge

Let's finish our exploration of the Linux bridge by showing a few examples of how to manually work with it.

We can start by showing the bridge on the host by running the following command:

```
root@ubuntu:~# brctl show
bridge name    bridge id           STP enabled  interfaces
lxcbr0         8000.000000000000   no
root@ubuntu:~#
```

To delete the bridge, the interface needs to be brought down first:

```
root@ubuntu:~# ifconfig lxcbr0 down
root@ubuntu:~# brctl delbr lxcbr0
root@ubuntu:~# brctl show
root@ubuntu:~#
```

Next, let's create a new bridge and add one of the containers' interfaces to it that is exposed on the host OS, veth366R6F, in this example:

```
root@ubuntu:~# brctl addbr lxcbr0
root@ubuntu:~# brctl show
bridge name    bridge id           STP enabled  interfaces
lxcbr0         8000.000000000000   no

root@ubuntu:~# brctl addif lxcbr0 veth366R6F
root@ubuntu:~# brctl show
bridge name    bridge id           STP enabled  interfaces
lxcbr0         8000.fe7a39cee87c   no           veth366R6F
root@ubuntu:~#
```

The bridge has been created, but the interface associated with it needs to be brought up as the error, as shown here:

```
root@ubuntu:~# ifconfig lxcrb0
lxcrb0: error fetching interface information: Device not found

root@ubuntu:~# ifconfig lxcbr0 up
root@ubuntu:~# ifconfig lxcbr0
lxcbr0    Link encap:EthernetHWaddr fe:7a:39:ce:e8:7c
inet6addr: fe80::fc7a:39ff:fece:e87c/64 Scope:Link
          UP BROADCAST RUNNING MULTICAST  MTU:1500  Metric:1
          RX packets:0 errors:0 dropped:0 overruns:0 frame:0
          TX packets:6 errors:0 dropped:0 overruns:0 carrier:0
          collisions:0 txqueuelen:0
          RX bytes:0 (0.0 B)  TX bytes:508 (508.0 B)
root@ubuntu:~#
```

Finally, let's assign an IP address to the bridge that the containers can use as their default gateway:

```
root@bridge:~# ifconfig lxcbr0 10.0.3.1 netmask 255.255.255.0
root@bridge:~#
```

Open vSwitch

Open vSwitch (OVS) is a software switch that allows for more advanced network configurations, such as policy routing, **Access Control Lists (ACLs)**, **Quality of Service (QoS)** policing, traffic monitoring, flow management, VLAN tagging, GRE tunneling, and more. OVS can be used as an alternative to the Linux bridge. In the next chapter, we'll build a software-defined network using OVS and GRE tunnels to isolate a group of LXC containers, but for now, let's demonstrate how to install and configure it in a way similar to the Linux bridge.

Let's start by installing the package on Ubuntu:

```
root@ubuntu:~# apt-get install openvswitch-switch
...
Setting up openvswitch-common (2.0.2-0ubuntu0.14.04.3) ...
Setting up openvswitch-switch (2.0.2-0ubuntu0.14.04.3) ...
openvswitch-switch start/running
...

root@ubuntu:~# ovs-vsctl --version
ovs-vsctl (Open vSwitch) 2.0.2
Compiled Dec  9 2015 14:08:08
root@ubuntu:~#
```

OVS uses a kernel module that should be loaded:

```
root@ubuntu:~# lsmod | grep switch
openvswitch            70989  0
vxlan                  37611  1 openvswitch
gre                    13796  1 openvswitch
libcrc32c              12644  1 openvswitch
root@ubuntu:~#
```

Next, let's confirm there are no switches configured:

```
root@bridge:~# ovs-vsctl show
4cf17055-87a7-4b01-a8eb-4a551c842342
ovs_version: "2.0.2"
root@bridge:~#
```

The following processes are started after installing the package:

```
root@bridge:~# pgrep -lfa switch
9424 ovsdb-server /etc/openvswitch/conf.db -vconsole:emer
-vsyslog:err -vfile:info --remote=punix:/var/run/openvswitch/db.sock
--private-key=db:Open_vSwitch,SSL,private_key
--certificate=db:Open_vSwitch,SSL,certificate
--bootstrap-ca-cert=db:Open_vSwitch,SSL,ca_cert --no-chdir
--log-file=/var/log/openvswitch/ovsdb-server.log
--pidfile=/var/run/openvswitch/ovsdb-server.pid --detach --monitor
9433 ovs-vswitchd: monitoring pid 9434 (healthy)
9434 ovs-vswitchdunix:/var/run/openvswitch/db.sock -vconsole:emer
-vsyslog:err -vfile:info --mlockall --no-chdir
--log-file=/var/log/openvswitch/ovs-vswitchd.log
--pidfile=/var/run/openvswitch/ovs-vswitchd.pid --detach --monitor
root@bridge:~#
```

The `ovsdb-server` is a database engine that uses JSON RPC and can run independent of OVS. The `ovsdb-server` accepts connections from the `ovs-vswitchd` daemon, which in turn can create and modify bridges, ports, network flows, and so on. As a quick example, we can list the databases managed by the `ovsdb-server` process and the various tables it contains:

```
root@ubuntu:~# ovsdb-client list-dbs
Open_vSwitch

root@ubuntu:~# ovsdb-client dump | grep table
Bridge table
Controller table
Flow_Sample_Collector_Set table
Flow_Table table
IPFIX table
Interface table
Manager table
Mirror table
NetFlow table
Open_vSwitch table
Port table
QoS table
Queue table
SSL table
sFlow table
root@ubuntu:~#
```

The `ovs-vswitchd` process is the main OVS application that controls all switches on the host OS.

Now it's time to create a switch and name it `lxcovs0`:

```
root@ubuntu:~# ovs-vsctl add-br lxcovs0
root@ubuntu:~# ovs-vsctl show
4cf17055-87a7-4b01-a8eb-4a551c842342
    Bridge "lxcovs0"
        Port "lxcovs0"
            Interface "lxcovs0"
                type: internal
ovs_version: "2.0.2"
root@ubuntu:~#
```

Next, assign an IP address and attach the container's virtual interface to it, by creating a port:

```
root@ubuntu:~# ifconfig lxcovs0 192.168.0.1 netmask 255.255.255.0
root@ubuntu:~# ovs-vsctl add-port lxcovs0 veth366R6F
root@ubuntu:~# ovs-vsctl show
4cf17055-87a7-4b01-a8eb-4a551c842342
    Bridge "lxcovs0"
        Port "lxcovs0"
            Interface "lxcovs0"
                type: internal
        Port "veth366R6F"
            Interface "veth366R6F"
ovs_version: "2.0.2"
root@ubuntu:~#
```

The `veth366R6F` interface belongs to the `br1` container we built earlier in this chapter. To test connectivity, attach to the container, and change the IP address and default gateway to be the port of the OVS network:

```
root@ubuntu:~# lxc-attach --name br1
root@br1:~# ifconfig eth0 192.168.0.10 netmask 255.255.255.0
root@br1:~# route add default gw 192.168.0.1
```

To avoid conflict with the Linux bridge, ensure the bridge is destroyed and the kernel module is unloaded:

```
root@ubuntu:~# ifconfig lxcbr0 down
root@ubuntu:~# brctl delbr lxcbr0
root@ubuntu:~# modprobe -r bridge
root@ubuntu:~#
```

Connecting LXC to the host network

There are three main modes of connecting LXC containers to the host network:

- Using a physical network interface on the host OS, which requires one physical interface on the host for each container
- Using a virtual interface connected to the host software bridge using NAT
- Sharing the same network namespace as the host, using the host network device in the container

The container configuration file provides the `lxc.network.type` option as we saw earlier in Table 5.1. Let's take a look at the available parameters for that configuration option:

Parameter	Description
none	The container will share the host's network namespace.
empty	LXC will create only the loopback interface.
veth	A virtual interface is created on the host and connected to interface inside the container's network namespace.
vlan	Creates a VLAN interface linked to the device specified with `lxc.network.link`. The VLAN ID is specified with the `lxc.network.vlan.id` option.
macvlan	Allows a single physical interface to be associated with multiple IPs and MAC addresses.
phys	Assigns a physical interface from the host to the container, using the `lxc.network.link` option.

Let's explore the network configurations in more details.

Configuring LXC using none network mode

In this mode, the container will share the same network namespace as the host. Let's configure the `br1` container we created in the beginning of this chapter for that mode:

```
root@ubuntu:~# vim /var/lib/lxc/br1/config
# Common configuration
lxc.include = /usr/share/lxc/config/ubuntu.common.conf
# Container specific configuration
lxc.rootfs = /var/lib/lxc/br1/rootfs
```

```
lxc.rootfs.backend = dir
lxc.utsname = br1
lxc.arch = amd64
# Network configuration
lxc.network.type = none
lxc.network.flags = up
```

Stop and start the container for the new network options to take effect, and attach to the container:

```
root@ubuntu:~# lxc-stop --name br1 && lxc-start --name br1
root@ubuntu:~# lxc-attach --name br1
root@br1:~#
```

Let's check the interface configuration and network routes inside the container:

```
root@br1:~# ifconfig
eth0      Link encap:EthernetHWaddr bc:76:4e:10:6a:31
inet addr:10.208.131.214  Bcast:10.208.255.255  Mask:255.255.128.0
inet6addr: fe80::be76:4eff:fe10:6a31/64 Scope:Link
          UP BROADCAST RUNNING MULTICAST  MTU:1500  Metric:1
          RX packets:35205 errors:0 dropped:0 overruns:0 frame:0
          TX packets:35251 errors:0 dropped:0 overruns:0 carrier:0
          collisions:0 txqueuelen:1000
          RX bytes:1621243 (1.6 MB)  TX bytes:1486058 (1.4 MB)
lo        Link encap:Local Loopback
inet addr:127.0.0.1  Mask:255.0.0.0
inet6addr: ::1/128 Scope:Host
          UP LOOPBACK RUNNING  MTU:65536  Metric:1
          RX packets:9 errors:0 dropped:0 overruns:0 frame:0
          TX packets:9 errors:0 dropped:0 overruns:0 carrier:0
          collisions:0 txqueuelen:0
          RX bytes:668 (668.0 B)  TX bytes:668 (668.0 B)
lxcovs0   Link encap:EthernetHWaddr b2:e1:c6:c8:e6:40
inet addr:192.168.0.1  Bcast:192.168.0.255  Mask:255.255.255.0
inet6addr: fe80::b0e1:c6ff:fec8:e640/64 Scope:Link
          UP BROADCAST RUNNING  MTU:1500  Metric:1
          RX packets:18557 errors:0 dropped:0 overruns:0 frame:0
          TX packets:678 errors:0 dropped:0 overruns:0 carrier:0
          collisions:0 txqueuelen:0
          RX bytes:6190048 (6.1 MB)  TX bytes:5641977 (5.6 MB)

root@br1:~# route -n
Kernel IP routing table
Destination     Gateway          Genmask          Flags Metric Ref   Use
Iface
```

```
0.0.0.0          10.208.128.1     0.0.0.0          UG    0       0       0
eth0
10.208.0.0       10.208.128.1     255.240.0.0      UG    0       0       0
eth0
10.208.128.0     0.0.0.0          255.255.128.0    U     0       0       0
eth0
root@br1:~#
```

Not surprisingly, the network interfaces and routes inside the container are the same as those on the host OS, since both share the same root network namespace.

Let's check the network connectivity while attached to the container:

```
root@br1:~# ping 8.8.8.8
PING 8.8.8.8 (8.8.8.8) 56(84) bytes of data.
64 bytes from 8.8.8.8: icmp_seq=1 ttl=48 time=11.7 ms
64 bytes from 8.8.8.8: icmp_seq=2 ttl=48 time=11.8 ms
root@br1:~# exit
root@ubuntu:~#
```

> Stopping the container in this mode will cause the host OS to shutdown, so be careful.

Configuring LXC using empty network mode

The `empty` mode only creates the loopback interface in the container. The configuration file looks similar to the following output:

```
root@ubuntu:~# vim /var/lib/lxc/br1/config
# Common configuration
lxc.include = /usr/share/lxc/config/ubuntu.common.conf
# Container specific configuration
lxc.rootfs = /var/lib/lxc/br1/rootfs
lxc.rootfs.backend = dir
lxc.utsname = br1
lxc.arch = amd64
# Network configuration
lxc.network.type = empty
lxc.network.flags = up
```

Restart the container and attach to it, so we can verify the loopback interface is the only device present:

```
root@ubuntu:~# lxc-stop --name br1 && sleep 5 && lxc-start --name br1
root@ubuntu:~# lxc-attach --name br1
root@br1:~#
```

Let's check the interface configuration and network routes inside the container:

```
root@br1:~# ifconfig
lo          Link encap:Local Loopback
inet addr:127.0.0.1  Mask:255.0.0.0
inet6addr:  ::1/128 Scope:Host
            UP LOOPBACK RUNNING  MTU:65536  Metric:1
            RX packets:0 errors:0 dropped:0 overruns:0 frame:0
            TX packets:0 errors:0 dropped:0 overruns:0 carrier:0
            collisions:0 txqueuelen:0
            RX bytes:0 (0.0 B)  TX bytes:0 (0.0 B)
root@br1:~# route -n
Kernel IP routing table
Destination     Gateway         Genmask         Flags Metric Ref    Use
Iface
root@br1:~# exit
root@ubuntu:~#
```

As expected, only the loopback interface is present and no routes are configured.

Configuring LXC using veth mode

The NAT mode is the default network mode when creating containers using the LXC template scripts or the libvirt userspace tools. In this mode, the container can reach the outside world using IP masquerading with iptables rules applied on the host. All examples we saw in previous chapters use the veth mode.

In this mode, LXC creates a virtual interface on the host named something like veth366R6F. This is one end of the virtual connection from the container and it should be connected to the software bridge. The other end of the connection is the interface inside the container, by default named eth0.

The following diagram helps visualize the network configuration:

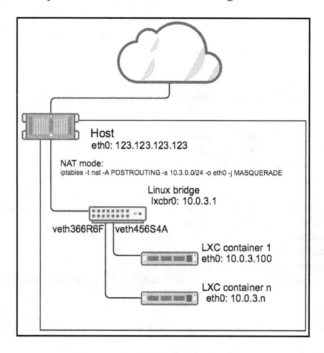

LXC in veth mode

The container configuration is displayed here:

```
root@ubuntu:~# cat /var/lib/lxc/br1/config
# Common configuration
lxc.include = /usr/share/lxc/config/ubuntu.common.conf
# Container specific configuration
lxc.rootfs = /var/lib/lxc/br1/rootfs
lxc.rootfs.backend = dir
lxc.utsname = br1
lxc.arch = amd64
# Network configuration
lxc.network.type = veth
lxc.network.link = lxcovs0
lxc.network.flags = up
lxc.network.hwaddr = 00:16:3e:39:cf:e9
root@ubuntu:~#
```

The `lxc.network.link` option specifies the network device on the host the virtual interface should connect to, in this case, the `lxcovs0` OVS switch that was created earlier.

Notice the `iptables` masquerade rule that was applied on the host:

```
root@ubuntu:~# iptables -L -n -t nat
Chain PREROUTING (policy ACCEPT)
target       prot opt source              destination
Chain INPUT (policy ACCEPT)
target       prot opt source              destination
Chain OUTPUT (policy ACCEPT)
target       prot opt source              destination
Chain POSTROUTING (policy ACCEPT)
target       prot opt source              destination
MASQUERADE   all  --  10.0.3.0/24         !10.0.3.0/24
root@ubuntu:~#
```

> If for some reason the `iptables` rule is not present, or you would like to build a container that is on a different subnet, adding a new rule can be done with the `iptables -t nat -A POSTROUTING -s 10.3.0.0/24 -o eth0 -j MASQUERADE` command.

Configuring LXC using phys mode

In this mode, we specify a physical interface from the host with the `lxc.network.link` configuration option, which will get assigned to the network namespace of the container and then make it unavailable for use by the host.

The following diagram helps visualize the network configuration:

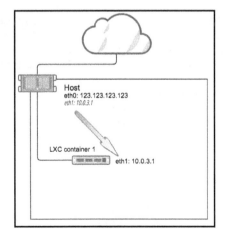

LXC in phys mode

Let's take a look at the configuration file:

```
root@ubuntu:~# vim /var/lib/lxc/br1/config
# Common configuration
lxc.include = /usr/share/lxc/config/ubuntu.common.conf
# Container specific configuration
lxc.rootfs = /var/lib/lxc/br1/rootfs
lxc.rootfs.backend = dir
lxc.utsname = br1
lxc.arch = amd64
# Network configuration
lxc.network.type = phys
lxc.network.link = eth1
lxc.network.ipv4 = 10.208.131.214/24
lxc.network.hwaddr = bc:76:4e:10:6a:31
lxc.network.flags = up
root@ubuntu:~#
```

We specify phys as the mode of networking, eth1 as the interface from the host that will be moved in the container's namespace, and the IP and MAC addresses of eth1. Let's take a look at all network interfaces on the host first:

```
root@ubuntu:~# ip a s
1: lo: <LOOPBACK,UP,LOWER_UP>mtu 65536 qdiscnoqueue state UNKNOWN group
default
    link/loopback 00:00:00:00:00:00 brd 00:00:00:00:00:00
      inet 127.0.0.1/8 scope host lo
        valid_lft forever preferred_lft forever
      inet6 ::1/128 scope host
        valid_lft forever preferred_lft forever
2: eth0: <BROADCAST,MULTICAST,UP,LOWER_UP>mtu 1500 qdiscpfifo_fast state UP
group default qlen 1000
    link/ether bc:76:4e:10:57:b8 brdff:ff:ff:ff:ff:ff
      inet 192.168.167.122/24 brd 192.237.167.255 scope global eth0
        valid_lft forever preferred_lft forever
      inet6 fe80::be76:4eff:fe10:57b8/64 scope link
        valid_lft forever preferred_lft forever
3: eth1: <BROADCAST,MULTICAST,UP,LOWER_UP>mtu 1500 qdiscpfifo_fast state UP
group default qlen 1000
    link/ether bc:76:4e:10:6a:31 brdff:ff:ff:ff:ff:ff
      inet 10.208.131.214/17 brd 10.208.255.255 scope global eth1
        valid_lft forever preferred_lft forever
      inet6 fe80::be76:4eff:fe10:6a31/64 scope link
        valid_lft forever preferred_lft forever
4: lxcbr0: <BROADCAST,MULTICAST,UP,LOWER_UP>mtu 1500 qdiscnoqueue state
UNKNOWN group default
    link/ether 52:26:ad:1d:1a:7f brdff:ff:ff:ff:ff:ff
      inet 10.0.3.1/24 scope global lxcbr0
```

```
        valid_lft forever preferred_lft forever
      inet6 fe80::5026:adff:fe1d:1a7f/64 scope link
        valid_lft forever preferred_lft forever
5: ovs-system: <BROADCAST,MULTICAST>mtu 1500 qdiscnoop state DOWN group
default
   link/ether c2:05:a1:f4:7f:89 brdff:ff:ff:ff:ff:ff
6: lxcovs0: <BROADCAST,UP,LOWER_UP>mtu 1500 qdiscnoqueue state UNKNOWN
group default
   link/ether b2:e1:c6:c8:e6:40 brdff:ff:ff:ff:ff:ff
      inet6 fe80::b0e1:c6ff:fec8:e640/64 scope link
        valid_lft forever preferred_lft forever
root@ubuntu:~#
```

Notice that the `eth1` interface is present on the host. Let's restart the `br1` container and list the host interfaces again:

```
root@ubuntu:~# lxc-stop --name br1 && lxc-start --name br1
root@ubuntu:~# ip a s
1: lo: <LOOPBACK,UP,LOWER_UP>mtu 65536 qdiscnoqueue state UNKNOWN group
default
   link/loopback 00:00:00:00:00:00 brd 00:00:00:00:00:00
      inet 127.0.0.1/8 scope host lo
        valid_lft forever preferred_lft forever
      inet6 ::1/128 scope host
        valid_lft forever preferred_lft forever
2: eth0: <BROADCAST,MULTICAST,UP,LOWER_UP>mtu 1500 qdiscpfifo_fast state UP
group default qlen 1000
   link/ether bc:76:4e:10:57:b8 brdff:ff:ff:ff:ff:ff
      inet 192.168.167.122/24 brd 192.237.167.255 scope global eth0
        valid_lft forever preferred_lft forever
      inet6 fe80::be76:4eff:fe10:57b8/64 scope link
        valid_lft forever preferred_lft forever
4: lxcbr0: <BROADCAST,MULTICAST,UP,LOWER_UP>mtu 1500 qdiscnoqueue state
UNKNOWN group default
   link/ether 52:26:ad:1d:1a:7f brdff:ff:ff:ff:ff:ff
      inet 10.0.3.1/24 scope global lxcbr0
        valid_lft forever preferred_lft forever
      inet6 fe80::5026:adff:fe1d:1a7f/64 scope link
        valid_lft forever preferred_lft forever
5: ovs-system: <BROADCAST,MULTICAST>mtu 1500 qdiscnoop state DOWN group
default
   link/ether c2:05:a1:f4:7f:89 brdff:ff:ff:ff:ff:ff
6: lxcovs0: <BROADCAST,UP,LOWER_UP>mtu 1500 qdiscnoqueue state UNKNOWN
group default
   link/ether b2:e1:c6:c8:e6:40 brdff:ff:ff:ff:ff:ff
      inet6 fe80::b0e1:c6ff:fec8:e640/64 scope link
        valid_lft forever preferred_lft forever
root@ubuntu:~#
```

The eth1 interface is not showing on the host anymore. Let's attach to the container and examine its interfaces:

```
root@ubuntu:~# lxc-attach --name br1
root@br1:~# ip a s
1: lo: <LOOPBACK,UP,LOWER_UP>mtu 65536 qdiscnoqueue state UNKNOWN group
default
    link/loopback 00:00:00:00:00:00 brd 00:00:00:00:00:00
        inet 127.0.0.1/8 scope host lo
          valid_lft forever preferred_lft forever
        inet6 ::1/128 scope host
          valid_lft forever preferred_lft forever
3: eth1: <BROADCAST,MULTICAST,UP,LOWER_UP>mtu 1500 qdiscpfifo_fast state UP
group default qlen 1000
    link/ether bc:76:4e:10:6a:31 brdff:ff:ff:ff:ff:ff
        inet 10.208.131.214/24 brd 10.208.131.255 scope global eth1
          valid_lft forever preferred_lft forever
        inet6 fe80::be76:4eff:fe10:6a31/64 scope link
          valid_lft forever preferred_lft forever
root@br1:~#
```

The eth1 interface is now a part of the container, with the same IP and MAC address as the original eth1 interface from the host, because we explicitly specified them in the container's configuration file.

If we need to have multiple containers using the phys mode, then we'll need that many physical interfaces, which is not always practical.

Configuring LXC using vlan mode

The vlan network mode allows us to create a **Virtual LAN (VLAN)** tagged interface inside the container's network namespace. A VLAN is a broadcast domain that is isolated at the data link layer from the rest of the network.

The lxc.network.link configuration option specifies the interface the container should be linked to from the host and lxc.network.vlan.id is the tag that will be applied to the network traffic by the container's interface.

This mode is useful when there are multiple containers running on hosts and the traffic needs to be isolated between subsets of containers, thus creating a logical network separation. We demonstrated similar concepts with VLAN tags when we talked about network namespaces in Chapter 1, *Introduction to Linux Containers*.

To create a container that will be tagging Ethernet packets, the configuration should look similar to the following:

```
root@ubuntu:~# cat /var/lib/lxc/br1/config
# Common configuration
lxc.include = /usr/share/lxc/config/ubuntu.common.conf
# Container specific configuration
lxc.rootfs = /var/lib/lxc/br1/rootfs
lxc.rootfs.backend = dir
lxc.utsname = br1
lxc.arch = amd64
# Network configuration
lxc.network.type = vlan
lxc.network.vlan.id = 100
lxc.network.link = eth1
lxc.network.flags = up
root@ubuntu:~#
```

We specify a VLAN ID of `100` and `eth1` as the interface the container will be paired with. Restart the container and attach to it:

```
root@ubuntu:~# lxc-stop --name br1 && lxc-start --name br1
root@ubuntu:~# lxc-attach --name br1
root@br1:~#
```

Let's examine the `eth0` interface from the container and ensure it's configured to tag packets with a VLAN ID of `100`:

```
root@br1:~# ip -d link show eth0
10: eth0@if3: <BROADCAST,MULTICAST,UP,LOWER_UP>mtu 1500 qdiscnoqueue state
UP mode DEFAULT group default
    link/ether bc:76:4e:10:6a:31 brdff:ff:ff:ff:ff:ff promiscuity 0
vlan protocol 802.1Q id 100 <REORDER_HDR>
root@br1:~#
```

Notice how the `eth0` interface is named `eth0@if3`. Here, `if3` means that the container's interface is paired with the host interface that has an ID of `3`, in our case `eth1`. We can see that by running the following command on the host:

```
root@br1:~# exit
root@ubuntu:~# ip -d link show eth1
3: eth1: <BROADCAST,MULTICAST,UP,LOWER_UP> mtu 1500 qdisc pfifo_fast state
UP mode DEFAULT group default qlen 1000
    link/ether bc:76:4e:10:6a:31 brd ff:ff:ff:ff:ff:ff promiscuity 0
root@ubuntu:~#
```

Now you can configure eth0 inside the container to be part of the same subnet as the eth1 interface on the host.

Configuring LXC using macvlan mode

The macvlan network mode allows for a single physical interface on the host to be associated with multiple virtual interfaces having different IP and MAC addresses. There are three modes that macvlan can operate in:

- **Private**: This mode disallows communication between LXC containers
- **Virtual Ethernet Port Aggregator** (**VEPA**): This mode disallows communication between LXC containers unless there's a switch that works as a reflective relay
- **Bridge**: This mode creates a simple bridge (not to be confused with the Linux bridge or OVS), which allows containers to talk to each other, but it isolates them from the host.

Let's configure the br1 container to use macvlan in bridge mode:

```
root@ubuntu:~# cat /var/lib/lxc/br1/config
# Common configuration
lxc.include = /usr/share/lxc/config/ubuntu.common.conf
# Container specific configuration
lxc.rootfs = /var/lib/lxc/br1/rootfs
lxc.rootfs.backend = dir
lxc.utsname = br1
lxc.arch = amd64
# Network configuration
lxc.network.type = macvlan
lxc.network.macvlan.mode = bridge
lxc.network.link = lxcmacvlan0
lxc.network.flags = up
```

The device that we specify with lxc.network.link is the bridged interface we are going to create next:

```
root@ubuntu:~# iplink add lxcmacvlan0 link eth1 type macvlan mode bridge
root@ubuntu:~# ifconfig lxcmacvlan0 up
root@ubuntu:~# ip -d link show lxcmacvlan0
12: lxcmacvlan0@eth1: <BROADCAST,MULTICAST,UP,LOWER_UP>mtu 1500
qdiscnoqueue state UNKNOWN mode DEFAULT group default
  link/ether ae:de:56:01:2f:b6 brdff:ff:ff:ff:ff:ff promiscuity 0
macvlan  mode bridge
root@ubuntu:~#
```

With the `macvlan` bridged interface up, we can start the container and examine its network interfaces:

```
root@ubuntu:~# lxc-stop --name br1 && lxc-start --name br1
root@ubuntu:~# lxc-attach --name br1
root@br1:~# ip -d link show eth0
13: eth0@if3: <BROADCAST,MULTICAST,UP,LOWER_UP>mtu 1500 qdiscnoqueue state
UNKNOWN mode DEFAULT group default
    link/ether aa:6e:cb:74:0c:fc brdff:ff:ff:ff:ff:ff promiscuity 0
macvlan  mode bridge
root@br1:~#
```

Notice the `if3` ID of the `eth0` interface in the container matches the `eth1` ID on the host. We can now assign an IP address to the `eth0` interface from the same subnet as `eth1` on the host and be able to reach other containers in the same subnet. This mode is similar to using the Linux bridge or OVS, but without the overhead of each. Also notice that the containers will not be able to communicate with the host directly.

Summary

In this chapter, you became familiar with the Linux Bridge and learned how to connect LXC containers to it. We also looked at Open vSwitch as an alternative to the Linux bridge. We then explored the various network configuration options that LXC presents and saw few examples.

We ended the chapter by demonstrating how to connect LXC to the host network and to other containers using, NAT, VLAN, direct connect, and more advanced nodes such as MAC VLAN.

In the next chapter, we are going to put all the knowledge you gained so far into practice, by building a highly available and scalable application deployment using LXC and HAProxy.

6
Clustering and Horizontal Scaling with LXC

Running applications inside LXC containers provides for a convenient way of allocating and limiting resources, as we saw in earlier chapters. LXC is also great for creating clusters of applications, for example, a web-server farm that can be scaled horizontally or vertically.

Horizontal scaling is a way of adding more computing power to a cluster or a group of resources performing a common task. This is usually accomplished by adding more servers, virtual machines, or in the case of LXC, more containers to run the applications. In contrast, vertical scaling is done by adding more hardware or virtual resources, such as CPU and memory, to physical servers, VMs, or containers.

In this chapter, we are going to put all the knowledge you've gained so far toward do the following:

- Creating a simple Apache cluster, running LXC on a minimal root filesystem with libvirt
- Implementing a multinode web cluster with Apache and HAProxy using Open vSwitch and a mesh of GRE tunnels
- Demonstrating how to add more containers by reusing the filesystem of existing LXC instances

Scaling applications with LXC

LXC is pretty well-suited for virtual machine replacement in sense that it can contain a complete root filesystem for a Linux distribution, in which case, the only shared component with the host OS is the kernel. Applications can be installed in the container's root filesystem so that the host or other containers cannot share them. This isolation is useful if we want to run different versions of the same application and its dependencies, or different Linux distributions altogether.

On the other hand, libvirt LXC allows for the execution of a single process or a group of processes from a binary which is shared from the host OS by all containers. In this case, the containers share the host filesystem and only abstract certain directories. This helps in scenarios where the application might not need its own dedicated filesystem, if, for example, the Linux distribution in the container is the same as the host OS. Scaling such applications is a matter of ensuring that the service is installed on the host and the necessary config files are present on the minimal root filesystem in the container. We can then make a copy of the container's configuration file and the minimal root filesystem, and start it without many changes.

In the next two sections, we'll explore both scenarios. We'll start by building minimal root filesystem Apache containers with libvirt and load balancing them with HAProxy, and then move on to build an Apache cluster with LXC, and dedicated filesystems and network isolation with Open vSwitch with a mesh of GRE tunnels.

Scaling Apache in minimal root filesystem with libvirt LXC

In this section, we'll demonstrate how to run multiple Apache servers on the same host using libvirt LXC and a minimal root filesystem for each container. The Apache binary and libraries will be shared among containers. Even though this approach may not be most suitable for Apache, but rather simpler single-threaded processes, it will help us demonstrate this concept in a more practical manner.

For this example, we'll use Ubuntu, but the same instructions apply to CentOS, as we demonstrated in `Chapter 2`, *Installing and Running LXC on Linux Systems*. Following are the steps for the example:

1. Let's begin by updating the OS and ensure it's running the latest kernel:

```
root@ubuntu:~# apt-get update && apt-get upgrade --yes && reboot
root@lxc:~# lsb_release -a 2>/dev/null
Distributor ID:    Ubuntu
Description:        Ubuntu 16.04.1 LTS
Release:    16.04
Codename:    xenial
root@ubuntu:~#

root@ubuntu:~# uname -r
4.4.0-38-generic
root@ubuntu:~#
```

2. The latest libvirt package on Ubuntu Xenial as of this writing is shown here:

```
root@ubuntu:~# apt-cache policy libvirt-bin
libvirt-bin:
Installed:
Candidate: 1.3.1-1ubuntu10.5
Version table:
*** 1.3.1-1ubuntu10.5 500
        500 http://rackspace.clouds.archive.ubuntu.com/ubuntu
        xenial-updates/main amd64 Packages
        100 /var/lib/dpkg/status
    1.3.1-1ubuntu10 500
        500 http://rackspace.clouds.archive.ubuntu.com/ubuntu
        xenial/main amd64 Packages
root@ubuntu:~#
```

3. Next, install the libvirt packages:

```
root@ubuntu:~# apt-get install libvirt-bin virtinst
root@ubuntu:~# dpkg --list | grep libvirt
ii  libvirt-bin      1.3.1-1ubuntu10.5        amd64
programs for the libvirt library
ii  libvirt0:amd64      1.3.1-1ubuntu10.5        amd64
library for interfacing with different virtualization systems
ii  python-libvirt      1.3.1-1ubuntu1        amd64
libvirt Python bindings
root@ubuntu:~#
```

4. Conveniently, libvirt created the bridge for us:

```
root@ubuntu:~# brctl show
bridge name       bridge id               STP enabled   interfaces
virbr0            8000.5254003d3c43   yes               virbr0-nic
root@ubuntu:~#
```

5. We'll be using the `default` libvirt network; let's ensure it is present:

```
root@ubuntu:~# export LIBVIRT_DEFAULT_URI=lxc:///
root@ubuntu:~# virsh net-list --all
Name              State       Autostart     Persistent
----------------------------------------------------------------
default           active      yes           yes
root@ubuntu:~#
```

6. To examine the `default` network and gateway that libvirt will use, run the following command:

```
root@ubuntu:~# virsh net-dumpxml default
<network>
  <name>default</name>
  <uuid>6585ac5b-3d81-4071-bb61-3aa22007834e</uuid>
  <forward mode='nat'>
    <nat>
      <port start='1024' end='65535'/>
    </nat>
  </forward>
  <bridge name='virbr0' stp='on' delay='0'/>
  <mac address='52:54:00:3d:3c:43'/>
  <ip address='192.168.122.1' netmask='255.255.255.0'>
    <dhcp>
      <range start='192.168.122.2' end='192.168.122.254'/>
    </dhcp>
  </ip>
</network>
root@ubuntu:~#
```

7. The libvirt toolkit also started `dnsmasq`, which will assign the network settings to the LXC containers if we configure them to use DHCP:

```
root@ubuntu:~# ps axfww
5310 ?          Ssl     0:00 /usr/sbin/libvirtd
5758 ?          S       0:00 /usr/sbin/dnsmasq
--conf-file=/var/lib/libvirt/dnsmasq/default.conf
--leasefile-ro
--dhcp-script=/usr/lib/libvirt/libvirt_leaseshelper
5759 ?          S       0:00  \_ /usr/sbin/dnsmasq
--conf-file=/var/lib/libvirt/dnsmasq/default.conf
--leasefile-ro
--dhcp-script=/usr/lib/libvir/libvirt_leaseshelper
```

8. We'll be using the default `dnsmasq` config, but let's ensure the DHCP range matches what `libvirt-net` knows from the preceding output:

```
root@ubuntu:~# cat /var/lib/libvirt/dnsmasq/default.conf
| grep -vi "#"
strict-order
user=libvirt-dnsmasq
pid-file=/var/run/libvirt/network/default.pid
except-interface=lo
bind-dynamic
interface=virbr0
dhcp-range=192.168.122.2,192.168.122.254
dhcp-no-override
dhcp-lease-max=253
dhcp-hostsfile=/var/lib/libvirt/dnsmasq/default.hostsfile
addn-hosts=/var/lib/libvirt/dnsmasq/default.addnhosts
root@ubuntu:~#
```

Creating the minimal root filesystem for the containers

For this example, we are not going to use the provided templates or use the `debootstrap` command to build a full-fledged filesystem for the container, but instead create a minimal directory structure to host the configuring files for Apache and the container. The rest will be in the same `mount` namespace as the host OS, with the exception of a few directories that we are going to bind to the container.

Follow these steps to create the minimal root filesystem for the containers:

1. Let's start by creating the directories; copy the necessary files and install Apache on the host:

```
root@ubuntu:~# cd /opt/
root@ubuntu:/opt# mkdir -p containers/http1/etc
root@ubuntu:/opt# mkdir -p containers/http1/var/www/html
root@ubuntu:/opt# apt-get install --yes apache2
...
root@ubuntu:/opt# cp -r /etc/apache2/ /opt/containers/http1/etc/
root@ubuntu:/opt# cp -r /etc/passwd /opt//containers/http1/etc/
root@ubuntu:/opt# cp -r /etc/shadow /opt//containers/http1/etc/
root@ubuntu:/opt# cp -r /etc/group /opt//containers/http1/etc/
root@ubuntu:/opt# cp -r /etc/mime.types /opt//containers/http1/etc/
root@ubuntu:/opt# cp -r /etc/init.d/ /opt//containers/http1/etc/
root@ubuntu:/opt# cp -r /etc/resolv.conf /opt/containers/http1/etc/
root@ubuntu:/opt# cp -r /etc/fstab /opt/containers/http1/etc/
root@ubuntu:/opt# cp -r /etc/apache2/ /opt/containers/http1/etc/
root@ubuntu:/opt# cp -r /etc/network/ /opt/containers/http1/etc/
```

2. Next, create the index.html page for Apache and configure the web server with its own unique PID file, which will later allow us to start multiple Apache processes:

```
root@ubuntu:/opt# echo "Apache in LXC http1" >
/opt/containers/http1/var/www/html/index.html
root@ubuntu:/opt# cd containers/
root@ubuntu:/opt/containers# sed -i
's/\${APACHE_PID_FILE}/\/var\/run\/apache2\/apache2_http1.pid/g'
http1/etc/apache2/apache2.conf
```

3. Configure the network interfaces file to use DHCP, so we can leverage the dnsmasq server that libvirtd started earlier:

```
root@ubuntu:/opt/containers# cat http1/etc/network/interfaces
auto lo
iface lo inet loopback
auto eth0
iface eth0 inet dhcp
root@ubuntu:/opt/containers#
```

Defining the Apache libvirt container

In order to build LXC containers with libvirt, we need to create the configuration file that contains the attributes of the containers. With the directory structure in place from the previous steps and Apache installed on the host, we can define the configuration file of the containers. We already saw a similar config when we talked about libvirt in Chapter 3, *Command-Line Operations Using Native and Libvirt Tools*. To view the configuration, run the following:

```
root@ubuntu:/opt/containers# cat http1.xml
<domain type='lxc'>
  <name>http1</name>
  <memory>102400</memory>
  <os>
    <type>exe</type>
    <init>/opt/containers/startup.sh</init>
  </os>
  <vcpu>1</vcpu>
  <on_poweroff>destroy</on_poweroff>
  <on_reboot>restart</on_reboot>
  <on_crash>destroy</on_crash>
  <devices>
    <emulator>/usr/lib/libvirt/libvirt_lxc</emulator>
    <filesystem type='mount'>
      <source dir='/opt/containers/http1/etc/apache2/'/>
      <target dir='/etc/apache2'/>
    </filesystem>
    <filesystem type='mount'>
      <source dir='/opt/containers/http1/var/www/html/'/>
      <target dir='/var/www/html'/>
    </filesystem>
    <filesystem type='mount'>
      <source dir='/opt/containers/http1/etc/'/>
      <target dir='/etc'/>
    </filesystem>
    <interface type='network'>
      <source network='default'/>
    </interface>
    <console type='pty'/>
  </devices>
</domain>
root@ubuntu:/opt/containers#
```

What is new in the preceding configuration is that, instead of specifying /sbin/init as the type of init system, we configure libvirt to use a custom script—startup.sh. The script can be anything we like; in this case, it will start the networking in the container, configure the shell, execute dhclient to obtain the network settings from dnsmasq, and then start Apache and bash:

```
root@ubuntu:/opt/containers# cat startup.sh
#!/bin/bash

export
PATH=$PATH:/usr/local/sbin:/usr/local/bin:/sbin:/bin:/usr/sbin:/usr/bin:/ro
ot/bin
export PS1="[\u@\h \W]\\$"

echo "Starting Networking" >> /var/log/messages
/etc/init.d/networking start
/sbin/dhclient eth0
echo "Starting httpd" >> /var/log/messages
/etc/init.d/apache2 start
/bin/bash
root@ubuntu:/opt/containers#
```

Next, make the script executable:

```
root@ubuntu:/opt/containers# chmod u+x startup.sh
root@ubuntu:/opt/containers#
```

The root directory of the container should look like the following:

```
root@ubuntu:/opt/containers# ls -la http1
total 16
drwxr-xr-x 4 root root 4096 Oct 31 17:25 .
drwxr-xr-x 3 root root 4096 Oct 31 17:32 ..
drwxr-xr-x 4 root root 4096 Oct 31 17:27 etc
drwxr-xr-x 3 root root 4096 Oct 31 17:25 var
root@ubuntu:/opt/containers#
```

Only two directories are present! We are now ready to define the container:

```
root@ubuntu:/opt/containers# virsh define http1.xml
Domain http1 defined from http1.xml
root@ubuntu:/opt/containers#
```

Starting the Apache libvirt container

With all the necessary components in place, let's start the container and confirm that it's running:

```
root@ubuntu:/opt/containers# virsh start http1
Domain http1 started
root@ubuntu:/opt/containers# virsh list --all
 Id    Name                          State
--------------------------------------------------
 19032 http1                         running
root@ubuntu:/opt/containers# ps axfww
...
10592 ?        S      0:00 /usr/lib/libvirt/libvirt_lxc --name http1
--console 23 --security=apparmor --handshake 26 --veth vnet1
10594 ?        S      0:00  \_ /bin/bash /opt/containers/startup.sh
10668 ?        Ss     0:00      \_ /sbin/dhclient eth0
10694 ?        Ss     0:00      \_ /usr/sbin/apache2 -k start
10698 ?        Sl     0:00      |   \_ /usr/sbin/apache2 -k start
10699 ?        Sl     0:00      |   \_ /usr/sbin/apache2 -k start
10697 ?        S      0:00      \_ /bin/bash
root@ubuntu:/opt/containers#
```

When listing the processes on the host, notice how the container was started from the `libvirt_lxc` script, which is the parent process of the `startup.sh` script, which in turn launched Apache.

Connect to the container and ensure it was able to obtain an IP address and default gateway from `dnsmasq`:

```
root@ubuntu:/opt/containers# virsh console http1
[root@ubuntu /]#ip a s
1: lo: <LOOPBACK,UP,LOWER_UP> mtu 65536 qdisc noqueue state UNKNOWN group
default qlen 1
    link/loopback 00:00:00:00:00:00 brd 00:00:00:00:00:00
    inet 127.0.0.1/8 scope host lo
       valid_lft forever preferred_lft forever
    inet6 ::1/128 scope host
       valid_lft forever preferred_lft forever
14: eth0@if15: <BROADCAST,MULTICAST,UP,LOWER_UP> mtu 1500 qdisc noqueue
state UP group default qlen 1000
    link/ether 52:54:00:92:cf:12 brd ff:ff:ff:ff:ff:ff link-netnsid 0
    inet 192.168.122.216/24 brd 192.168.122.255 scope global eth0
       valid_lft forever preferred_lft forever
    inet6 fe80::5054:ff:fe92:cf12/64 scope link
       valid_lft forever preferred_lft forever
```

```
[root@ubuntu /]#ip r s
default via 192.168.122.1 dev eth0
192.168.122.0/24 dev eth0  proto kernel  scope link  src 192.168.122.10
[root@ubuntu /]# Ctrl + ]
```

Let's connect to Apache from the host OS:

```
root@ubuntu:/opt/containers# curl 192.168.122.216
Apache in LXC http1
root@ubuntu:/opt/containers#
```

 The 192.168.122.70 IP address is what dnsmasq assigned to the container; you might need to replace it with whatever is the correct address on your system.

Scaling Apache with libvirt LXC and HAProxy

For scaling Apache with libvirt LXC and HAProxy, follow these steps:

1. With one Apache container running, let's quickly create a second one by copying the simple directory structure and libvirt config from the http1 container:

```
root@ubuntu:/opt/containers# cp -r http1 http2
root@ubuntu:/opt/containers# cp http1.xml http2.xml
root@ubuntu:/opt/containers#
```

2. All we need to change is the name of the container, the PID file for Apache, and its index file:

```
root@ubuntu:/opt/containers# sed -i 's/http1/http2/g'
http2.xml
```

```
root@ubuntu:/opt/containers# sed -i 's/http1/http2/g'
http2/etc/apache2/apache2.conf
```

```
root@ubuntu:/opt/containers# echo "Apache in LXC http2" >
/opt/containers/http2/var/www/html/index.html
```

3. Define the new container and examine the directory structure that contains the root filesystem and the configuration files for both containers:

```
root@ubuntu:/opt/containers# virsh define http2.xml
Domain http2 defined from http2.xml
```

```
root@ubuntu:/opt/containers# ls -la
total 28
drwxr-xr-x 4 root root 4096 Oct 31 19:57 .
drwxr-xr-x 3 root root 4096 Oct 31 17:32 ..
drwxr-xr-x 4 root root 4096 Oct 31 17:25 http1
-rw-r--r-- 1 root root  868 Oct 31 17:31 http1.xml
drwxr-xr-x 4 root root 4096 Oct 31 19:56 http2
-rw-r--r-- 1 root root  868 Oct 31 19:57 http2.xml
-rwxr--r-- 1 root root  418 Oct 31 19:44 startup.sh
root@ubuntu:/opt/containers#
```

4. Let's start the new container and ensure both instances are running:

```
root@ubuntu:/opt/containers# virsh start http2
Domain http2 started

root@ubuntu:/opt/containers# virsh list --all
 Id    Name                           State
----------------------------------------------------
 10592 http1                          running
 11726 http2                          running
root@ubuntu:~#
```

5. To obtain more information about the Apache containers, run the following command:

```
root@ubuntu:~# virsh dominfo http1
Id:             15720
Name:           http1
UUID:           defd17d7-f220-4dca-9be9-bdf40b4d9164
OS Type:        exe
State:          running
CPU(s):         1
CPU time:       35.8s
Max memory:     102400 KiB
Used memory:    8312 KiB
Persistent:     yes
Autostart:      disable
Managed save:   no
Security model: apparmor
Security DOI:   0
Security label: libvirt-defd17d7-f220-4dca-9be9-bdf40b4d9164
(enforcing)

root@ubuntu:~# virsh dominfo http2
Id:             16126
Name:           http2
UUID:           a62f9e9d-4de3-415d-8f2d-358a1c8bc0bd
```

```
OS Type:         exe
State:           running
CPU(s):          1
CPU time:        36.5s
Max memory:      102400 KiB
Used memory:     8300 KiB
Persistent:      yes
Autostart:       disable
Managed save:    no
Security model:  apparmor
Security DOI:    0
Security label:  libvirt-a62f9e9d-4de3-415d-8f2d-358a1c8bc0bd
(enforcing)
root@ubuntu:~#
```

The `dominfo` output provides useful information about the container's memory and CPU utilization, which we can use for monitoring, alerting, and autoscaling, as we'll see in `Chapter 7`, *Monitoring and Backups in a Containerized World*. Note that the `OS Type` is set to `exe`, because the container's init system is a script.

6. Let's test connectivity to Apache in the new container; replace the IP of the instance as necessary:

```
root@ubuntu:/opt/containers# curl 192.168.122.242
Apache in LXC http2
root@ubuntu:/opt/containers#
```

7. Both Apache processes are accessible from the host OS because of the common bridge they are all connected to. In order to access them from outside the host OS, we can install HAProxy on the server, with the IP addresses of the containers as its backend servers:

```
root@ubuntu:~# echo "nameserver 8.8.8.8" > /etc/resolv.conf
root@ubuntu:~# apt-get install --yes haproxy
root@ubuntu:~# cat /etc/haproxy/haproxy.cfg
global
        log /dev/log    local0
        log /dev/log    local1 notice
        chroot /var/lib/haproxy
        stats socket /run/haproxy/admin.sock mode 660 level admin
        stats timeout 30s
        user haproxy
        group haproxy
        daemon
        ca-base /etc/ssl/certs
```

```
        crt-base /etc/ssl/private
        ssl-default-bind-ciphers
        ECDH+AESGCM:DH+AESGCM:ECDH+AES256:DH+AES256:ECDH+AES128
        :DH+AES:ECDH+3DES:DH+3DES:RSA+AESGCM:RSA+AES
        :RSA+3DES:!aNULL:!MD5:!DSS
        ssl-default-bind-options no-sslv3
defaults
        log    global
        mode   http
        option   httplog
        option   dontlognull
        timeout connect 5000
        timeout client  50000
        timeout server  50000
frontend http
        bind :80
        reqadd X-Forwarded-Proto:\ http
        default_backend http_nodes
backend http_nodes
        mode http
        balance roundrobin
        option httpclose
        option forwardfor
        option redispatch
        option httpchk GET /
        cookie JSESSIONID prefix
        server http1 192.168.122.216:80 check inter 5000
        server http1 192.168.122.242:80 check inter 5000
root@ubuntu:~#
```

The IP addresses specified in the server lines of the `backend` section of the HAProxy config are those of the libvirt LXC containers. Update the files as needed.

In the `frontend` section of the config, we tell HAProxy to listen on port `80` and bind to all interfaces. In the `backend` section, we specify the IPs of both LXC containers. You might need to replace the IPs of the containers with those that `dnsmasq` provided on your system.

8. Restart HAProxy, since on Ubuntu, it starts automatically after package installation:

```
root@ubuntu:~# service haproxy restart
root@ubuntu:~#
```

9. Then, ensure HAProxy is running and listening on port 80 on the host:

```
root@ubuntu:~# pgrep -lfa haproxy
1957 /usr/sbin/haproxy-systemd-wrapper -f /etc/haproxy
/haproxy.cfg -p /run/haproxy.pid
1958 /usr/sbin/haproxy -f /etc/haproxy/haproxy.cfg -p
/run/haproxy.pid -Ds
1960 /usr/sbin/haproxy -f /etc/haproxy/haproxy.cfg -p
/run/haproxy.pid -Ds
root@ubuntu:~#

root@ubuntu:~# netstat -antup | grep -i listen | grep -w 80
tcp        0      0 0.0.0.0:80       0.0.0.0:*
LISTEN         1960/haproxy
tcp6       0      0 :::80            :::*
LISTEN         9693/apache2
root@ubuntu:~#
```

10. We configured HAProxy to use round robin for selecting backend nodes; let's connect to it a few times and confirm we connected to Apache in each LXC container:

```
root@ubuntu:~# curl localhost
Apache in LXC http1

root@ubuntu:~# curl localhost
Apache in LXC http2
root@ubuntu:~#
```

11. Finally, we can stop one of the containers and ensure HAproxy will remove it from rotation:

```
root@ubuntu:~# virsh destroy http2
Domain http2 destroyed
root@ubuntu:~# virsh list --all
Id    Name                    State
----------------------------------------------------
15720 http1                   running
-     http2                   shut off
root@ubuntu:~# curl localhost
Apache in LXC http1
root@ubuntu:~# curl localhost
Apache in LXC http1
root@ubuntu:~#
```

Apache might not be the best application to run in multiple containers on the same host. Nevertheless, it helps to demonstrate how easy it is to scale applications running in minimal LXC containers with libvirt LXC, behind a proxy, or how to build a multitenant environment. The added benefit in using shared binaries from all containers is that upgrading them will not require changes in each LXC instance, but rather changes on the host OS that will be visible from all containers on that server. The preceding setup might seem simple, but it provides a powerful way to scale services in lightweight LXC containers that will not require much disk space.

Scaling Apache with a full LXC root filesystem and OVS GRE tunnels

Running multiple containers on the same host with a minimal filesystem for each is great in some scenarios, but let's focus on a more complex multiserver deployment example next. The following diagram shows the deployment we are going to build in this section:

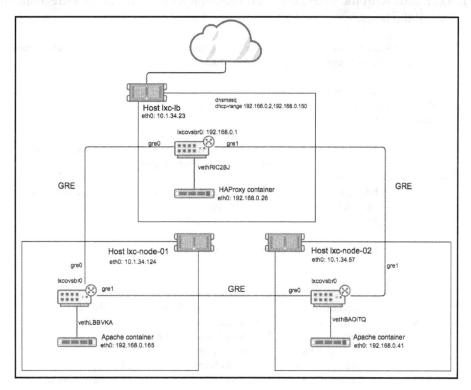

Multiserver LXC deployment with LXC and GRE tunnels

We are going to use three servers—lxc-lb, lxc-node-01, and lxc-node-02. Each one will have LXC and OVS installed. The lxc-lb host will host a container running HAProxy, and later, HAProxy on the server itself. The lxc-node-01 and lxc-node-02 servers will have containers running Apache. All LXC instances will communicate on a dedicated private network through a mesh of GRE tunnels connected to OVS. The OVS GRE mesh will create network isolation between the containers and the hosts, and potentially other containers and their networks. All containers will obtain their network configurations from dnsmasq running on the lxc-lb host.

For this deployment, we'll use three EC2 instances from AWS, running the latest Ubuntu Xenial release.

Configuring the load-balancer host

To configure the load balancer host, follow these steps:

1. Let's start with the lxc-lb server. Examine what LXC versions are available and install the latest:

```
root@lxc-lb:~# apt-get update && apt-get upgrade --yes && reboot
root@lxc-lb:~# apt-cache policy lxc
lxc:
  Installed: (none)
  Candidate: 2.0.5-0ubuntu1~ubuntu16.04.2
  Version table:
     2.0.5-0ubuntu1~ubuntu16.04.2 500
        500 http://us-east-1.ec2.archive.ubuntu.com/ubuntu
        xenial-updates/main amd64 Packages
     2.0.0-0ubuntu2 500
        500 http://us-east-1.ec2.archive.ubuntu.com/ubuntu
        xenial/main amd64 Packages
root@lxc-lb:~#

root@lxc-lb:~# apt-get install --yes lxc
...

root@lxc-lb:~# dpkg --list | grep lxc
ii          liblxc1       2.0.5-0ubuntu1~ubuntu16.04.2
amd64       Linux Containers userspace tools (library)
ii          lxc           2.0.5-0ubuntu1~ubuntu16.04.2
all         Transitional package for lxc1
ii          lxc-common    2.0.5-0ubuntu1~ubuntu16.04.2
amd64       Linux Containers userspace tools (common tools)
ii          lxc-templates 2.0.5-0ubuntu1~ubuntu16.04.2
amd64       Linux Containers userspace tools (templates)
```

```
ii              lxc1            2.0.5-0ubuntu1~ubuntu16.04.2
amd64           Linux Containers userspace tools
ii              lxcfs           2.0.4-0ubuntu1~ubuntu16.04.1
amd64           FUSE based filesystem for LXC
ii              python3-lxc     2.0.5-0ubuntu1~ubuntu16.04.2

amd64
Linux Containers userspace tools (Python 3.x bindings)
root@lxc-lb:~#

root@lxc-lb:~# lxc-create --version
2.0.5
root@lxc-lb:~#
```

2. After installing the LXC packages and templates, we ended up with the Linux bridge as well, however, we are not going to use it:

```
root@lxc-lb:~# brctl show
bridge name      bridge id            STP enabled interfaces
lxcbr0           8000.000000000000    no
root@lxc-lb:~#
```

3. Next, install OVS and create a new bridge named lxcovsbr0:

```
root@lxc-lb:~# apt-get install --yes openvswitch-switch
...
root@lxc-lb:~# ovs-vsctl add-br lxcovsbr0
root@lxc-lb:~# ovs-vsctl show
482cf359-a59e-4482-8a71-02b0884d016d
    Bridge "lxcovsbr0"
        Port "lxcovsbr0"
            Interface "lxcovsbr0"
                type: internal
    ovs_version: "2.5.0"
root@lxc-lb:~#
```

4. The default LXC network uses the 10.0.3.0/24 subnet; we are going to replace it with 192.168.0.0/24. This helps in cases where there's already an existing LXC network, and we would like to start a new one and isolate certain sets of containers, and also help demonstrate the concept:

```
root@lxc-lb:~# cat /etc/default/lxc-net | grep -vi "#"
USE_LXC_BRIDGE="true"
LXC_BRIDGE="lxcbr0"
LXC_ADDR="10.0.3.1"
LXC_NETMASK="255.255.255.0"
LXC_NETWORK="10.0.3.0/24"
```

```
LXC_DHCP_RANGE="10.0.3.2,10.0.3.254"
LXC_DHCP_MAX="253"

root@lxc-lb:~# cat /etc/lxc/default.conf
lxc.network.type = veth
lxc.network.link = lxcbr0
lxc.network.flags = up
lxc.network.hwaddr = 00:16:3e:xx:xx:xx
root@lxc-lb:~#
```

5. Replace the name of the default Linux bridge with the OVS bridge we just created, and change the network:

```
root@lxc-lb:~# sed -i 's/lxcbr0/lxcovsbr0/g' /etc/default/lxc-net
root@lxc-lb:~# sed -i 's/10.0.3/192.168.0/g' /etc/default/lxc-net
root@lxc-lb:~# sed -i 's/lxcbr0/lxcovsbr0/g' /etc/lxc/default.conf
```

6. The dnsmasq service is configured for the 10.0.3.0/24 network, but after a restart, it should listen on the new subnet we specified earlier. Let's reboot the server to ensure the changes will persist:

```
root@lxc-lb:~# pgrep -lfa dnsmasq
10654 dnsmasq -u lxc-dnsmasq --strict-order --bind-interfaces
--pid-file=/run/lxc/dnsmasq.pid --listen-address 10.0.3.1
--dhcp-range 10.0.3.2,10.0.3.254 --dhcp-lease-max=253
--dhcp-no-override --except-interface=lo --interface=lxcbr0
--dhcp-leasefile=/var/lib/misc/dnsmasq.lxcbr0.leases
--dhcp-authoritative
root@lxc-lb:~#
root@lxc-lb:~# reboot
```

7. As expected, dnsmasq will now offer IPs from the 192.168.0.0/24 subnet:

```
root@lxc-lb:~# pgrep -lfa dnsmasq
1354 dnsmasq -u lxc-dnsmasq --strict-order --bind-interfaces
--pid-file=/run/lxc/dnsmasq.pid --listen-address 192.168.0.1
--dhcp-range 192.168.0.2,192.168.0.254 --dhcp-lease-max=253
--dhcp-no-override --except-interface=lo --interface=lxcovsbr0
--dhcp-leasefile=/var/lib/misc/dnsmasq.lxcovsbr0.leases
--dhcp-authoritative
root@lxc-lb:~#
```

8. Examine the OVS bridge; it should be up and configured with an IP:

```
root@lxc-lb:~# ip a s lxcovsbr0
4: lxcovsbr0: <BROADCAST,MULTICAST,UP,LOWER_UP> mtu 1500 qdisc
noqueue state UNKNOWN group default qlen 1
    link/ether ee:b0:a2:42:22:4e brd ff:ff:ff:ff:ff:ff
    inet 192.168.0.1/24 scope global lxcovsbr0
       valid_lft forever preferred_lft forever
    inet6 fe80::ecb0:a2ff:fe42:224e/64 scope link
       valid_lft forever preferred_lft forever
root@lxc-lb:~#
```

Creating the load-balancer container

To create the load-balancer container, follow these steps:

1. We are going to use the Ubuntu template to create the root filesystem of the
   HAProxy container:

```
root@lxc-lb:~# lxc-create --name haproxy --template ubuntu
root@lxc-lb:~# lxc-start --name haproxy
root@lxc-lb:~#
```

2. The OVS bridge should now have the containers interfaces added as a port—the
   vethUY97FY, in this example:

```
root@lxc-lb:~# ovs-vsctl show
482cf359-a59e-4482-8a71-02b0884d016d
    Bridge "lxcovsbr0"
        Port "lxcovsbr0"
            Interface "lxcovsbr0"
                type: internal
        Port "vethUY97FY"
            Interface "vethUY97FY"
    ovs_version: "2.5.0"
root@lxc-lb:~#

root@lxc-lb:~# ip a s vethUY97FY
6: vethUY97FY@if5: <BROADCAST,MULTICAST,UP,LOWER_UP> mtu 1500 qdisc
noqueue master ovs-system state UP group default qlen 1000
    link/ether fe:d1:f3:ca:9e:83 brd ff:ff:ff:ff:ff:ff link-netnsid 0
    inet6 fe80::fcd1:f3ff:feca:9e83/64 scope link
       valid_lft forever preferred_lft forever
root@lxc-lb:~#
```

3. Attach to the new container and make sure it received an IP address from the DHCP server running on the same host:

```
root@lxc-lb:~# lxc-attach --name haproxy
root@haproxy:~# ifconfig
eth0      Link encap:Ethernet  HWaddr 00:16:3e:76:92:0a
          inet addr:192.168.0.26  Bcast:192.168.0.255
          Mask:255.255.255.0
          inet6 addr: fe80::216:3eff:fe76:920a/64 Scope:Link
          UP BROADCAST RUNNING MULTICAST  MTU:1500  Metric:1
          RX packets:16 errors:0 dropped:0 overruns:0 frame:0
          TX packets:12 errors:0 dropped:0 overruns:0 carrier:0
          collisions:0 txqueuelen:1000
          RX bytes:1905 (1.9 KB)  TX bytes:1716 (1.7 KB)
lo        Link encap:Local Loopback
          inet addr:127.0.0.1  Mask:255.0.0.0
          inet6 addr: ::1/128 Scope:Host
          UP LOOPBACK RUNNING  MTU:65536  Metric:1
          RX packets:0 errors:0 dropped:0 overruns:0 frame:0
          TX packets:0 errors:0 dropped:0 overruns:0 carrier:0
          collisions:0 txqueuelen:1
          RX bytes:0 (0.0 B)  TX bytes:0 (0.0 B)
root@haproxy:~# route -n
Kernel IP routing table
Destination     Gateway         Genmask         Flags Metric Ref  Use Iface
0.0.0.0         192.168.0.1     0.0.0.0         UG    0      0      0 eth0
192.168.0.0     0.0.0.0         255.255.255.0   U     0      0      0 eth0
root@haproxy:~#
```

4. The container should have connectivity to the host and the Internet. Let's test that before moving on:

```
root@haproxy:~# ping -c 3 192.168.0.1
PING 192.168.0.1 (192.168.0.1) 56(84) bytes of data.
64 bytes from 192.168.0.1: icmp_seq=1 ttl=64 time=0.218 ms
64 bytes from 192.168.0.1: icmp_seq=2 ttl=64 time=0.045 ms
64 bytes from 192.168.0.1: icmp_seq=3 ttl=64 time=0.046 ms
--- 192.168.0.1 ping statistics ---
3 packets transmitted, 3 received, 0% packet loss, time 2000ms
rtt min/avg/max/mdev = 0.045/0.103/0.218/0.081 ms
root@haproxy:~# ping google.com -c 3
PING google.com (216.58.217.110) 56(84) bytes of data.
64 bytes from iad23s42-in-f14.1e100.net (216.58.217.110): icmp_seq=1
ttl=48 time=2.55 ms
64 bytes from iad23s42-in-f14.1e100.net (216.58.217.110): icmp_seq=2
ttl=48 time=2.11 ms
64 bytes from iad23s42-in-f14.1e100.net (216.58.217.110): icmp_seq=3
```

```
ttl=48 time=2.39 ms
--- google.com ping statistics ---
3 packets transmitted, 3 received, 0% packet loss, time 2002ms
rtt min/avg/max/mdev = 2.113/2.354/2.555/0.191 ms
root@haproxy:~# exit
exit
root@lxc-lb:~#
```

If connectivity is not working, make sure the dnsmasq server properly assigned an IP address and that the container is connected to the OVS bridge, and the bridge interface is up with an IP address itself.

Building the GRE tunnels

Generic Routing Encapsulation (**GRE**) is a tunneling protocol that allows for building virtual point-to-point networks over the **Internet Protocol** (**IP**). We can use it to create a network mesh between the OVS switches on the three hosts, thus connecting the LXC containers to an isolated network. Each server (or EC2 instance in this example) will connect to each other. The OVS provides a convenient way for establishing the GRE tunnels.

While still on the load-balancer host, create two GRE tunnels to the other two servers, replacing the IPs as necessary:

```
root@lxc-lb:~# ovs-vsctl add-port lxcovsbr0 gre0 -- set interface gre0
type=gre options:remote_ip=10.1.34.124
root@lxc-lb:~# ovs-vsctl add-port lxcovsbr0 gre1 -- set interface gre1
type=gre options:remote_ip=10.1.34.57
root@lxc-lb:~#
```

 Notice that preceding IP addresses are those of the actual servers, not the containers.

Listing all ports on the bridge will now show the GRE ports as well:

```
root@lxc-lb:~# ovs-vsctl show
482cf359-a59e-4482-8a71-02b0884d016d
    Bridge "lxcovsbr0"
        Port "gre1"
            Interface "gre1"
                type: gre
                options: {remote_ip="10.1.34.57"}
        Port "vethRIC2BJ"
            Interface "vethRIC2BJ"
```

```
        Port "lxcovsbr0"
            Interface "lxcovsbr0"
                type: internal
        Port "gre0"
            Interface "gre0"
                type: gre
                options: {remote_ip="10.1.34.124"}
    ovs_version: "2.5.0"
root@lxc-lb:~#
```

Since we are creating a network mesh between OVS, packet loops may occur. To prevent topology loops, we need to enable the **Spanning Tree Protocol** (**STP**) on OVS. STP is a layer-2 protocol that prevents network loops when creating redundant and interconnected links between switches. To enable it on the OVS switch, execute the following command:

```
root@lxc-lb:~# ovs-vsctl set bridge lxcovsbr0 stp_enable=true
root@lxc-lb:~#
```

With all of the preceding steps completed, the first host is now configured. In the next section, we are going to configure the rest of the servers in a similar way.

Configuring the Apache nodes

To configure the Apache nodes, follow these steps:

1. On the first Apache node, install LXC and OVS, and create the bridge:

    ```
    root@lxc-node-01:~# apt-get update && apt-get --yes upgrade && reboot
    root@lxc-node-01:~# apt-get install --yes lxc
    root@lxc-node-01:~# apt-get install --yes openvswitch-switch
    root@lxc-node-01:~# ovs-vsctl add-br lxcovsbr0
    root@lxc-node-01:~# ifconfig lxcovsbr0 up
    ```

2. Replace the name of the bridge and change the subnet:

    ```
    root@lxc-node-01:~# sed -i 's/lxcbr0/lxcovsbr0/g'
    /etc/lxc/default.conf
    root@lxc-node-01:~# sed -i 's/lxcbr0/lxcovsbr0/g'
    /etc/default/lxc-net
    root@lxc-node-01:~# sed -i 's/10.0.3/192.168.0/g'
    /etc/default/lxc-net
    ```

3. Create the GRE tunnels to the other two servers, replacing the IPs as needed:

```
root@lxc-node-01:~# ovs-vsctl add-port lxcovsbr0 gre0 -- set
interface gre0 type=gre options:remote_ip=10.1.34.23
root@lxc-node-01:~# ovs-vsctl add-port lxcovsbr0 gre1 -- set
interface gre1 type=gre options:remote_ip=10.1.34.57
root@lxc-node-01:~# ovs-vsctl show
625928b0-b57a-46b2-82fe-77d541473f29
    Bridge "lxcovsbr0"
        Port "gre0"
            Interface "gre0"
                type: gre
                options: {remote_ip="10.1.34.23"}
        Port "gre1"
            Interface "gre1"
                type: gre
                options: {remote_ip="10.1.34.57"}
        Port "lxcovsbr0"
            Interface "lxcovsbr0"
                type: internal
    ovs_version: "2.5.0"
root@lxc-node-01:~#
```

4. Enable STP on the bridge:

```
root@lxc-node-01:~# ovs-vsctl set bridge lxcovsbr0 stp_enable=true
root@lxc-node-01:~#
```

5. Next, let's create an Ubuntu container named apache:

```
root@lxc-node-01:~# lxc-create --name apache --template ubuntu
root@lxc-node-01:~# lxc-start --name apache
```

6. Time to configure the last node in a similar fashion:

```
root@lxc-node-02:~# apt-get update && apt-get upgrade --yes && reboot
root@lxc-node-02:~# apt-get install --yes lxc
root@lxc-node-02:~# apt-get install --yes openvswitch-switch
root@lxc-node-02:~# ovs-vsctl add-br lxcovsbr0
root@lxc-node-02:~# ifconfig lxcovsbr0 up
root@lxc-node-02:~# sed -i 's/lxcbr0/lxcovsbr0/g'
/etc/lxc/default.conf
root@lxc-node-02:~# sed -i 's/lxcbr0/lxcovsbr0/g'
/etc/default/lxc-net
root@lxc-node-02:~# sed -i 's/10.0.3/192.168.0/g'
/etc/default/lxc-net
```

7. Create the GRE tunnels:

```
root@lxc-node-02:~# ovs-vsctl add-port lxcovsbr0 gre0 -- set
interface gre0 type=gre options:remote_ip=10.1.34.23
root@lxc-node-02:~# ovs-vsctl add-port lxcovsbr0 gre1 -- set
interface gre1 type=gre options:remote_ip=10.1.34.124
root@lxc-node-02:~# ovs-vsctl show
7b8574ce-ed52-443e-bcf2-6b1ddbedde4c
    Bridge "lxcovsbr0"
        Port "gre0"
            Interface "gre0"
                type: gre
                options: {remote_ip="10.1.34.23"}
        Port "gre1"
            Interface "gre1"
                type: gre
                options: {remote_ip="10.1.34.124"}
        Port "lxcovsbr0"
            Interface "lxcovsbr0"
                type: internal
    ovs_version: "2.5.0"
root@lxc-node-02:~#
```

8. Also, enable STP on the switch:

```
root@lxc-node-02:~# ovs-vsctl set bridge lxcovsbr0 stp_enable=true
root@lxc-node-02:~#
```

9. Finally, create and start the Apache container:

```
root@lxc-node-02:~# lxc-create --name apache --template ubuntu
root@lxc-node-02:~# lxc-start --name apache
```

Installing Apache and HAProxy, and testing connectivity

With all the servers configured, the containers started, and the GRE tunnels established, let's test the connectivity between each LXC instance. Since all containers are part of the same network, connected to each other through the OVS switches with the GRE tunnels, they should be able to communicate with each other. Most importantly, the Apache containers will obtain their network configuration through DHCP from the dnsmasq service running on the lxc-lb server.

To verify that each container received a lease, we can examine the dnsmasq lease file by executing the following command:

```
root@lxc-lb:~# cat /var/lib/misc/dnsmasq.lxcovsbr0.leases
1478111141 00:16:3e:84:cc:f3 192.168.0.41 apache *
1478111044 00:16:3e:74:b3:8c 192.168.0.165 * *
1478110360 00:16:3e:76:92:0a 192.168.0.26 haproxy *
root@lxc-lb:~#
```

1. Getting a lease might take a few seconds; you might need to check the file a few times before any IP is recorded. Once all containers have IPs, we should be able to see them when listing the containers on each server:

```
root@lxc-lb:~# lxc-ls -f
NAME      STATE    AUTOSTART GROUPS IPV4           IPV6
haproxy RUNNING 0              -        192.168.0.26 -
root@lxc-lb:~#
root@lxc-node-01:~# lxc-ls -f
NAME      STATE    AUTOSTART GROUPS IPV4           IPV6
apache RUNNING 0               -        192.168.0.165 -
root@lxc-node-01:~#
root@lxc-node-02:~# lxc-ls -f
NAME      STATE    AUTOSTART GROUPS IPV4           IPV6
apache RUNNING 0               -        192.168.0.41 -
root@lxc-node-02:~#
```

2. Next, let's install HAProxy in the haproxy container on the node lxc-lb server and test connectivity between containers:

```
root@lxc-lb:~# lxc-attach --name haproxy
root@haproxy:~# ping -c3 192.168.0.165
PING 192.168.0.165 (192.168.0.165) 56(84) bytes of data.
64 bytes from 192.168.0.165: icmp_seq=1 ttl=64 time=0.840 ms
64 bytes from 192.168.0.165: icmp_seq=2 ttl=64 time=0.524 ms
64 bytes from 192.168.0.165: icmp_seq=3 ttl=64 time=0.446 ms
--- 192.168.0.165 ping statistics ---
3 packets transmitted, 3 received, 0% packet loss, time 1999ms
rtt min/avg/max/mdev = 0.446/0.603/0.840/0.171 ms
root@haproxy:~# ping -c3 192.168.0.41
PING 192.168.0.41 (192.168.0.41) 56(84) bytes of data.
64 bytes from 192.168.0.41: icmp_seq=1 ttl=64 time=1.26 ms
64 bytes from 192.168.0.41: icmp_seq=2 ttl=64 time=0.939 ms
64 bytes from 192.168.0.41: icmp_seq=3 ttl=64 time=1.05 ms
--- 192.168.0.41 ping statistics ---
3 packets transmitted, 3 received, 0% packet loss, time 2001ms
rtt min/avg/max/mdev = 0.939/1.086/1.269/0.142 ms
root@haproxy:~#
```

```
root@haproxy:~# apt-get update && apt-get install haproxy
...
```

 If you are building this example deployment on a cloud provider and `apt-get update` hangs, try reducing the MTU setting of the `eth0` interface inside the LXC containers as follows: `ifconfig eth0 mtu 1400`.

3. Let's view the `haproxy.cfg` configuration file:

```
root@haproxy:~# cat /etc/haproxy/haproxy.cfg
global
        log /dev/log local0
        log /dev/log local1 notice
        chroot /var/lib/haproxy
        stats socket /run/haproxy/admin.sock mode 660 level admin
        stats timeout 30s
        user haproxy
        group haproxy
        daemon

        ca-base /etc/ssl/certs

        crt-base /etc/ssl/private
        ssl-default-bind-ciphers
        ECDH+AESGCM:DH+AESGCM:ECDH+AES256:DH+AES256:ECDH+
        AES128:DH+AES:ECDH+3DES:DH+3DES:RSA+AESGCM:RSA+AES:
        RSA+3DES:!aNULL:!MD5:!DSS
        ssl-default-bind-options no-sslv3
defaults
        log global
        mode http
        option httplog
        option dontlognull
        timeout connect 5000
        timeout client 50000
        timeout server 50000
frontend http
        bind :80
        reqadd X-Forwarded-Proto:\ http
        default_backend http_nodes
        backend http_nodes
        mode http
        balance roundrobin
        option httpclose
        option forwardfor
        option redispatch
```

```
        option httpchk GET /
        cookie JSESSIONID prefix
        server http1 192.168.0.165:80 check inter 5000
        server http1 192.168.0.41:80 check inter 5000
root@haproxy:~#
```

The HAProxy configuration is almost identical to the one we used earlier in this chapter.

 Note that the IP addresses in the `backend` section of the HAProxy configuration file are those of the Apache containers running on the `lxc-node-01/02` servers.

4. Restart HAProxy and ensure it's running:

```
root@haproxy:~# service haproxy restart
root@haproxy:~# ps axfww
  PID TTY        STAT   TIME COMMAND
    1 ?          Ss     0:00 /sbin/init
   38 ?          Ss     0:00 /lib/systemd/systemd-journald
   59 ?          Ss     0:00 /usr/sbin/cron -f
   62 ?          Ssl    0:00 /usr/sbin/rsyslogd -n
  143 ?          Ss     0:00 /sbin/dhclient -1 -v -pf
/run/dhclient.eth0.pid
-lf /var/lib/dhcp/dhclient.eth0.leases -I -df
/var/lib/dhcp/dhclient6.eth0.leases eth0
  167 ?          Ss     0:00 /usr/sbin/sshd -D
  168 pts/2      Ss+    0:00 /sbin/agetty --noclear
--keep-baud pts/2 115200 38400 9600 vt220
  169 lxc/console Ss+   0:00 /sbin/agetty --noclear
--keep-baud console 115200 38400 9600 vt220
  412 ?          Ss     0:00 /usr/sbin/haproxy-systemd-wrapper -f
/etc/haproxy/haproxy.cfg -p /run/haproxy.pid
  413 ?          S      0:00  \_ /usr/sbin/haproxy -f
/etc/haproxy/haproxy.cfg -p /run/haproxy.pid -Ds
  414 ?          Ss     0:00      \_ /usr/sbin/haproxy -f
/etc/haproxy/haproxy.cfg -p /run/haproxy.pid -Ds
root@haproxy:~#
```

Notice, from the preceding output how, unlike the previous example with libvirt LXC we saw earlier in the chapter, the init process is the parent process in the container now.

5. Install Apache in the other two containers and create an `index.html` page for each:

```
root@lxc-node-01:~# lxc-attach --name apache
root@apache:~# apt-get install --yes apache2
root@apache:~# echo "Apache on LXC container on host lxc-node-01" >
/var/www/html/index.html
root@lxc-node-02:~# lxc-attach --name apache
root@apache:~# apt-get install --yes apache2
root@apache:~# echo "Apache on LXC container on host lxc-node-02" >
/var/www/html/index.html
```

6. From within the `haproxy` container, connect to port `80` that HAProxy is listening on, and the load balancer should forward the requests to the Apache containers:

```
root@haproxy:~# apt-get install --yes curl
root@haproxy:~# curl localhost
Apache on LXC container on host lxc-node-01
root@haproxy:~# curl localhost
Apache on LXC container on host lxc-node-02
root@haproxy:~# exit
exit
root@lxc-lb:~#
```

7. We should be able to connect to HAProxy from the `lxc-lb` host as well, since the host OS can talk to the containers through the OVS switch:

```
root@lxc-lb:~# apt-get install curl
root@lxc-lb:~# curl 192.168.0.26
Apache on LXC container on host lxc-node-01
root@lxc-lb:~# curl 192.168.0.26
Apache on LXC container on host lxc-node-02
root@lxc-lb:~#
```

The preceding `192.168.0.26` address is the IP of the `haproxy` container; replace it with whatever `dnsmasq` assigned on your system.

8. Finally, we can install HAProxy on the `lxc-lb` server itself, which will allow us to connect to the Apache servers from the outside world, if, for example, the `lxc-lb` host has a public IP. In this case, we don't have to run HAProxy in the container at all, though we can reuse the same config:

```
root@lxc-lb:~# apt-get install haproxy
...
root@lxc-lb:~#
```

Copy the config from the container (listed earlier in this section) and restart HAProxy:

```
root@lxc-lb:~# service haproxy restart
root@lxc-lb:~# curl 10.1.34.23
Apache on LXC container on host lxc-node-01
root@lxc-lb:~# curl 10.1.34.23
Apache on LXC container on host lxc-node-02
root@lxc-lb:~#
```

Note that the 10.1.34.23 IP address is the address of the lxc-lb server in this example. If your server has more than one IP address or a public one, you can use any of them, since we configured HAProxy to bind to all interfaces.

With this, we have a simple setup that can be used in production to create highly available services and scale them horizontally by adding more servers and containers, behind a load balancer such as HAProxy or Nginx.

Scaling the Apache service

Setups such as the preceding ones can be fully automated by creating snapshots of the container's filesystem and configuration files, with the services already installed; then use those copies to start new containers on demand.

To demonstrate how to manually scale Apache by adding more containers, follow these steps:

1. First, stop one of the Apache instances:

```
root@lxc-node-01:~# lxc-ls -f
NAME    STATE   AUTOSTART GROUPS IPV4 IPV6
apache RUNNING 0           -       -    -
root@lxc-node-01:~# lxc-stop --name apache
```

2. Next, copy its root filesystem and the LXC configuration file:

```
root@lxc-node-01:~# cd /var/lib/lxc
root@lxc-node-01:/var/lib/lxc# ls -alh
total 12K
drwx------   3 root root 4.0K Nov  2 16:53 .
drwxr-xr-x 43 root root 4.0K Nov  2 15:02 ..
drwxrwx---   3 root root 4.0K Nov  2 16:53 apache
root@lxc-node-01:/var/lib/lxc# cp -rp apache/ apache_new
root@lxc-node-01:/var/lib/lxc#
```

3. Change the name of the new container and remove the MAC address from the configuration file. LXC will dynamically assign a new one when the container starts:

```
root@lxc-node-01:/var/lib/lxc# sed -i 's/apache/apache_new/g'
apache_new/config
root@lxc-node-01:/var/lib/lxc# sed -i '/lxc.network.hwaddr/d'
apache_new/config
root@lxc-node-01:/var/lib/lxc#
```

4. We now have two containers on the host:

```
root@lxc-node-01:/var/lib/lxc# lxc-ls -f
NAME         STATE    AUTOSTART GROUPS IPV4 IPV6
apache       STOPPED 0          -       -    -
apache_new STOPPED 0           -       -    -
root@lxc-node-01:/var/lib/lxc#
```

5. Let's start them both:

```
root@lxc-node-01:/var/lib/lxc# lxc-start --name apache
root@lxc-node-01:/var/lib/lxc# lxc-start --name apache_new
root@lxc-node-01:/var/lib/lxc# lxc-ls -f
NAME         STATE    AUTOSTART GROUPS IPV4 IPV6
apache       RUNNING 0          -       -    -
apache_new RUNNING 0           -       -    -
root@lxc-node-01:/var/lib/lxc#
```

6. Since we copied the entire root filesystem from the original container, the Apache service is already installed in the new instance. Now, start it and ensure it's running:

```
root@lxc-node-01:/var/lib/lxc# lxc-attach --name apache_new
root@apache:/# /etc/init.d/apache2 start
[ ok ] Starting apache2 (via systemctl): apache2.service.
root@apache:/# ps ax
  PID TTY         STAT    TIME COMMAND
    1 ?           Ss      0:00 /sbin/init
   37 ?           Ss      0:00 /lib/systemd/systemd-journald
   50 ?           Ss      0:00 /sbin/ifup -a --read-environment
   60 ?           Ss      0:00 /usr/sbin/cron -f
   62 ?           Ssl     0:00 /usr/sbin/rsyslogd -n
   97 ?           S       0:00 /bin/sh -c /sbin/dhclient -1 -v -pf
/run/dhclient.eth0.pid -lf
/var/lib/dhcp/dhclient.eth0.leases -I
-df /var/lib/dhcp/dhclient6.eth0.leases eth0 ?
   98 ?           S       0:00 /sbin/dhclient -1 -v -pf
```

```
        /run/dhclient.eth0.pid -lf /var/lib/dhcp/dhclient.eth0.leases
        -I -df /var/lib/dhcp/dhclient6.eth0.leases eth0
   125 pts/3    Ss     0:00 /bin/bash
   168 ?        Ss     0:00 /usr/sbin/apache2 -k start
   171 ?        Sl     0:00 /usr/sbin/apache2 -k start
   172 ?        Sl     0:00 /usr/sbin/apache2 -k start
   246 pts/3    R+     0:00 ps ax
root@apache:/#
```

A similar process to this can be fully automated with services such as Jenkins and distributed between different servers to achieve a level of service autoscaling. We'll explore this setup in further detail in Chapter 7, *Monitoring and Backups in a Containerized World*.

Summary

Using LXC to scale various workloads requires a proxy service such as HAProxy or Nginx, and the actual service running in containers. Network connectivity and segmentation can be achieved using software-defined networks with OVS and GRE tunnels.

In this chapter, we looked at how to run Apache in simple libvirt-based LXC containers that do not require an entire root filesystem, but rather a minimal set of directories with the shared binaries and libraries from the host OS. We also created an Apache cluster behind a load balancer on multiple servers, and demonstrated a simple yet effective way of scaling it by duplicating an LXC container.

In the next chapter, we'll build on what you've learned so far, show how to monitor and back up LXC, and create an autoscaling service with Jenkins and Sensu.

7
Monitoring and Backups in a Containerized World

In the previous chapter, we looked at a few examples of how to scale applications running inside LXC containers, by creating multiple instances behind a proxy service such as HAProxy. This ensures the application has enough resources and can withstand failures, thus achieving a level of high availability.

For applications running in a single LXC instance, it's often desirable to perform periodic backups of the container, which includes the root filesystem and the container's configuration file. Depending on the backing store, there are a few available options that we are going to explore in this chapter.

Using a highly available or shared backend store can help with quickly recovering from failed hosts, or when one needs to migrate LXC containers between servers. We are going to look at how to create containers on an **Internet Small Computer Systems Interface (iSCSI)** target and migrate LXC between servers. We are also going to look at an example of how to use GlusterFS as a shared filesystem to host the root filesystem of containers, thus creating active-passive LXC deployments.

We are also going to go over how to monitor LXC containers and the services running inside them, with various tools such as Monit and Sensu; we will end the chapter with an example of creating a simple autoscaling solution based on monitoring triggers.

In this chapter, we are going to explore the following topics:

- Backing up LXC containers using `tar` and `rsync`
- Backing up LXC containers with the `lxc-copy` utility
- Creating LXC containers using the iSCSI target as a backend store and demonstrating how to migrate containers if the primary server goes down
- Demonstrating how to use GlusterFS as a shared filesystem for the root filesystem of containers and deploy active-passive LXC nodes
- Looking into what metrics LXC exposes, and how to monitor, alert, and act on them

Backing up and migrating LXC

Creating backups of LXC instances ensures that we can recover from events such as server crashes or corrupt backend stores. Backups also provide for a quick way of migrating instances between hosts or starting multiple similar containers, by just changing their config files.

Creating LXC backup using tar and rsync

In most use cases, we build containers from templates, or with tools such as debootstrap, which result in an entire root filesystem, for the instance. Creating backups in such cases is a matter of stopping the container, archiving its configuration file along with the actual root filesystem, then storing them on a remote server. Let's demonstrate this concept with a simple example:

1. Start by updating your Ubuntu distribution and installing LXC. For this example, we'll be using Ubuntu 16.04, but the instructions apply to any other Linux distribution:

```
root@ubuntu:~# apt-get update && apt-get -y upgrade && reboot
root@ubuntu:~# lsb_release -cd
Description: Ubuntu 16.04.1 LTS
Codename: xenial
root@ubuntu:~#
root@ubuntu:~# apt-get install -y lxc
```

2. Next, proceed by creating a container using the default directory backend store, and start it:

```
root@ubuntu:~# lxc-create --name dir_container --template ubuntu
root@ubuntu:~# lxc-start --name dir_container
```

3. Install an application inside LXC, in this case, Nginx, and create a custom index file:

```
root@ubuntu:~# lxc-attach --name dir_container
root@dir_container:~# apt-get install -y nginx
root@dir_container:~# echo "Original container" >
/var/www/html/index.nginx-debian.html
root@dir_container:~# exit
exit
root@ubuntu:~#
```

4. With the container running, ensure we can reach the HTTP service:

```
root@ubuntu:~# lxc-ls -f
NAME STATE AUTOSTART GROUPS IPV4 IPV6
dir_container RUNNING 0 - 10.0.3.107 -
root@ubuntu:~# curl 10.0.3.107
Original container
root@ubuntu:~#
```

5. Notice how the container's filesystem and its configuration file are self-contained in the /var/lib/lxc directory:

```
root@ubuntu:~# cd /var/lib/lxc
root@ubuntu:/var/lib/lxc# ls -lah
total 12K
drwx------ 3 root root 4.0K Nov 15 16:28 .
drwxr-xr-x 42 root root 4.0K Nov 15 16:17 ..
drwxrwx--- 3 root root 4.0K Nov 15 16:33 dir_container
root@ubuntu:/var/lib/lxc# ls -la dir_container/
total 16
drwxrwx--- 3 root root 4096 Nov 15 16:33 .
drwx------ 3 root root 4096 Nov 15 16:28 ..
-rw-r--r-- 1 root root 712 Nov 15 16:33 config
drwxr-xr-x 21 root root 4096 Nov 15 16:38 rootfs
root@ubuntu:/var/lib/lxc#
```

6. This is quite convenient for creating a backup using standard Linux utilities such as `tar` and `rsync`. Stop the container before we back it up:

```
root@ubuntu:/var/lib/lxc# lxc-stop --name dir_container
root@ubuntu:/var/lib/lxc# lxc-ls -f
NAME STATE AUTOSTART GROUPS IPV4 IPV6
dir_container STOPPED 0 - - -
root@ubuntu:/var/lib/lxc#
```

7. Create a `bzip` archive of the root filesystem and the configuration file, making sure to preserve the numeric owner IDs, so that we can later start it on a different server without creating user ID collisions:

```
root@ubuntu:/var/lib/lxc# tar --numeric-owner -jcvf
dir_container.tar.bz2 dir_container/
...
root@ubuntu:/var/lib/lxc# file dir_container.tar.bz2
dir_container.tar.bz2: bzip2 compressed data, block size = 900k
root@ubuntu:/var/lib/lxc#
```

8. Next, copy the archive to a different server, in this case, `ubuntu-backup`, and delete the archive from the original server:

```
root@ubuntu:/var/lib/lxc# rsync -vaz dir_container.tar.bz2
ubuntu-backup:/tmp
sending incremental file list
dir_container.tar.bz2
sent 148,846,592 bytes received 35 bytes 9,603,008.19 bytes/sec
total size is 149,719,493 speedup is 1.01
root@ubuntu:/var/lib/lxc# rm -f dir_container.tar.bz2
```

With the archive on the destination server, we are now ready to restore it when needed.

Restoring from the archived backup

To restore the container from the `bz2` backup, on the destination server, extract the archive in `/var/lib/lxc`:

```
root@ubuntu-backup:~# cd /var/lib/lxc
root@ubuntu-backup:/var/lib/lxc# ls -la
total 8
drwx------ 2 root root 4096 Oct 21 16:56 .
drwxr-xr-x 42 root root 4096 Nov 15 16:48 ..
root@ubuntu-backup:/var/lib/lxc#
root@ubuntu-backup:/var/lib/lxc# tar jxfv /tmp/dir_container.tar.bz2
```

. . .

```
root@ubuntu-backup:/var/lib/lxc# ls -la
total 12
drwx------  3 root root 4096 Nov 15 16:59 .
drwxr-xr-x 42 root root 4096 Nov 15 16:48 ..
drwxrwx---  3 root root 4096 Nov 15 16:33 dir_container
root@ubuntu-backup:/var/lib/lxc#
```

Notice how, after extracting the root filesystem and the configuration file, listing all containers will show the container we just restored, albeit in a stopped state:

```
root@ubuntu-backup:/var/lib/lxc# lxc-ls -f
NAME STATE AUTOSTART GROUPS IPV4 IPV6
dir_container STOPPED 0 - - -
root@ubuntu-backup:/var/lib/lxc#
```

Let's start it and hit the HTTP endpoint, ensuring we get the same result back as with the original LXC instance:

```
root@ubuntu-backup:/var/lib/lxc# lxc-start --name dir_container
root@ubuntu-backup:/var/lib/lxc# lxc-ls -f
NAME STATE AUTOSTART GROUPS IPV4 IPV6
dir_container RUNNING 0 - 10.0.3.107 -
root@ubuntu-backup:/var/lib/lxc# curl 10.0.3.107
Original container
root@ubuntu-backup:/var/lib/lxc#
```

To clean up, run the following commands:

```
root@ubuntu-backup:/var/lib/lxc# lxc-stop --name dir_container
root@ubuntu-backup:/var/lib/lxc# lxc-destroy --name dir_container
Destroyed container dir_container
root@ubuntu-backup:/var/lib/lxc# ls -la
total 8
drwx------  2 root root 4096 Nov 15 17:01 .
drwxr-xr-x 42 root root 4096 Nov 15 16:48 ..
root@ubuntu-backup:/var/lib/lxc#
```

Creating container backup using lxc-copy

Regardless of the backend store of the container, we can use the `lxc-copy` utility to create a full copy of the LXC instance. Follow these steps for creating container backup:

1. We start by specifying the name of the container on the original host we want to back up, and a name for the copy:

   ```
   root@ubuntu:/var/lib/lxc# lxc-copy --name dir_container --newname
   dir_container_backup
   root@ubuntu:/var/lib/lxc#
   ```

   This command created a new root filesystem and configuration file on the host:

   ```
   root@ubuntu:/var/lib/lxc# ls -la
   total 16
   drwx------  4 root root 4096 Nov 15 17:07 .
   drwxr-xr-x 42 root root 4096 Nov 15 16:17 ..
   drwxrwx---  3 root root 4096 Nov 15 16:33 dir_container
   drwxrwx---  3 root root 4096 Nov 15 17:07 dir_container_backup

   root@ubuntu:/var/lib/lxc# lxc-ls -f
   NAME STATE AUTOSTART GROUPS IPV4 IPV6
   dir_container STOPPED 0 - - -
   dir_container_backup STOPPED 0 - - -
   root@ubuntu:/var/lib/lxc#
   ```

2. Creating a full copy will update the configuration file of the new container with the newly specified name and location of the `rootfs`:

   ```
   root@ubuntu:/var/lib/lxc# cat dir_container_backup/config | egrep
   "rootfs|utsname"
   lxc.rootfs = /var/lib/lxc/dir_container_backup/rootfs
   lxc.rootfs.backend = dir
   lxc.utsname = dir_container_backup
   root@ubuntu:/var/lib/lxc#
   ```

   Notice the container's name and directory have changed from the original instance. Now we can archive and store remotely, as shown in the previous section, with `tar` and `rsync`. Using this method is convenient, if we need to ensure the name of the container and the location of its `rootfs` differ from the original, in the case where we would like to keep the backup on the same server, or on hosts with the same LXC name.

---

3. Finally, to clean up, execute the following command:

```
root@ubuntu:/var/lib/lxc# lxc-destroy --name dir_container_backup
Destroyed container dir_container_backup
root@ubuntu:/var/lib/lxc# lxc-destroy --name dir_container
Destroyed container dir_container
root@ubuntu:/var/lib/lxc#
```

Migrating LXC containers on an iSCSI target

Moving containers from one host to another can be quite useful when performing server maintenance, or when redistributing server load. Cloud platforms such as OpenStack leverage schedulers that choose where an LXC instance should be created and tools to migrate them, based on certain criteria such as instance density, resource utilization, and others, as we'll see in the next chapter. Nevertheless, it helps to know how to manually migrate instances between hosts should the need arise.

Creating a backup or a copy of the container is easier when we use the default `dir` backing store with LXC; however, it is not as trivial when leveraging other types such as LVM, Btrfs, or ZFS, unless using a shared storage, such as GlusterFS, or iSCSI block devices, which we are going to explore next.

The iSCSI protocol has been around for a while, and lots of **Storage Area Networks** (**SAN**) solutions exist around it. It's a great way of providing access to block devices over a TCP/IP network.

Setting up the iSCSI target

The endpoint that exposes the block device is called the **target**. Creating an iSCSI target on Linux is quite trivial. All we need is a block device. In the following example, we are going to use two servers; one will be the iSCSI target that exposes a block device, and the other will be the initiator server, which will connect to the target and use the presented block device as the location for the LXC containers' root filesystem and configuration files.

Follow these steps for setting up the iSCSI target:

1. Let's start by installing the necessary package on Ubuntu, and then demonstrate the same on CentOS:

```
root@ubuntu-backup:~# apt-get install -y iscsitarget
root@ubuntu-backup:~#
```

2. With the package installed, enable the target functionality:

```
root@ubuntu-backup:~# sed -i
's/ISCSITARGET_ENABLE=false/ISCSITARGET_ENABLE=true/g'
/etc/default/iscsitarget
root@ubuntu-backup:~#
```

3. Next, let's create the target configuration file. The file is well-documented with comments; we are going to use a small subset of the available configuration options. We start by specifying an arbitrary identifier, `iqn.2001-04.com.example:lxc` in this example, a username and password, and, most importantly, the block device we are going to expose over iSCSI –`/dev/xvdb`. The iSCSI identifier is in the following form:

```
iqn.yyyy-mm.naming-authority:unique name
```

The description of this identifier is as follows:

- `yyyy-mm` : This is the year and month when the naming authority was established
- `naming-authority`: This is usually reverse syntax of the Internet domain name of the naming authority, or the domain name of the server
- `unique name`: This is any name you would like to use

With these in mind, the minimal working target configuration file is as follows:

```
root@ubuntu-backup:~# cat /etc/iet/ietd.conf
Target iqn.2001-04.com.example:lxc
IncomingUser lxc secret
OutgoingUser
Lun 0 Path=/dev/xvdb,Type=fileio
Alias lxc_lun
root@ubuntu-backup:~#
```

4. Next, specify which hosts or initiators are allowed to connect to the iSCSI target; replace the IP with that of the host that is going to connect to the target server:

```
root@ubuntu-backup:~# cat /etc/iet/initiators.allow
iqn.2001-04.com.example:lxc 10.208.129.253
root@ubuntu-backup:~#
```

5. Now, start the iSCSI target service:

```
root@ubuntu-backup:~# /etc/init.d/iscsitarget start
[ ok ] Starting iscsitarget (via systemctl): iscsitarget.service.
root@ubuntu-backup:~#
```

6. On CentOS, the process and configuration files are slightly different. To install the package, execute the following command:

```
[root@centos ~]# yum install scsi-target-utils
[root@centos ~]#
```

7. The configuration file has the following format:

```
[root@centos ~]# cat /etc/tgt/targets.conf
default-driver iscsi
<target iqn.2001-04.com.example:lxc>
backing-store /dev/xvdb
initiator-address 10.208.5.176
incominguser lxc secret
</target>
[root@centos ~]#
```

8. To start the service, run the following command:

```
[root@centos ~]# service tgtd restart
```

9. Let's list the exposed target by running the following command:

```
[root@centos ~]# tgt-admin --show
Target 1: iqn.2001-04.com.example:lxc
System information:
Driver: iscsi
State: ready
I_T nexus information:
LUN information:
...
LUN: 1
Type: disk
SCSI ID: IET 00010001
SCSI SN: beaf11
Size: 80531 MB, Block size: 512
Online: Yes
Removable media: No
Prevent removal: No
Readonly: No
SWP: No
```

```
Thin-provisioning: No
Backing store type: rdwr
Backing store path: /dev/xvdb
Backing store flags:
Account information:
ACL information:
10.208.5.176
[root@centos ~]#
```

Setting up the iSCSI initiator

The initiator is the server that will connect to the target and access the exposed block device over the iSCSI protocol.

1. To install the initiator tools on Ubuntu, run the following command:

   ```
   root@ubuntu:~# apt-get install -y open-iscsi
   ```

   On CentOS, the package name is different:

   ```
   [root@centos ~]# yum install iscsi-initiator-utils
   ```

2. Next, enable the service and start the iSCSI daemon:

   ```
   root@ubuntu:~# sed -i 's/node.startup = manual/node.startup =
   automatic/g'   /etc/iscsi/iscsid.conf
   root@ubuntu:~# /etc/init.d/open-iscsi restart
   [ ok ] Restarting open-iscsi (via systemctl): open-iscsi.service.
   root@ubuntu:~#
   ```

3. The `iscsiadm` command is the userspace tool that we can use from the initiating server to ask the target for available devices. From the initiator host, let's ask the target server we configured earlier what block devices are available:

   ```
   root@ubuntu:~# iscsiadm -m discovery -t sendtargets -p 10.208.129.201
   10.208.129.201:3260,1 iqn.2001-04.com.example:lxc
   192.237.179.19:3260,1 iqn.2001-04.com.example:lxc
   10.0.3.1:3260,1 iqn.2001-04.com.example:lxc
   root@ubuntu:~#
   ```

   From the preceding output, we can see that the target server presented one target identified by the **iSCSI Qualified Name (IQN)** of `iqn.2001-04.com.example:lxc`. In this case, the target server has three IP addresses, thus the three lines from the output.

4. Earlier, we configured the target to use a username and a password. We need to configure the initiator host to present the same credentials to the target host in order to access the resources:

```
root@ubuntu:~# iscsiadm -m node -T iqn.2001-04.com.example:lxc -p
10.208.129.201:3260 --op=update --name node.session.auth.authmethod
--value=CHAP
root@ubuntu:~# iscsiadm -m node -T iqn.2001-04.com.example:lxc -p
10.208.129.201:3260 --op=update --name node.session.auth.username
--value=lxc
root@ubuntu:~# iscsiadm -m node -T iqn.2001-04.com.example:lxc -p
10.208.129.201:3260 --op=update --name node.session.auth.password
--value=secret
root@ubuntu:~#
```

5. After updating the initiator's configuration, we can check that the credentials have been applied by examining the configuration file that was automatically created:

```
root@ubuntu:~# cat
/etc/iscsi/nodes/iqn.2001-04.com.example\:lxc/10.208.129.201\,3260\,1
/default | grep auth
node.session.auth.authmethod = CHAP
node.session.auth.username = lxc
node.session.auth.password = secret
node.conn[0].timeo.auth_timeout = 45
root@ubuntu:~#
```

Logging in to the iSCSI target using the presented block device as rootfs for LXC

With the initiator host configured, we are now ready to log in to the iSCSI target and use the presented block device:

1. To log in, from the initiator host run the following command:

```
root@ubuntu:~# iscsiadm -m node -T iqn.2001-04.com.example:lxc -p
10.208.129.201:3260 --login
Logging in to [iface: default, target: iqn.2001-04.com.example:lxc,
portal:10.208.129.201,3260] (multiple)
Login to [iface: default, target: iqn.2001-04.com.example:lxc,
portal:10.208.129.201,3260] successful.
root@ubuntu:~#
```

2. Let's verify that the initiator host now contains an iSCSI session:

```
root@ubuntu:~# iscsiadm -m session
tcp: [2] 10.208.129.201:3260,1 iqn.2001-04.com.example:lxc
(non-flash)
root@ubuntu:~#
```

3. The initiator host should now have a new block device available for use:

```
root@ubuntu:~# ls -la /dev/disk/by-path/
total 0
drwxr-xr-x 2 root root 60 Nov 15 20:23 .
drwxr-xr-x 6 root root 120 Nov 15 20:23 ..
lrwxrwxrwx 1 root root 9 Nov 15 20:23
ip-10.208.129.201:3260-iscsi-iqn.2001-04.com.example:lxc-lun-0
-> ../../sda
root@ubuntu:~#
```

4. This new block device can be used as a regular storage device. Let's create a filesystem on it:

```
root@ubuntu:~# mkfs.ext4 /dev/disk/by-path/ip-10.208.129.201\
:3260-iscsi-iqn.2001-04.com.example\:lxc-lun-0
root@ubuntu:~#
```

5. With the filesystem present, let's use the block device as the default location for the LXC filesystem, by mounting it at /var/lib/lxc:

```
root@ubuntu:~# mount /dev/disk/by-path/ip-10.208.129.201\
:3260-iscsi-iqn.2001-04.com.example\:lxc-lun-0 /var/lib/lxc
root@ubuntu:~# df -h | grep lxc
/dev/sda 74G 52M 70G 1% /var/lib/lxc
root@ubuntu:~#
```

Since we mounted the iSCSI device at the default location for the root filesystem of the LXC containers, next time we build one, its root filesystem will be on the iSCSI device. As we'll see shortly, this is useful if the initiator host needs to undergo maintenance, or becomes unavailable for whatever reason, because we can mount the same iSCSI target to a new host and just start the same containers there with no configuration changes on the LXC side.

Building the iSCSI container

Create a new LXC container as usual, start it, and ensure it's running:

```
root@ubuntu:~# lxc-create --name iscsi_container --template ubuntu
root@ubuntu:~# lxc-start --name iscsi_container
root@ubuntu:~# lxc-ls -f
NAME STATE AUTOSTART GROUPS IPV4 IPV6
iscsi_container RUNNING 0 - 10.0.3.162 -
root@ubuntu:~#
```

Even though the root filesystem is now on the new iSCSI block device, from the perspective of the host OS, nothing is different:

```
root@ubuntu:~# ls -la /var/lib/lxc/iscsi_container/
total 16
drwxrwx--- 3 root root 4096 Nov 15 21:01 .
drwxr-xr-x 4 root root 4096 Nov 15 21:01 ..
-rw-r--r-- 1 root root 716 Nov 15 21:01 config
drwxr-xr-x 21 root root 4096 Nov 15 21:01 rootfs
root@ubuntu:~#
```

Since the `rootfs` of the container now resides on a block device that is remote, depending on the network connection between the LXC initiator host and the ISCSI target host, some latency might be present. In production deployments, an isolated low-latency network is preferred between the iSCSI target and the initiator hosts.

To migrate the container to a different host, we need to stop it, unmount the disk, then log out the block device from the iSCSI target:

```
root@ubuntu:~# lxc-stop --name iscsi_container
root@ubuntu:~# umount /var/lib/lxc
root@ubuntu:~# iscsiadm -m node -T iqn.2001-04.com.example:lxc -p
10.208.129.201:3260 --logout
Logging out of session [sid: 6, target: iqn.2001-04.com.example:lxc,
portal: 10.208.129.201,3260]
Logout of [sid: 6, target: iqn.2001-04.com.example:lxc, portal:
10.208.129.201,3260] successful.
root@ubuntu:~#
```

Restoring the iSCSI container

To restore the iSCI container, follow these steps:

1. On a new host that is configured as an initiator, we can log in the same target as we saw earlier:

```
root@ubuntu-backup:~# iscsiadm -m node -T iqn.2001-04.com.example:lxc
-p 10.208.129.201:3260 --login
Logging in to [iface: default, target: iqn.2001-04.com.example:lxc,
portal: 10.208.129.201,3260] (multiple)
Login to [iface: default, target: iqn.2001-04.com.example:lxc,
portal: 10.208.129.201,3260] successful.
root@ubuntu-backup:~#
```

2. Ensure that a new block device has been presented after logging in to the iSCSI target:

```
root@ubuntu-backup:~# ls -la /dev/disk/by-path/
total 0
drwxr-xr-x 2 root root 60 Nov 15 21:31 .
drwxr-xr-x 6 root root 120 Nov 15 21:31 ..
lrwxrwxrwx 1 root root 9 Nov 15 21:31 ip-10.208.129.201:
3260-iscsi-iqn.2001-04.com.example:lxc-lun-0 -> ../../sda
root@ubuntu-backup:~#
```

When logging in the iSCSI target on a new host, keep in mind that the name of the presented block device might be different from what it was on the original server.

3. Next, mount the block device to the default location of LXC root filesystem:

```
root@ubuntu-backup:~# mount /dev/disk/by-path/ip-10.208.129.201\
:3260-iscsi-iqn.2001-04.com.example\:lxc-lun-0 /var/lib/lxc
root@ubuntu-backup:~#
```

4. If we list all available containers now, we'll see that the container we created on the previous host is now present on the new server, just by mounting the iSCSI target:

```
root@ubuntu-backup:~# lxc-ls -f
NAME STATE AUTOSTART GROUPS IPV4 IPV6
iscsi_container STOPPED 0 - - -
root@ubuntu-backup:~#
```

5. Finally, we can start the container as usual:

```
root@ubuntu-backup:~# lxc-start --name iscsi_container
root@ubuntu-backup:~# lxc-ls -f
NAME STATE AUTOSTART GROUPS IPV4 IPV6
iscsi_container RUNNING 0 - 10.0.3.162 -
root@ubuntu-backup:~#
```

If the container is configured with a static IP address, the same IP will be present on the new host; however, if the container obtains its network configuration dynamically, its IP might change. Keep this in mind if there is an associated A record in DNS for the container you are migrating.

LXC active backup with replicated GlusterFS storage

In the previous section, we saw how to use a remote block device as a local storage for LXC by means of exporting it over iSCSI. We formatted the block device with a filesystem that does not allow shared access from multiple servers. If you log in the target device to more than one server and they try to write to it at the same time, corruption will occur. Using iSCSI devices on a single node to host the LXC containers provides for an excellent way of achieving a level of redundancy should the LXC server go down; we just log in the same block device on a new initiator server and start the containers. We can consider this as a form of cold backup, since there will be downtime while moving the iSCSI block device to the new host, logging in to it, and starting the container.

There's an alternative way, where we can use a shared filesystem that can be attached and accessed from multiple servers at the same time, with the same LXC containers running on multiple hosts, with different IP addresses. Let's explore this scenario using the scalable network filesystem GlusterFS as the remotely shared filesystem of choice.

Creating the shared storage

GlusterFS has two main components - a server component that runs the GlusterFS daemon, which exports local block devices called **bricks**, and a client component that connects to the servers with a custom protocol over TCP/IP network and creates aggregate virtual volumes that can then be mounted and used as a regular filesystem.

There are three types of volumes:

- **Distributed**: These are volumes that distribute files throughout the cluster
- **Replicated**: These are volumes that replicate data across two or more nodes in the storage cluster
- **Striped**: These stripe files across multiple storage nodes

To achieve high availability of the LXC containers running on such shared volumes, we are going to use the replicated volumes on two GlusterFS servers. For this example, we are going to use a block device on each GlusterFS server with LVM.

1. On the first storage node, let's create the PV, the VG, and the LV on the /dev/xvdb block device:

```
root@node1:~# pvcreate /dev/xvdb
Physical volume "/dev/xvdb" successfully created
root@node1:~# vgcreate vg_node /dev/xvdb
Volume group "vg_node" successfully created
root@node1:~# lvcreate -n node1 -L 10g vg_node
Logical volume "node1" created.
root@node1:~#
```

2. Next, let's create a filesystem on the LVM device and mount it. XFS performs quite well with GlusterFS:

```
root@node1:~# mkfs.xfs -i size=512 /dev/vg_node/node1
meta-data=/dev/vg_node/node1    isize=512         agcount=4,
agsize=655360 blks
        =                       sectsz=512        attr=2,
projid32bit=1
        =                       crc=1             finobt=1,
sparse=0
   data =                       bsize=4096        blocks=2621440,
imaxpct=25
        =                       sunit=0           swidth=0
blks
naming =version 2              bsize=4096        ascii-ci=0
ftype=1
log      =internal log          bsize=4096        blocks=2560,
version=2
        =                       sectsz=512        sunit=0 blks,
lazy-count=1
realtime =none                 extsz=4096        blocks=0,
rtextents=0
root@node1:~# mount /dev/vg_node/node1 /mnt/
root@node1:~# mkdir /mnt/bricks
```

3. Finally, let's install the GlusterFS service:

```
root@node1:~# apt-get install -y glusterfs-server
```

Repeat the preceding steps on the second GlusterFS node, replacing node1 with node2 as necessary.

4. Once we have the GlusterFS daemon running on both nodes, it's time to probe from node1 to see if we can see any peers:

```
root@node1:~# gluster peer status
Number of Peers: 0
root@node1:~# gluster peer probe node2
peer probe: success.
root@node1:~# gluster peer status
Number of Peers: 1
Hostname: node2
Uuid: 65a480ba-e841-41a2-8f28-9d8f58f344ce
State: Peer in Cluster (Connected)
root@node1:~#
```

By probing from node1, we can now see that both node1 and node2 are part of a cluster.

5. The next step is to create the replicated volume by specifying the mount path of the LV we created and mounted earlier. Since we are using two nodes in the storage cluster, the replication factor is going to be 2. The following commands create the replicated volume, which will contain block devices from both node1 and node2 and list the created volume:

```
root@node1:~# gluster volume create lxc_glusterfs replica 2 transport
tcp node1:/mnt/bricks/node1 node2:/mnt/bricks/node2
volume create: lxc_glusterfs: success: please start the volume to
access data
root@node1:~# gluster volume list
lxc_glusterfs
root@node1:~#
```

6. To start the newly created replicated volume, run the following commands:

```
root@node1:~# gluster volume start lxc_glusterfs
volume start: lxc_glusterfs: success
```

To create and start the volume, we only need to run the preceding commands from one of the storage nodes.

7. To obtain information about the new volume, run this command on any of the nodes:

```
root@node1:~# gluster volume info
Volume Name: lxc_glusterfs
Type: Replicate
Volume ID: 9f11dc99-19d6-4644-87d2-fa6e983bcb83
Status: Started
Number of Bricks: 1 x 2 = 2
Transport-type: tcp
Bricks:
Brick1: node1:/mnt/bricks/node1
Brick2: node2:/mnt/bricks/node2
Options Reconfigured:
performance.readdir-ahead: on
root@node1:~#
```

From the preceding output, notice both bricks from node1 and node2. We can see them on both nodes as well:

```
root@node1:~# ls -la /mnt/bricks/node1/
total 0
drwxr-xr-x 4 root root  41 Nov 16 21:33 .
drwxr-xr-x 3 root root  19 Nov 16 21:33 ..
drw------- 6 root root 141 Nov 16 21:34 .glusterfs
drwxr-xr-x 3 root root  25 Nov 16 21:33 .trashcan
root@node1:~#
```

We see the following on node2:

```
root@node2:~# ls -la /mnt/bricks/node1/
total 0
drwxr-xr-x 4 root root  41 Nov 16 21:33 .
drwxr-xr-x 3 root root  19 Nov 16 21:33 ..
drw------- 6 root root 141 Nov 16 21:34 .glusterfs
drwxr-xr-x 3 root root  25 Nov 16 21:33 .trashcan
root@node2:~#
```

We should see the same files because we are using the replicated volume. Creating files on one of the mounted volumes should appear on the other, although, as with the iSCSI setup earlier, the network latency is important, since the data needs to be transferred over the network.

Building the GlusterFS LXC container

With the GlusterFS cluster ready, let's use a third server to mount the replicated volume from the storage cluster and use it as the LXC root filesystem and configuration location:

1. First, let's install the GlusterFS client:

   ```
   root@lxc1:~# apt-get install -y glusterfs-client attr
   ```

2. Next, mount the replicated volume from the storage cluster to the LXC host:

   ```
   root@lxc1:~# mount -t glusterfs node2:/lxc_glusterfs /var/lib/lxc
   ```

   In the preceding command, we are using `node2` as the target from which we are mounting; however, we can use `node1` in exactly the same way. The name of the target device we specify in the `lxc_glusterfs` mount command is what we specified as the name of the replicated volume earlier.

3. Now that the replicated GlusterFS volume has been mounted to the default LXC location, let's create and start a container:

   ```
   root@lxc1:~# lxc-create --name glusterfs_lxc --template ubuntu
   root@lxc1:~# lxc-start --name glusterfs_lxc
   ```

4. Attach to the container and install Nginx so we can later test connectivity from multiple servers:

   ```
   root@lxc1:~# lxc-attach --name glusterfs_lxc
   root@glusterfs_lxc:~# apt-get -y install nginx
   . . .
   root@glusterfs_lxc:~# echo "Nginx on GlusterFS LXC" >
   /var/www/html/index.nginx-debian.html
   root@glusterfs_lxc:~# exit
   exit
   root@lxc1:~#
   ```

5. Obtain the IP address of the container and ensure we can connect to Nginx from the host OS:

   ```
   root@lxc1:~# lxc-ls -f
   NAME STATE AUTOSTART GROUPS IPV4 IPV6
   glusterfs_lxc RUNNING 0 - 10.0.3.184 -
   root@lxc1:~# curl 10.0.3.184
   Nginx on GlusterFS LXC
   root@lxc1:~#
   ```

6. With the container created, the root filesystem and configuration file will be visible on both storage nodes:

```
root@node1:~# ls -la /mnt/bricks/node1/
total 12
drwxr-xr-x 5 root root 62 Nov 16 21:53 .
drwxr-xr-x 3 root root 19 Nov 16 21:33 ..
drw------- 261 root root 8192 Nov 16 21:54 .glusterfs
drwxrwx--- 3 root root 34 Nov 16 21:53 glusterfs_lxc
drwxr-xr-x 3 root root 25 Nov 16 21:33 .trashcan
root@node1:~#
```

7. The following will be visible on `node2`:

```
root@node2:~# ls -la /mnt/bricks/node2/
total 12
drwxr-xr-x 5 root root 62 Nov 16 21:44 .
drwxr-xr-x 3 root root 19 Nov 16 21:33 ..
drw------- 261 root root 8192 Nov 16 21:44 .glusterfs
drwxrwx--- 3 root root 34 Nov 16 21:47 glusterfs_lxc
drwxr-xr-x 3 root root 25 Nov 16 21:33 .trashcan
root@node2:~#
```

Depending on your network bandwidth and latency, replicating the data between both storage nodes might take some time. This will also affect how long it takes for the LXC container to build, start, and stop.

Restoring the GlusterFS container

Let's create a second LXC host, install the GlusterFS client, and mount the replicated volume in the same way we did earlier:

```
root@lxc2:~# apt-get install -y glusterfs-client attr
root@lxc2:~# mount -t glusterfs node1:/lxc_glusterfs /var/lib/lxc
root@lxc2:~# lxc-ls -f
NAME STATE AUTOSTART GROUPS IPV4 IPV6
glusterfs_lxc STOPPED 0 - - -
root@lxc2:~#
```

Notice how, just by mounting the GlusterFS volume, the host now sees the container in a stopped state. This is exactly the same container as the running one on `node1` - same config and root filesystem, that is. Since we are using a shared filesystem, we can start the container on multiple hosts without worrying about data corruption, unlike the case with iSCSI:

```
root@lxc2:~# lxc-start --name glusterfs_lxc
root@lxc2:~# lxc-ls -f
NAME STATE AUTOSTART GROUPS IPV4 IPV6
glusterfs_lxc RUNNING 0 - 10.0.3.184 -
root@lxc2:~#
```

Since we are using DHCP to dynamically assign IP addresses to the containers, the same container on the new hosts gets a new IP. Notice how connecting to Nginx running in the container gives us the same result, since the container shares its filesystem and configuration file across multiple LXC nodes:

```
root@lxc2:~# curl 10.0.3.184
Nginx on GlusterFS LXC
root@lxc2:~#
```

This setup in a sense implements a hot standby backup, where we can use both containers behind a proxy service such as HAProxy, with the second node only being used when the first node goes down, ensuring that any configuration changes are immediately available. As an alternative, both LXC containers can be used at the same time, but keep in mind that they'll write to the same filesystem, so the Nginx logs in this case will be written from both LXC containers on the lxc1 and lxc2 nodes.

Monitoring and alerting on LXC metrics

Monitoring LXC containers is not much different than monitoring a VM or a server - we can run a monitoring client inside the container, or on the actual host that runs LXC. Since the root filesystem of the containers is exposed on the host and LXC uses cgroups and namespaces, we can collect various information directly from the host OS, if we would rather not run a monitoring agent in the container. Before we look at two examples of LXC monitoring, let's first see how we can gather various metrics that we can monitor and alert on.

Gathering container metrics

LXC provides a few simple tools that can be used to monitor the state of the container and its resource utilization. The information they provide, as you are going to see next, is not that verbose; however, we can utilize the cgroup filesystem and collect even more information from it. Let's explore each of these options.

Using lxc-monitor to track container state

The `lxc-monitor` tool can be used to track containers, state changes – when they start or stop.

To demonstrate this, open two terminals; in one, create a new container and in the other, run the `lxc-monitor` command. Start the container and observe the output in the second terminal:

```
root@ubuntu:~# lxc-create --name monitor_lxc --template ubuntu
root@ubuntu:~# lxc-start --name monitor_lxc
root@ubuntu:~# lxc-monitor --name monitor_lxc
'monitor_lxc' changed state to [STARTING]
'monitor_lxc' changed state to [RUNNING]
```

Stop the container and notice the state change:

```
root@ubuntu:~# lxc-stop --name monitor_lxc
root@ubuntu:~#
'monitor_lxc' changed state to [STARTING]
'monitor_lxc' changed state to [RUNNING]
'monitor_lxc' exited with status [0]
'monitor_lxc' changed state to [STOPPING]
'monitor_lxc' changed state to [STOPPED]
root@ubuntu:~# lxc-start --name monitor_lxc
```

Using lxc-top to obtain CPU and memory utilization

The `lxc-top` tool is similar to the standard `top` Linux command; it shows CPU, memory, and I/O utilization. To start it, execute the following command:

```
root@ubuntu:~# lxc-top --name monitor_lxc
Container    CPU     CPU     CPU     BlkIO     Mem
Name                 Used    Sys     User
Total    Used
monitor_lxc          0.52    0.26    0.16      0.00
12.71 MB
TOTAL 1 of 1         0.52    0.26    0.16      0.00
12.71 MB
```

Using lxc-info to gather container information

We can use the `lxc-info` tool to periodically poll for information such as CPU, memory, I/O, and network utilization:

```
root@ubuntu:~# lxc-info --name monitor_lxc
Name:         monitor_lxc
State:        RUNNING
PID:          19967
IP:           10.0.3.88
CPU use:      0.53 seconds
BlkIO use:    0 bytes
Memory use:   12.74 MiB
KMem use:     0 bytes
Link:         veth8OX0PW
TX bytes:     1.34 KiB
RX bytes:     1.35 KiB
Total bytes:  2.69 KiB
root@ubuntu:~#
```

Leveraging cgroups to collect memory metrics

In `Chapter 1`, *Introduction to Linux Containers* we explored cgroups in great details and saw how LXC creates a directory hierarchy in the cgroup virtual filesystem for each container it starts. To find where the cgroup hierarchy for the container we built earlier is, run the following command:

```
root@ubuntu:~# find /sys/fs/ -type d -name monitor_lxc
/sys/fs/cgroup/freezer/lxc/monitor_lxc
/sys/fs/cgroup/cpuset/lxc/monitor_lxc
/sys/fs/cgroup/net_cls,net_prio/lxc/monitor_lxc
/sys/fs/cgroup/devices/lxc/monitor_lxc
/sys/fs/cgroup/perf_event/lxc/monitor_lxc
/sys/fs/cgroup/hugetlb/lxc/monitor_lxc
/sys/fs/cgroup/blkio/lxc/monitor_lxc
/sys/fs/cgroup/pids/lxc/monitor_lxc
/sys/fs/cgroup/memory/lxc/monitor_lxc
/sys/fs/cgroup/cpu,cpuacct/lxc/monitor_lxc
/sys/fs/cgroup/systemd/lxc/monitor_lxc
root@ubuntu:~#
```

We can use the files in the memory group to set and obtain metrics that we can monitor and alert on. For example, to set the memory of the container to 512 MB, run the following command:

```
root@ubuntu:~# lxc-cgroup --name monitor_lxc memory.limit_in_bytes
536870912
root@ubuntu:~#
```

To read the current memory utilization for the container, execute the following command:

```
root@ubuntu:~# cat
/sys/fs/cgroup/memory/lxc/monitor_lxc/memory.usage_in_bytes
13361152
root@ubuntu:~#
```

To collect more information about the container's memory, read from the following file:

```
root@ubuntu:~# cat /sys/fs/cgroup/memory/lxc/monitor_lxc/memory.stat
cache 8794112
rss 4833280
rss_huge 0
mapped_file 520192
dirty 0
...
root@ubuntu:~#
```

Using cgroups to collect CPU statistics

To collect CPU usage, we can read from the `cpuacct` cgroup subsystem:

```
root@ubuntu:~# cat /sys/fs/cgroup/cpu,cpuacct/lxc/monitor_lxc/cpuacct.usage
627936278
root@ubuntu:~#
```

Collecting network metrics

Each container creates a virtual interface on the host; the output from the `lxc-info` command earlier displayed it as `veth8OX0PW`. We can collect information about the packets sent and received, error rates, and so on, by running the following command:

```
root@ubuntu:~# ifconfig veth8OX0PW
veth8OX0PW Link encap:Ethernet HWaddr fe:4d:bf:3f:17:8f
          inet6 addr: fe80::fc4d:bfff:fe3f:178f/64 Scope:Link
          UP BROADCAST RUNNING MULTICAST MTU:1500 Metric:1
          RX packets:125645 errors:0 dropped:0 overruns:0 frame:0
```

```
        TX packets:129909 errors:0 dropped:0 overruns:0 carrier:0
        collisions:0 txqueuelen:1000
        RX bytes:20548005 (20.5 MB) TX bytes:116477293 (116.4 MB)
root@ubuntu:~#
```

Alternatively, we can connect to the container's network namespace and obtain the information that way. The following three commands demonstrate how to execute commands in the container's network namespace. Note the PID of 19967; it can be obtained from the lxc-info command:

```
root@ubuntu:~# mkdir -p /var/run/netns
root@ubuntu:~# ln -sf /proc/19967/ns/net /var/run/netns/monitor_lxc
root@ubuntu:~# ip netns exec monitor_lxc ip a s
1: lo: <LOOPBACK,UP,LOWER_UP> mtu 65536 qdisc noqueue state UNKNOWN group
default qlen 1
    link/loopback 00:00:00:00:00:00 brd 00:00:00:00:00:00
    inet 127.0.0.1/8 scope host lo
        valid_lft forever preferred_lft forever
    inet6 ::1/128 scope host
        valid_lft forever preferred_lft forever
17: eth0@if18: <BROADCAST,MULTICAST,UP,LOWER_UP> mtu 1500 qdisc noqueue
state UP group default qlen 1000
    link/ether 00:16:3e:01:b7:8b brd ff:ff:ff:ff:ff:ff link-netnsid 0
        inet 10.0.3.88/24 brd 10.0.3.255 scope global eth0
    valid_lft forever preferred_lft forever
        inet6 fe80::216:3eff:fe01:b78b/64 scope link
    valid_lft forever preferred_lft forever
root@ubuntu:~#
```

Notice how we can see the network interfaces that are inside the LXC container, even though we ran the commands on the host.

Simple container monitoring and alerting with Monit

Now that we've demonstrated how to gather various monitoring data points, let's actually set up a system to monitor and alert on them. In this section, we are going to install a simple monitoring solution utilizing the monit daemon. Monit is an easy-to-configure service that uses scripts that can be automatically executed, based on certain monitoring events and thresholds.

Let's look at a few examples next:

1. To install `monit`, run the following command:

```
root@ubuntu:~# apt-get install -y monit mailutils
```

2. Next, create a minimal configuration file. The config that is packaged with the installation is documented quite well:

```
root@ubuntu:~# cd /etc/monit/
root@ubuntu:/etc/monit# cat monitrc | grep -vi "#"
set daemon 120
set logfile /var/log/monit.log
set idfile /var/lib/monit/id
set statefile /var/lib/monit/state
set eventqueue
basedir /var/lib/monit/events
slots 100
set httpd port 2812 and
allow admin:monit
include /etc/monit/conf.d/*
include /etc/monit/conf-enabled/*
root@ubuntu:/etc/monit#
```

The preceding config starts a web interface that can be reached on port 2812 with the specified credentials. It also defines two more directories where config files can be read.

3. Next, let's create a monitoring configuration that checks whether a container is running. Executing a script, which we'll write next, performs the actual check:

```
root@ubuntu:/etc/monit# cat conf.d/container_state.cfg
check program container_status with path
"/etc/monit/container_running.sh
monitor_lxc"
if status == 1
then exec "/bin/bash -c '/etc/monit/alert.sh'"
group lxc
root@ubuntu:/etc/monit#
```

The preceding configuration tells monit to run the container_running.sh script periodically and, if the exit status is 1, to execute a second script called alert.sh that will alert us. Simple enough. The container_running.sh script follows:

```
root@ubuntu:/etc/monit# cat container_running.sh
#!/bin/bash
CONTAINER_NAME=$1
CONTAINER_STATE=$(lxc-info --state --name $CONTAINER_NAME
| awk '{print $2}')
if [ "$CONTAINER_STATE" != "RUNNING" ]
then
  exit 1
else
  exit 0
fi
root@ubuntu:/etc/monit#
```

We can see that we are utilizing the lxc-info command to check the status of the container. The alert.sh script is even simpler:

```
root@ubuntu:/etc/monit# cat alert.sh
#!/bin/bash
echo "LXC container down" | mail -s "LXC container Alert"
youremail@example.com
root@ubuntu:/etc/monit#
```

4. Reload the monit service and check the status of the new monitoring service that we named container_status earlier in the configuration file:

```
root@ubuntu:/etc/monit# monit reload
Reinitializing monit daemon
The Monit daemon 5.16 uptime: 15h 43m
root@ubuntu:/etc/monit# monit status container_status
The Monit daemon 5.16 uptime: 15h 47m
Program 'container_status'
status Status ok
monitoring status Monitored
last started Fri, 18 Nov 2016 15:03:24
last exit value 0
data collected Fri, 18 Nov 2016 15:03:24
root@ubuntu:/etc/monit#
```

We can also connect to the web interface on port 2812 and see the newly defined monitoring target:

Monit Service Manager

Monit is running on ubuntu with uptime, 15h 47m and monitoring:

System	Status	Load	CPU	Memory	Swap
ubuntu	Running	[0.00] [0.00] [0.00]	0.1%us, 0.1%sy, 0.0%wa	40.3% [806.1 MB]	0.0% [0 B]

Program	Status	Output	Last started	Exit value
container_status	Status ok	no output	18 Nov 2016 15:03:24	0

5. Let's stop the container and check the status of `monit`:

```
root@ubuntu:/etc/monit# lxc-stop --name monitor_lxc
root@ubuntu:/etc/monit# monit status container_status
The Monit daemon 5.16 uptime: 15h 53m
Program 'container_status'
status Status failed
monitoring status Monitored
last started Fri, 18 Nov 2016 15:09:24
last exit value 1
data collected Fri, 18 Nov 2016 15:09:24
root@ubuntu:/etc/monit#
```

Monit Service Manager

Monit is running on ubuntu with uptime, 15h 38m and monitoring:

System	Status	Load	CPU	Memory	Swap
ubuntu	Running	[0.00] [0.00] [0.00]	0.0%us, 0.1%sy, 0.0%wa	39.6% [791.7 MB]	0.0% [0 B]

Program	Status	Output	Last started	Exit value
container_status	Status failed	no output	18 Nov 2016 14:54:40	1

Notice from the output of the command and the web interface that the status of the `container_status` service is now `failed`. Since we set up `monit` to send an e-mail when the service we are monitoring is failing, check the mail log. You should have received an e-mail from `monit`, which will most likely end up in your `spam` folder:

```
root@ubuntu:/etc/monit# tail -5 /var/log/mail.log
Nov 18 15:13:51 ubuntu postfix/pickup[26069]: 8AB30177CB3: uid=0
from=<root@ubuntu>
Nov 18 15:13:51 ubuntu postfix/cleanup[31295]: 8AB30177CB3: message-
id=<20161118151351.8AB30177CB3@ubuntu>
```

```
Nov 18 15:13:51 ubuntu postfix/qmgr[5392]: 8AB30177CB3: from=<root@ubuntu>,
size=340, nrcpt=1 (queue active)
Nov 18 15:13:51 ubuntu postfix/smtp[31297]: 8AB30177CB3: to=<
youremail@example.com >, relay=gmail-smtp-in.1.google.com[74.125.70.26]:25,
delay=0.22, delays=0.01/0.01/0.08/0.13, dsn=2.0.0, status=sent (250 2.0.0
OK 1479482031 u74si2324555itu.40 - gsmtp)
Nov 18 15:13:51 ubuntu postfix/qmgr[5392]: 8AB30177CB3: removed
root@ubuntu:/etc/monit#
```

For more information on Monit, refer to `https://mmonit.com/monit/documentation/monit.html`.

Monit is a quick and easy way to set up monitoring for LXC containers per server. It is agentless, and thanks to the exposed metrics from the cgroup hierarchies, it is easy to alert on various data points, without the need to attach or run anything extra in the containers.

Container monitoring and alert triggers with Sensu

Monit is a great tool for monitoring and alerting in a decentralized setup. However, for a more robust and feature-rich way of deploying centralized-based monitoring, other monitoring tools such as Sensu can be leveraged. There are two main ways to implement monitoring with Sensu - with an agent in each container, or on the LXC host with standalone checks collecting data from sources such as cgroups, in a way similar to Monit.

Sensu uses the client-server architecture, in the sense that the server publishes checks in a messaging queue that is provided by RabbitMQ, and the clients subscribe to the topic in that queue and execute checks and alerts based on set thresholds. State and historical data is stored in a Redis server.

Let's demonstrate a Sensu deployment with an agent inside the LXC container first, then move on to an agentless monitoring.

Monitoring LXC containers with Sensu agent and server

We need to install the required services that Sensu will use, Redis and RabbitMQ:

1. Let's start with the Redis server, and, once it's installed, ensure it's running:

```
root@ubuntu:~# apt-get -y install redis-server
root@ubuntu:~# redis-cli ping
PONG
```

```
root@ubuntu:~#
```

2. Installing RabbitMQ is just as easy:

```
root@ubuntu:~# apt-get install -y rabbitmq-server
```

3. Once installed, we need to create the virtual host that the agents will be subscribing to and reading messages from:

```
root@ubuntu:~# rabbitmqctl add_vhost /sensu
Creating vhost "/sensu" ...
root@ubuntu:~#
```

4. Next, create a username and a password to connect to that topic:

```
root@ubuntu:~# rabbitmqctl add_user sensu secret
Creating user "sensu" ...
root@ubuntu:~# rabbitmqctl set_permissions -p
/sensu sensu ".*" ".*" ".*"
Setting permissions for user "sensu" in vhost "/sensu" ...
root@ubuntu:~#
```

5. Time to install the Sensu server and client:

```
root@ubuntu:~# wget -q
https://sensu.global.ssl.fastly.net/apt/pubkey.gpg -O-
| sudo apt-key add -
OK
root@ubuntu:~# echo
"deb https://sensu.global.ssl.fastly.net/apt sensu main"
| sudo tee /etc/apt/sources.list.d/sensu.list
deb https://sensu.global.ssl.fastly.net/apt sensu main
root@ubuntu:~# apt-get update
root@ubuntu:~# apt-get install -y sensu
root@ubuntu:~# cd /etc/sensu/conf.d/
```

At a minimum, we need five configuration files, one for the Sensu API endpoint, two that specify what transport we are using - RabbitMQ in this case - the Redis config file for Sensu, and a client config file, for the Sensu client running on the same server. The following config files are pretty much self-explanatory - we specify the IP addresses and ports of the RabbitMQ and Redis servers, along with the API service:

```
root@ubuntu:/etc/sensu/conf.d# cat api.json
{
  "api": {
    "host": "localhost",
    "bind": "0.0.0.0",
```

```
      "port": 4567
    }
  }

root@ubuntu:/etc/sensu/conf.d#
root@ubuntu:/etc/sensu/conf.d# cat transport.json
{
  "transport": {
    "name": "rabbitmq",
    "reconnect_on_error": true
  }
}

root@ubuntu:/etc/sensu/conf.d#
root@ubuntu:/etc/sensu/conf.d# cat rabbitmq.json
{
  "rabbitmq": {
    "host": "10.208.129.253",
    "port": 5672,
    "vhost": "/sensu",
    "user": "sensu",
    "password": "secret"
  }
}

root@ubuntu:/etc/sensu/conf.d#
root@ubuntu:/etc/sensu/conf.d# cat redis.json
{
  "redis": {
    "host": "localhost",
    "port": 6379
  }
}

root@ubuntu:/etc/sensu/conf.d# cat client.json
{
  "client": {
    "name": "ubuntu",
    "address": "127.0.0.1",
    "subscriptions": [
      "base"
    ],
    "socket": {
      "bind": "127.0.0.1",
      "port": 3030
    }
  }
}
```

```
root@ubuntu:/etc/sensu/conf.d#
```

For more information on Sensu, refer to https://sensuapp.org/docs/.

Before we start the Sensu server, we can install a web-based frontend called Uchiwa:

```
root@ubuntu:~# apt-get install -y uchiwa
```

In the configuration file, we specify the address and port of the Sensu API service – localhost and port 4567 - and the port Uchiwa will be listening on - 3000 - in this case:

```
root@ubuntu:/etc/sensu/conf.d# cat /etc/sensu/uchiwa.json
{
  "sensu": [
    {
      "name": "LXC Containers",
      "host": "localhost",
      "ssl": false,
      "port": 4567,
      "path": "",
      "timeout": 5000
    }
  ],
  "uchiwa": {
    "port": 3000,
    "stats": 10,
    "refresh": 10000
  }
}
root@ubuntu:/etc/sensu/conf.d#
```

With all of the configuration in place, let's start the Sensu services:

```
root@ubuntu:~# /etc/init.d/sensu-server start
* Starting sensu-server [ OK ]
root@ubuntu:~# /etc/init.d/sensu-api start
* Starting sensu-api [ OK ]
root@ubuntu:/etc/sensu/conf.d# /etc/init.d/sensu-client start
* Starting sensu-client [ OK ]
root@ubuntu:/etc/sensu/conf.d#
root@ubuntu:~# /etc/init.d/uchiwa restart
uchiwa stopped.
uchiwa started.
root@ubuntu:~#
```

With the Sensu server now fully configured, we need to attach to a container on the host and install the Sensu agent:

```
root@ubuntu:~# lxc-attach --name monitor_lxc
root@monitor_lxc:~# apt-get install -y wget
root@monitor_lxc:~# wget -q
https://sensu.global.ssl.fastly.net/apt/pubkey.gpg -O- | sudo apt-key add -
OK
root@monitor_lxc:~# echo "deb https://sensu.global.ssl.fastly.net/apt sensu
main" | sudo tee /etc/apt/sources.list.d/sensu.list
deb https://sensu.global.ssl.fastly.net/apt sensu main
root@monitor_lxc:~# apt-get update
root@monitor_lxc:~# apt-get install -y sensu
root@monitor_lxc:/# cd /etc/sensu/conf.d/
```

To configure the Sensu agent, we need to edit the client config, where we specify the IP address and the name of the container:

```
root@monitor_lxc:/etc/sensu/conf.d# cat client.json
{
  "client": {
    "name": "monitor_lxc",
    "address": "10.0.3.2",
    "subscriptions": ["base"]
  }
}
root@monitor_lxc:/etc/sensu/conf.d#
```

We tell the agent how to connect to the RabbitMQ server on the host, by providing its IP address, port, and the credentials we created earlier:

```
root@monitor_lxc:/etc/sensu/conf.d# cat rabbitmq.json
{
  "rabbitmq": {
    "host": "10.0.3.1",
    "port": 5672,
    "vhost": "/sensu",
    "user": "sensu",
    "password": "secret"
  }
}
root@monitor_lxc:/etc/sensu/conf.d#
```

Then, specify the transport mechanism:

```
root@monitor_lxc:/etc/sensu/conf.d# cat transport.json
{
  "transport": {
```

```
        "name": "rabbitmq",
        "reconnect_on_error": true
    }
}
root@monitor_lxc:/etc/sensu/conf.d#
```

With the preceding three files in place, let's start the agent:

```
root@monitor_lxc:/etc/sensu/conf.d# /etc/init.d/sensu-client start
* Starting sensu-client [ OK ]
root@monitor_lxc:/etc/sensu/conf.d#
```

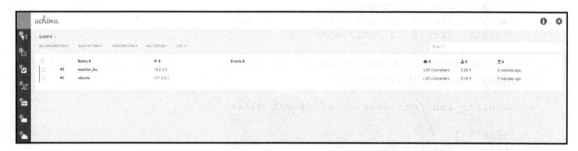

To verify that all services are running normally and that the Sensu agent can connect to the server, we can connect to the Uchiwa interface on port 3000 using the host IP, as shown earlier.

While still attached to the LXC container, let's install a Sensu check. Sensu checks are available as gems, or can be written manually. Let's search the gem repository for any memory checks instead of writing our own:

```
root@monitor_lxc:/etc/sensu/conf.d# apt-get install -y rubygems
root@monitor_lxc:/etc/sensu/conf.d# gem search sensu | grep plugins | grep
memory
sensu-plugins-memory (0.0.2)
sensu-plugins-memory-checks (1.0.2)
root@monitor_lxc:/etc/sensu/conf.d#
```

Install the memory check and restart the agent:

```
root@monitor_lxc:/etc/sensu/conf.d# gem install sensu-plugins-memory-checks
root@monitor_lxc:/etc/sensu/conf.d# /etc/init.d/sensu-client restart
configuration is valid
* Stopping sensu-client [ OK ]
* Starting sensu-client [ OK ]
root@monitor_lxc:/etc/sensu/conf.d#
```

On the Sensu server host (and not on the container), we need to define the new memory check so that the Sensu server can tell the agent to execute it. We do that by creating a new checks file:

```
root@ubuntu:/etc/sensu/conf.d# cat check_memory.json
{
  "checks": {
    "memory_check": {
      "command": "/usr/local/bin/check-memory-percent.rb -w 80 -c 90",
      "subscribers": ["base"],
      "handlers": ["default"],
      "interval": 300
    }
  }
}
root@ubuntu:/etc/sensu/conf.d#
```

We specify the path and the name of the check that needs to be run from the Sensu agent, in this case, the Ruby script that we installed in the container from the gem. Restart the Sensu services for the changes to take effect:

```
root@ubuntu:/etc/sensu/conf.d# /etc/init.d/sensu-server restart
configuration is valid
* Stopping sensu-server [ OK ]
* Starting sensu-server [ OK ]

root@ubuntu:/etc/sensu/conf.d# /etc/init.d/sensu-api restart
configuration is valid
* Stopping sensu-api [ OK ]
* Starting sensu-api [ OK ]

root@ubuntu:/etc/sensu/conf.d# /etc/init.d/uchiwa restart
Killing uchiwa (pid 15299) with SIGTERM
Waiting uchiwa (pid 15299) to die...
Waiting uchiwa (pid 15299) to die...
uchiwa stopped.
uchiwa started.
root@ubuntu:/etc/sensu/conf.d#
```

Checking the Uchiwa interface, we can see that the memory check is now active:

We can install multiple Sensu check scripts from gems inside the LXC container; define them on the Sensu server just like we would on a normal server or a virtual machine, and end up with a full-fledged monitoring solution.

There are a few caveats when running an agent inside the container:

- The agent consumes resources; if we are trying to run lightweight containers with a minimum amount of memory, this might not be the best solution.
- When measuring CPU load, the load inside the container will reflect the general load on the host itself, since the containers are not isolated from the host by a hypervisor. The best way to measure CPU utilization is by obtaining the data from the cgroups, or with the `lxc-info` command on the host.
- If using a shared root filesystem such as the one we saw in the previous chapter, monitoring the disk space inside the container might reflect the total space on the server.

If running a Sensu agent inside the LXC container is not desired, we can perform standalone checks from the Sensu server on the same host instead. Let's explore this setup next.

Monitoring LXC containers using standalone Sensu checks

On servers that run LXC containers, we can install the Sensu agent directly on the host OS, instead of inside each container, just like we did earlier in this chapter. We can also leverage Sensu's standalone checks, which provide a decentralized way of monitoring, meaning that the Sensu agent defines and schedules the checks instead of the Sensu server. This provides us with the benefit of not having to install agents and monitoring scripts inside the containers, and having the Sensu agents run the checks on each server.

Let's demonstrate how to create a standalone check on the LXC host we've been using so far:

```
root@ubuntu:/etc/sensu/conf.d# cat check_memory_no_agent.json
{
  "checks": {
    "check_memory_no_agent": {
      "command": "check_memory_no_agent.sh -n monitor_lxc -w 943718400
      -e 1048576000",
      "standalone": true,
      "subscribers": [
        "base"
```

```
            ],
            "interval": 300
        }
    }
}
root@ubuntu:/etc/sensu/conf.d#
```

The main difference when defining a standalone check is the presence of the
`"standalone"`: true stanza, as shown from the preceding output. In the command
section of the check configuration, we specify what script to execute to perform the actual
check and the thresholds it should alert on. The script can be anything, as long as it exits
with error code 2 for Critical alerts, error code 1 for Warning, and 0 if all is OK.

This is a very simple bash script that uses the memory.usage_in_bytes cgroup file to
collect metrics on the memory usage and alert on it if the specified threshold is reached:

```
root@ubuntu:/etc/sensu/conf.d# cd ../plugins/
root@ubuntu:/etc/sensu/plugins# cat check_memory_no_agent.sh
#!/bin/bash
# Checks memory usage for an LXC container from cgroups

usage()
{
  echo "Usage: `basename $0` -n|--name monitor_lxc -w|--warning
  5000 -e|--error 10000"
  exit 2
}
sanity_check()
{
  if [ "$CONTAINER_NAME" == "" ] || [ "$WARNING" == "" ] || [ "$ERROR"
  == "" ]
  then
    usage
  fi
}
report_result()
{
  if [ "$MEMORY_USAGE" -ge "$ERROR" ]
  then
    echo "CRITICAL - Memory usage too high at $MEMORY_USAGE"
    exit 2
  elif [ "$MEMORY_USAGE" -ge "$WARNING" ]
  then
    echo "WARNING - Memory usage at $MEMORY_USAGE"
    exit 1
  else
    echo "Memory Usage OK at $MEMROY_USAGE"
```

```
        exit 0
    fi
}
get_memory_usage()
{
    declare -g -i MEMORY_USAGE=0
    MEMORY_USAGE=$(cat
    /sys/fs/cgroup/memory/lxc/$CONTAINER_NAME/memory.usage_in_bytes)
}
main()
{
    sanity_check
    get_memory_usage
    report_result
}
while [[ $# > 1 ]]
do
    key=$1

    case $key in
      -n|--name)
        CONTAINER_NAME=$2
        shift
    ;;
    -w|--warning)
      WARNING=$2
      shift
    ;;
    -e|--error)
      ERROR=$2
      shift
    ;;
    *)
      usage
    ;;
    esac
    shift
done
main
root@ubuntu:/etc/sensu/plugins#
```

The preceding script, albeit simple, should be a good starting point for the reader to start writing more useful Sensu checks that operate on various LXC metrics. Looking at the script, we can see that it has three basic functions. First, it checks for the provided container name, and warning and error thresholds in the `sanitiy_check()` function. Then it gets the memory usage in bites from the cgroup file in the `get_memory_usage()` function, and finally, reports the results in the `report_result()` function, by returning the appropriate error code, as described earlier.

Change the permissions and the execution flag of the script, reload Sensu services, and make sure the check is showing in Uchiwa:

```
root@ubuntu:/etc/sensu/plugins# chown sensu:sensu check_memory_no_agent.sh
root@ubuntu:/etc/sensu/plugins# chmod u+x check_memory_no_agent.sh
root@ubuntu:/etc/sensu/plugins# echo "sensu ALL=(ALL) NOPASSWD:ALL" >
/etc/sudoers.d/sensu
root@ubuntu:/etc/sensu/plugins# /etc/init.d/sensu-client restart
```

Just like Monit, Sensu provides handlers that get triggered when an alert is fired. This can be a custom script that sends an e-mail, makes a call to an external service such as PagerDuty, and so on. All of this provides the capability for an automated and proactive way of handling LXC alerts.

For more information on Sensu handlers, refer to the documentation at `https://sensuapp.org/docs/latest/reference/handlers.html`.

Simple autoscaling pattern with LXC, Jenkins, and Sensu

In Chapter 6, *Clustering and Horizontal Scaling with LXC*, we looked at how to horizontally scale services with LXC and HAProxy, by provisioning more containers on multiple hosts. In this chapter, we explored different ways of monitoring the resource utilization of LXC containers and triggering actions based on the alerts. With all of this knowledge in place, we can now implement a commonly used autoscaling pattern, as shown in the following diagram:

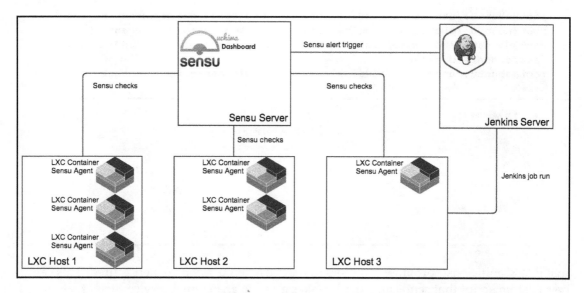

The pattern uses Jenkins as a build system, controlled by the Sensu alert handlers. When a Sensu agent running inside an LXC container receives a scheduled check from the Sensu server, for example, a memory check, it executes the script and returns either OK, Warning, or a Critical status, depending on the configured alert thresholds. If the Critical status is returned, then a configured Sensu handler, which can be as simple as a curl command, makes an API call to the Jenkins server, which in turn executes a preconfigured job. The Jenkins job can be a script that selects an LXC host from a list of hosts, based on a set of criteria that either builds a new container, or increases the available memory on the alerting LXC container, if possible. This is one of the simplest autoscaling design patterns, utilizing a monitoring system and a RESTful build service such as Jenkins.

In the next chapter, we are going to explore a full OpenStack deployment that utilizes a smart scheduler to select compute hosts on which to provision new LXC containers, based on available memory or just the number of already running containers.

We have already looked at some examples of how to implement most of the components and interactions in the preceding diagram. Let's quickly touch on Jenkins and set up a simple job that creates new LXC containers when called through the REST API remotely. The rest will be left to the reader to experiment with.

To install Jenkins on Ubuntu, run the following commands:

```
root@ubuntu: ~# wget -q -O -
https://pkg.jenkins.io/debian/jenkins-ci.org.key | sudo apt-key add -
root@ubuntu:~# sh -c 'echo deb http://pkg.jenkins.io/debian-stable binary/
> /etc/apt/sources.list.d/jenkins.list'
root@ubuntu:~# apt-get update
root@ubuntu:~# apt-get install jenkins
```

Jenkins listens on port 8080. The following two iptables rules forward port 80 to port 8080, making it easier to connect:

```
root@ubuntu:~# iptables -t nat -A PREROUTING -p tcp --dport 80 -j REDIRECT
--to-ports 8080
root@ubuntu:~# iptables -t nat -I OUTPUT -p tcp -d 127.0.0.1 --dport 80 -j
REDIRECT --to-ports 8080
```

Make sure to add the jenkins user to the sudoers file:

```
root@ubuntu:~# cat /etc/sudoers | grep jenkins
jenkins ALL=(ALL) NOPASSWD:ALL
root@ubuntu:~#
```

Once installed, Jenkins will start and be accessible over HTTP. Open the Jenkins web page and paste the content of the following file as requested:

```
root@ubuntu:~# cat /var/lib/jenkins/secrets/initialAdminPassword
32702ecf076e439c8d58c51f1247776d
root@ubuntu:~#
```

After installing the recommended plugins, do the following:

1. Create a new job named `LXC Provision`.
2. In **Build Triggers**, select **Trigger builds remotely (e.g., from scripts)** and type a random string, for example, `somesupersecrettoken`.
3. In the **Build** section, click on **Add build step** and select **Execute shell**.
4. In the **Command** window, add the following simple bash script:

```
set +x
echo "Building new LXC container"
sudo lxc-create --template ubuntu --name $(cat /dev/urandom |
tr -cd 'a-z' | head -c 10)
```

5. Finally, click on **Save**.

The Jenkins job should look similar to the following screenshot:

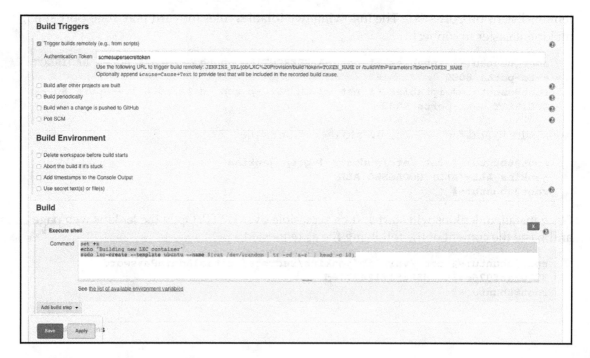

To trigger the job remotely, run the following, replacing the username, password, and IP address with those configured on your host:

```
root@ubuntu:~# curl
http://user:password@192.237.167.103:8080/job/LXC%20Provision/build?token=s
omesupersecrettoken
root@ubuntu:~#
```

This will trigger the Jenkins job, which in turn will create a new LXC container with a random name:

```
root@ubuntu:~# lxc-ls -f
NAME STATE AUTOSTART GROUPS IPV4 IPV6
ifjvdlpvnv STOPPED 0 - - -
root@ubuntu:~#
```

Now, all that is left is to create a Sensu handler (or a `monit` trigger script) for a check, or set of checks, which in turn can execute a similar `curl` command as the preceding one. Of course, this deployment is only meant to scratch the surface of what is possible by combining Sensu, Jenkins, and LXC for autoscaling services running inside containers.

Summary

In this chapter, we looked at how to back up LXC containers using Linux native tools such as `tar` and `rsync`, and LXC utilities such as `lxc-copy`. We looked at examples of how to create cold and hot standby LXC container backups using the iSCSI target as the LXC root filesystem and configuration files store. We also looked at how to deploy a shared network filesystem using GlusterFS, and the benefits of running multiple containers on the same filesystem, but on different hosts.

We also touched on how to monitor the state, health, and resource utilization of LXC containers using tools such as Monit and Sensu, and how to trigger actions, such as running a script to act on those alerts.

Finally, we reviewed one of the common autoscaling patterns, combining several tools to automatically create new containers based on alert events.

In the next chapter, we are going to look at a complete OpenStack deployment, which will allow us to create LXC containers utilizing smart schedulers.

8
Using LXC with OpenStack

In previous chapters, we looked at examples of common design patterns that help autoscale services running inside LXC containers by leveraging tools such as Jenkins, custom REST-based APIs, and monitoring tools. In this chapter, we'll explore a fully automated way of provisioning LXC containers on a set of servers, using OpenStack.

OpenStack is a cloud operating system that allows for the provisioning of virtual machines, LXC containers, load balancers, databases, and storage and network resources in a centralized, yet modular and extensible way. It's ideal for managing a set of compute resources (servers) and selecting the best candidate target to provision services on, based on criteria such as CPU load, memory utilization, and VM/container density, to name just a few.

In this chapter, we'll cover the following OpenStack components and services:

- Deploying the Keystone identity service, which will provide a central directory of users and services, and a simple way to authenticate using tokens
- Installing the Nova compute controller, which will manage a pool of servers and provision LXC containers on them
- Configuring the Glance image repository, which will store the LXC images
- Provisioning the Neutron networking service that will manage DHCP, DNS, and the network bridging on the compute hosts
- Finally, we'll provision an LXC container using the libvirt OpenStack driver

Deploying OpenStack with LXC support on Ubuntu

An OpenStack deployment may consist of multiple components that interact with each other through exposed APIs, or a message bus such as RabbitMQ, as shown in the following figure:

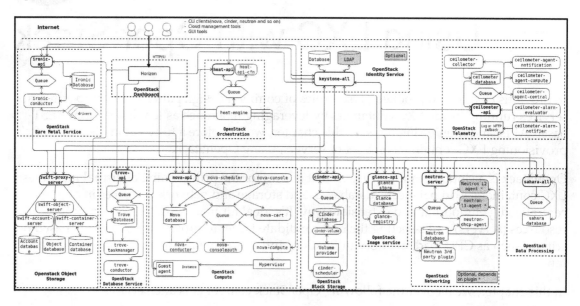

In this chapter, we'll deploy a minimum set of those components - Keystone, Glance, Nova, and Neutron - which will be sufficient to provision LXC containers and still take advantage of the scheduler logic and scalable networking that OpenStack provides.

For this tutorial, we are going to be using Ubuntu Xenial, and as of the time of this writing, the latest Newton OpenStack release. What is the name of that OpenStack release?

Preparing the host

To simplify things, we are going to use a single server to host all services with a minimum of 16 GB of RAM. In production environments, it's a common approach to separate each service into its own set of servers, for scalability and high availability. By following the steps in this chapter, you can easily deploy on multiple hosts by replacing the IP addresses and hostnames as needed.

> If using multiple servers, you need to make sure the time is synchronized on all hosts using services such as `ntpd`.

Let's begin by ensuring we have the latest packages, and installing the repository that contains the Newton OpenStack release:

```
root@controller:~# apt install -y software-properties-common
root@controller:~# add-apt-repository cloud-archive:newton
. . .
Press [ENTER] to continue or ctrl-c to cancel adding it
. . .
OK
root@controller:~# apt update && apt dist-upgrade -y
root@controller:~# reboot
root@controller:~# apt install -y python-openstackclient
```

Make sure to add the name of the server, in this example, `controller`, to `/etc/hosts`.

Installing the database service

The services we are going to deploy use a MariaDB database as their backend store. Install it by running the following command:

```
root@controller:~# apt install -y mariadb-server python-pymysql
```

A minimal configuration file should look like the following:

```
root@controller:~# cat /etc/mysql/mariadb.conf.d/99-openstack.cnf
[mysqld]
bind-address = 10.208.130.36
default-storage-engine = innodb
innodb_file_per_table
max_connections = 4096
collation-server = utf8_general_ci
character-set-server = utf8
root@controller:~#
```

Replace the IP address the service binds to with whatever is on your server, then start the service and run the script that will secure the installation:

```
root@controller:~# service mysql restart
root@controller:~# mysql_secure_installation
```

The preceding command will prompt for a new root password. For simplicity, we'll use `lxcpassword` as a password for all services, for the rest of the chapter.

Verify that MySQL is set up correctly and that you can connect to it:

```
root@controller:~# mysql -u root -h 10.208.130.36 -p
Enter password: [lxcpassword]
Welcome to the MariaDB monitor. Commands end with; or \g.
Your MariaDB connection id is 47
Server version: 10.0.28-MariaDB-0ubuntu0.16.04.1 Ubuntu 16.04
Copyright (c) 2000, 2016, Oracle, MariaDB Corporation Ab and others.
Type 'help;' or '\h' for help. Type '\c' to clear the current input
statement.
MariaDB [(none)]> [quit]
```

Installing the message queue service

OpenStack supports the following message queues - RabbitMQ, Qpid, and ZeroMQ - which facilitate interprocess communication between services. We are going to use RabbitMQ:

```
root@controller:~# apt install -y rabbitmq-server
```

Add a new user and password:

```
root@controller:~# rabbitmqctl add_user openstack lxcpassword
Creating user "openstack" ...
root@controller:~#
```

Also, grant permissions for that user:

```
root@controller:~# rabbitmqctl set_permissions openstack ".*" ".*" ".*"
Setting permissions for user "openstack" in vhost "/" ...
root@controller:~#
```

Installing the caching service

The identity service Keystone caches authentication tokens using Memcached. To install it, execute the following command:

```
root@controller:~# apt install -y memcached python-memcache
```

Replace the localhost address with the IP address of your server:

```
root@controller:~# sed -i 's/127.0.0.1/10.208.130.36/g' /etc/memcached.conf
```

The config file should look similar to the following:

```
root@controller:~# cat /etc/memcached.conf | grep -vi "#" | sed '/^$/d'
-d
logfile /var/log/memcached.log
-m 64
-p 11211
-u memcache
-l 10.208.130.36
root@controller:~# service memcached restart
```

Installing and configuring the identity service

The Keystone identity service provides a centralized point for managing authentication and authorization for the rest of the OpenStack components. Keystone also keeps a catalog of services and the endpoints they provide, which the user can locate by querying it.

To deploy Keystone, first create a database and grant permissions to the `keystone` user:

```
root@controller:~# mysql -u root -plxcpassword
MariaDB [(none)]> CREATE DATABASE keystone;
Query OK, 1 row affected (0.01 sec)
MariaDB [(none)]> GRANT ALL PRIVILEGES ON keystone.* TO
'keystone'@'localhost' IDENTIFIED BY 'lxcpassword';
Query OK, 0 rows affected (0.00 sec)
MariaDB [(none)]> GRANT ALL PRIVILEGES ON keystone.* TO 'keystone'@'%'
IDENTIFIED BY 'lxcpassword';
Query OK, 0 rows affected (0.01 sec)
MariaDB [(none)]> exit
Bye
root@controller:~#
```

Next, install the identity service components:

```
root@controller:~# apt install -y keystone
```

The following is a minimal working configuration for Keystone:

```
root@controller:~# cat /etc/keystone/keystone.conf
[DEFAULT]
log_dir = /var/log/keystone
[assignment]
[auth]
[cache]
[catalog]
[cors]
[cors.subdomain]
[credential]
[database]
connection = mysql+pymysql://keystone:lxcpassword@controller/keystone
[domain_config]
[endpoint_filter]
[endpoint_policy]
[eventlet_server]
[federation]
[fernet_tokens]
[identity]
[identity_mapping]
[kvs]
[ldap]
[matchmaker_redis]
[memcache]
[oauth1]
[os_inherit]
[oslo_messaging_amqp]
[oslo_messaging_notifications]
[oslo_messaging_rabbit]
[oslo_messaging_zmq]
[oslo_middleware]
[oslo_policy]
[paste_deploy]
[policy]
[profiler]
[resource]
[revoke]
[role]
[saml]
[security_compliance]
[shadow_users]
[signing]
[token]
provider = fernet
[tokenless_auth]
[trust]
```

```
[extra_headers]
Distribution = Ubuntu
root@controller:~#
```

If you are using the same hostname and password as in this tutorial, no changes are required.

Next, populate the `keystone` database by running the following command:

```
root@controller:~# su -s /bin/sh -c "keystone-manage db_sync" keystone
...
root@controller:~#
```

Keystone uses tokens to authenticate and authorize users and services. There are different token formats available, such as UUID, PKI, and Fernet tokens. For this example deployment, we are going to use the Fernet tokens, which, unlike the other types, do not need to be persisted in a backend. To initialize the Fernet key repositories, run the following:

```
root@controller:~# keystone-manage fernet_setup --keystone-user keystone --
keystone-group keystone
root@controller:~# keystone-manage credential_setup --keystone-user
keystone --keystone-group keystone
root@controller:~#
```

 For more information on the available identity tokens, refer to `http://doc s.openstack.org/admin-guide/identity-tokens.html`.

Perform the basic bootstrap process by executing the following command:

```
root@controller:~# keystone-manage bootstrap --bootstrap-password
lxcpassword --bootstrap-admin-url http://controller:35357/v3/ --bootstrap-
internal-url http://controller:35357/v3/ --bootstrap-public-url
http://controller:5000/v3/ --bootstrap-region-id RegionOne
root@controller:~#
```

We are going to use Apache with the WSGI module to drive Keystone. Add the following stanza in the Apache config file and restart it:

```
root@controller:~# cat /etc/apache2/apache2.conf
...
ServerName controller
...
root@controller:~# service apache2 restart
```

Delete the default SQLite database that Keystone ships with:

```
root@controller:~# rm -f /var/lib/keystone/keystone.db
```

Let's create the administrative account by defining the following environment variables:

```
root@controller:~# export OS_USERNAME=admin
root@controller:~# export OS_PASSWORD=lxcpassword
root@controller:~# export OS_PROJECT_NAME=admin
root@controller:~# export OS_USER_DOMAIN_NAME=default
root@controller:~# export OS_PROJECT_DOMAIN_NAME=default
root@controller:~# export OS_AUTH_URL=http://controller:35357/v3
root@controller:~# export OS_IDENTITY_API_VERSION=3
```

Time to create our first project in Keystone. Projects represent a unit of ownership, where all resources are owned by a project. The `service` project we are going to create next will be used by all the services we are going to deploy in this chapter:

```
root@controller:~# openstack project create --domain default --description
"LXC Project" service
+-------------+------------------------------------+
| Field | Value |
+-------------+------------------------------------+
| description | LXC Project |
| domain_id | default |
| enabled | True |
| id | 9a1a863fe41b42b2955b313f2cca0ef0 |
| is_domain | False |
| name | service |
| parent_id | default |
+-------------+------------------------------------+
root@controller:~#
```

To list the available projects, run the following command:

```
root@controller:~# openstack project list
+----------------------------------+---------+
| ID | Name |
+----------------------------------+---------+
| 06f4e2d7e384474781803395b24b3af2 | admin |
| 9a1a863fe41b42b2955b313f2cca0ef0 | service |
+----------------------------------+---------+
root@controller:~#
```

Let's create an unprivileged project and user, which can be used by regular users instead of
the OpenStack services:

```
root@controller:~# openstack project create --domain default --description
"LXC User Project" lxc
+-------------+--------------------------------------+
| Field | Value |
+-------------+--------------------------------------+
| description | LXC User Project |
| domain_id | default |
| enabled | True |
| id | eb9cdc2c2b4e4f098f2d104752970d52 |
| is_domain | False |
| name | lxc |
| parent_id | default |
+-------------+--------------------------------------+
root@controller:~#
root@controller:~# openstack user create --domain default --password-prompt
lxc
User Password:
Repeat User Password:
+---------------------+--------------------------------------+
| Field | Value |
+---------------------+--------------------------------------+
| domain_id | default |
| enabled | True |
| id | 1e83e0c8ca194f2e9d8161eb61d21030 |
| name | lxc |
| password_expires_at | None |
+---------------------+--------------------------------------+
root@controller:~#
```

Next, create a `user` role, and associate it with the `lxc` project and the user we created in the
previous two steps:

```
root@controller:~# openstack role create user
+-----------+----------------------------------+
| Field | Value |
+-----------+----------------------------------+
| domain_id | None |
| id | 331c0b61e9784112874627264f03a058 |
| name | user |
+-----------+----------------------------------+
root@controller:~# openstack role add --project lxc --user lxc user
root@controller:~#
```

Use the following file to configure the **Web Service Gateway Interface (WSGI)** middleware pipeline for Keystone:

```
root@controller:~# cat /etc/keystone/keystone-paste.ini
# Keystone PasteDeploy configuration file.
[filter:debug]
use = egg:oslo.middleware#debug

[filter:request_id]
use = egg:oslo.middleware#request_id

[filter:build_auth_context]
use = egg:keystone#build_auth_context

[filter:token_auth]
use = egg:keystone#token_auth

[filter:admin_token_auth]
use = egg:keystone#admin_token_auth

[filter:json_body]
use = egg:keystone#json_body

[filter:cors]
use = egg:oslo.middleware#cors
oslo_config_project = keystone

[filter:http_proxy_to_wsgi]
use = egg:oslo.middleware#http_proxy_to_wsgi

[filter:ec2_extension]
use = egg:keystone#ec2_extension

[filter:ec2_extension_v3]
use = egg:keystone#ec2_extension_v3

[filter:s3_extension]
use = egg:keystone#s3_extension

[filter:url_normalize]
use = egg:keystone#url_normalize

[filter:sizelimit]
use = egg:oslo.middleware#sizelimit

[filter:osprofiler]
use = egg:osprofiler#osprofiler
```

```
[app:public_service]
use = egg:keystone#public_service

[app:service_v3]
use = egg:keystone#service_v3

[app:admin_service]
use = egg:keystone#admin_service

[pipeline:public_api]
pipeline = cors sizelimit http_proxy_to_wsgi osprofiler url_normalize
request_id build_auth_context token_auth json_body ec2_extension
public_service

[pipeline:admin_api]
pipeline = cors sizelimit http_proxy_to_wsgi osprofiler url_normalize
request_id build_auth_context token_auth json_body ec2_extension
s3_extension admin_service

[pipeline:api_v3]
pipeline = cors sizelimit http_proxy_to_wsgi osprofiler url_normalize
request_id build_auth_context token_auth json_body ec2_extension_v3
s3_extension service_v3

[app:public_version_service]
use = egg:keystone#public_version_service

[app:admin_version_service]
use = egg:keystone#admin_version_service

[pipeline:public_version_api]
pipeline = cors sizelimit osprofiler url_normalize public_version_service

[pipeline:admin_version_api]
pipeline = cors sizelimit osprofiler url_normalize admin_version_service

[composite:main]
use = egg:Paste#urlmap
/v2.0 = public_api
/v3 = api_v3
/ = public_version_api

[composite:admin]
use = egg:Paste#urlmap
/v2.0 = admin_api
/v3 = api_v3
/ = admin_version_api
root@controller:~#
```

Let's test the configuration so far, by requesting a token for the `admin` and the `lxc` users:

```
root@controller:~# openstack --os-auth-url http://controller:35357/v3 --os-
project-domain-name default --os-user-domain-name default --os-project-name
admin --os-username admin token issue
Password:
...
root@controller:~# openstack --os-auth-url http://controller:5000/v3 --os-
project-domain-name default --os-user-domain-name default --os-project-name
lxc --os-username lxc token issue
Password:
...
root@controller:~#
```

We can create two files, which will contain the `admin` and `user` credentials we configured earlier:

```
root@controller:~# cat rc.admin
export OS_PROJECT_DOMAIN_NAME=default
export OS_USER_DOMAIN_NAME=default
export OS_PROJECT_NAME=admin
export OS_USERNAME=admin
export OS_PASSWORD=lxcpassword
export OS_AUTH_URL=http://controller:35357/v3
export OS_IDENTITY_API_VERSION=3
export OS_IMAGE_API_VERSION=2
root@controller:~#
root@controller:~# cat rc.lxc
export OS_PROJECT_DOMAIN_NAME=default
export OS_USER_DOMAIN_NAME=default
export OS_PROJECT_NAME=lxc
export OS_USERNAME=lxc
export OS_PASSWORD=lxcpassword
export OS_AUTH_URL=http://controller:5000/v3
export OS_IDENTITY_API_VERSION=3
export OS_IMAGE_API_VERSION=2
root@controller:~#
```

To use the `admin` user, for example, source the file as follows:

```
root@controller:~# . rc.admin
```

Notice the new environment variables:

```
root@controller:~# env | grep ^OS
OS_USER_DOMAIN_NAME=default
OS_IMAGE_API_VERSION=2
OS_PROJECT_NAME=admin
```

```
OS_IDENTITY_API_VERSION=3
OS_PASSWORD=lxcpassword
OS_AUTH_URL=http://controller:35357/v3
OS_USERNAME=admin
OS_PROJECT_DOMAIN_NAME=default
root@controller:~#
```

With the admin credentials loaded, let's request an authentication token that we can use later with the other OpenStack services:

```
root@controller:~# openstack token issue
+-------------+--------------------------------------------------------
--------------------------------------------------------------------
-----------------------------------------------+
| Field | Value |
+-------------+--------------------------------------------------------
--------------------------------------------------------------------
-----------------------------------------------+
| expires | 2016-12-02 19:49:07+00:00 |
| id |
gAAAAABYQcIj7eKEfCMTWY43EXZbqZ8UdeZ8CZIb2l2sqIFHFBV_bv6LHO4CFbFLdh7kUEw_Zk-
MzQrl5mbq7g8RXPAZ31iBDpDie2-xIAMgRqsxkAh7PJ2kdhcHAxkBj-
Uq65rHmjYmPZTUlUTONOP3_dId0_8DsdLkFWoardxG0FAotrlH-2s |
| project_id | 06f4e2d7e384474781803395b24b3af2 |
| user_id | 5c331f397597439faef5a1199cdf354f |
+-------------+--------------------------------------------------------
--------------------------------------------------------------------
-----------------------------------------------+
root@controller:~#
```

Installing and configuring the image service

The image service provides an API for users to discover, register, and obtain images for virtual machines, or images that can be used as the root filesystem for LXC containers. Glance supports multiple storage backends, but for simplicity we are going to use the file store that will keep the LXC image directly on the filesystem.

To deploy Glance, first create a database and a user, like we did for Keystone:

```
root@controller:~# mysql -u root -plxcpassword
MariaDB [(none)]> CREATE DATABASE glance;
Query OK, 1 row affected (0.00 sec)
MariaDB [(none)]> GRANT ALL PRIVILEGES ON glance.* TO 'glance'@'localhost'
IDENTIFIED BY 'lxcpassword';
Query OK, 0 rows affected (0.00 sec)
MariaDB [(none)]> GRANT ALL PRIVILEGES ON glance.* TO 'glance'@'%'
```

```
IDENTIFIED BY 'lxcpassword';
Query OK, 0 rows affected (0.00 sec)
MariaDB [(none)]> exit
Bye
root@controller:~#
```

Next, create the `glance` user and add it to the `admin` role:

```
root@controller:~# openstack user create --domain default --password-prompt
glance
User Password:
Repeat User Password:
+---------------------+-------------------------------------+
| Field | Value |
+---------------------+-------------------------------------+
| domain_id | default |
| enabled | True |
| id | ce29b972845d4d77978b7e7803275d53 |
| name | glance |
| password_expires_at | None |
+---------------------+-------------------------------------+
root@controller:~# openstack role add --project service --user glance admin
root@controller:~#
```

Now it's time to create the `glance` service record:

```
root@controller:~# openstack service create --name glance --description
"OpenStack Image" image
+-------------+----------------------------------+
| Field | Value |
+-------------+----------------------------------+
| description | OpenStack Image |
| enabled | True |
| id | 2aa82fc0a0224baab8d259e4f5279907 |
| name | glance |
| type | image |
+-------------+----------------------------------+
root@controller:~#
```

Create the Glance API endpoints in Keystone:

```
root@controller:~# openstack endpoint create --region RegionOne image
public http://controller:9292
+-------------+----------------------------------+
| Field | Value |
+-------------+----------------------------------+
| enabled | True |
| id | aa26c33d456d421ca3555e6523c7814f |
```

```
| interface | public |
| region | RegionOne |
| region_id | RegionOne |
| service_id | 2aa82fc0a0224baab8d259e4f5279907 |
| service_name | glance |
| service_type | image |
| url | http://controller:9292 |
+--------------+---------------------------------+
root@controller:~#
```

OpenStack supports multiregion deployments for achieving high availability; however, for simplicity, we are going to deploy all services in the same region:

```
root@controller:~# openstack endpoint create --region RegionOne image
internal http://controller:9292
...
root@controller:~# openstack endpoint create --region RegionOne image admin
http://controller:9292
...
root@controller:~#
```

Now that Keystone knows about the `glance` service, let's install it:

```
root@controller:~# apt install -y glance
```

Use the following two minimal configuration files, replacing the password and hostname as needed:

```
root@controller:~# cat /etc/glance/glance-api.conf
[DEFAULT]
[cors]
[cors.subdomain]
[database]
connection = mysql+pymysql://glance:lxcpassword@controller/glance
[glance_store]
stores = file,http
default_store = file
filesystem_store_datadir = /var/lib/glance/images/
[image_format]
disk_formats = ami,ari,aki,vhd,vhdx,vmdk,raw,qcow2,vdi,iso,root-tar
[keystone_authtoken]
auth_uri = http://controller:5000
auth_url = http://controller:35357
memcached_servers = controller:11211
auth_type = password
project_domain_name = default
user_domain_name = default
project_name = service
```

```
username = glance
password = lxcpassword
[matchmaker_redis]
[oslo_concurrency]
[oslo_messaging_amqp]
[oslo_messaging_notifications]
[oslo_messaging_rabbit]
[oslo_messaging_zmq]
[oslo_middleware]
[oslo_policy]
[paste_deploy]
flavor = keystone
[profiler]
[store_type_location_strategy]
[task]
[taskflow_executor]
root@controller:~#
root@controller:~# cat /etc/glance/glance-registry.conf
[DEFAULT]
[database]
connection = mysql+pymysql://glance:GLANCE_DBPASS@controller/glance
[keystone_authtoken]
auth_uri = http://controller:5000
auth_url = http://controller:35357
memcached_servers = controller:11211
auth_type = password
project_domain_name = default
user_domain_name = default
project_name = service
username = glance
password = lxcpassword
[matchmaker_redis]
[oslo_messaging_amqp]
[oslo_messaging_notifications]
[oslo_messaging_rabbit]
[oslo_messaging_zmq]
[oslo_policy]
[paste_deploy]
flavor = keystone
[profiler]
root@controller:~#
```

Populate the `glance` database by running the following:

```
root@controller:~# su -s /bin/sh -c "glance-manage db_sync" glance
...
root@controller:~#
```

Start the Glance services:

```
root@controller:~# service glance-registry restart
root@controller:~# service glance-api restart
root@controller:~#
```

We can build an image for the LXC containers by hand, as we saw in Chapter 2, *Installing and Running LXC on Linux Systems,* or download a prebuilt image from an Ubuntu repository. Let's download an image and extract it:

```
root@controller:~# wget
http://uec-images.ubuntu.com/releases/precise/release/ubuntu-12.04-server-c
loudimg-amd64.tar.gz
root@controller:~# tar zxfv ubuntu-12.04-server-cloudimg-amd64.tar.gz
precise-server-cloudimg-amd64.img
precise-server-cloudimg-amd64-vmlinuz-virtual
precise-server-cloudimg-amd64-loader
precise-server-cloudimg-amd64-floppy
README.files
root@controller:~#
```

The file that contains the root filesystem has the `.img` extension. Let's add it to the image service:

```
root@controller:~# openstack image create "lxc_ubuntu_12.04" --file
precise-server-cloudimg-amd64.img --disk-format raw --container-format bare
--public
+------------------+--------------------------------------------------+
| Field | Value |
+------------------+--------------------------------------------------+
| checksum | b5e5895e85127d9cebbd2de32d9b193c |
| container_format | bare |
| created_at | 2016-12-02T19:01:28Z |
| disk_format | raw |
| file | /v2/images/f344646d-d293-4638-bab4-86d461f38233/file |
| id | f344646d-d293-4638-bab4-86d461f38233 |
| min_disk | 0 |
| min_ram | 0 |
| name | lxc_ubuntu_12.04 |
| owner | 06f4e2d7e384474781803395b24b3af2 |
| protected | False |
| schema | /v2/schemas/image |
| size | 1476395008 |
| status | active |
| tags | |
| updated_at | 2016-12-02T19:01:41Z |
| virtual_size | None |
| visibility | public |
```

```
+------------------+---------------------------------------------------+
root@controller:~#
```

 Note that LXC uses the `raw` disk and `bare` container formats.

The image is now stored at the location defined in the `glance-api.conf` as the `filesystem_store_datadir` parameter, as we saw in the preceding configuration example:

```
root@controller:~# ls -la /var/lib/glance/images/
total 1441804
drwxr-xr-x 2 glance glance 4096 Dec 2 19:01 .
drwxr-xr-x 4 glance glance 4096 Dec 2 18:53 ..
-rw-r----- 1 glance glance 1476395008 Dec 2 19:01 f344646d-d293-4638-
bab4-86d461f38233
root@controller:~#
```

Let's list the available images in Glance:

```
root@controller:~# openstack image list
+-------------------------------------+------------------+--------+
| ID | Name | Status |
+-------------------------------------+------------------+--------+
| f344646d-d293-4638-bab4-86d461f38233 | lxc_ubuntu_12.04 | active |
+-------------------------------------+------------------+--------+
root@controller:~#
```

Installing and configuring the compute service

The OpenStack compute service manages a pool of compute resources (servers) and various virtual machines, or containers running on said resources. It provides a scheduler service that takes a request for a new VM or container from the queue and decides on which compute host to create and start it.

 For more information on the various Nova services, refer to: `http://docs.openstack.org/developer/nova/`.

Let's begin by creating the nova database and user:

```
root@controller:~# mysql -u root -plxcpassword
MariaDB [(none)]> CREATE DATABASE nova_api;
Query OK, 1 row affected (0.00 sec)
MariaDB [(none)]> CREATE DATABASE nova;
Query OK, 1 row affected (0.00 sec)
MariaDB [(none)]> GRANT ALL PRIVILEGES ON nova_api.* TO 'nova'@'localhost'
IDENTIFIED BY 'lxcpassword';
Query OK, 0 rows affected (0.03 sec)
MariaDB [(none)]> GRANT ALL PRIVILEGES ON nova_api.* TO 'nova'@'%'
IDENTIFIED BY 'lxcpassword';
Query OK, 0 rows affected (0.00 sec)
MariaDB [(none)]> GRANT ALL PRIVILEGES ON nova.* TO 'nova'@'localhost'
IDENTIFIED BY 'lxcpassword';
Query OK, 0 rows affected (0.00 sec)
MariaDB [(none)]> GRANT ALL PRIVILEGES ON nova.* TO 'nova'@'%' IDENTIFIED
BY 'lxcpassword';
Query OK, 0 rows affected (0.00 sec)
MariaDB [(none)]> exit
Bye
root@controller:~#
```

Once the database is created and the user permissions granted, create the nova user and
add it to the admin role in the identity service:

```
root@controller:~# openstack user create --domain default --password-prompt
nova
User Password:
Repeat User Password:
+---------------------+----------------------------------+
| Field | Value |
+---------------------+----------------------------------+
| domain_id | default |
| enabled | True |
| id | a1305c903548431a80b608fadf78f287 |
| name | nova |
| password_expires_at | None |
+---------------------+----------------------------------+
root@controller:~# openstack role add --project service --user nova admin
root@controller:~#
```

Next, create the nova service and endpoints:

```
root@controller:~# openstack service create --name nova --description
"OpenStack Compute" compute
+-------------+----------------------------------+
| Field | Value |
```

```
+--------------+----------------------------------+
| description | OpenStack Compute |
| enabled | True |
| id | 779d2feb591545cf9d2acc18765a0ca5 |
| name | nova |
| type | compute |
+--------------+----------------------------------+
root@controller:~# openstack endpoint create --region RegionOne compute
public http://controller:8774/v2.1/%\(tenant_id\)s
+--------------+------------------------------------------------+
| Field | Value |
+--------------+------------------------------------------------+
| enabled | True |
| id | cccfd4d817a24f9ba58128901cbbb473 |
| interface | public |
| region | RegionOne |
| region_id | RegionOne |
| service_id | 779d2feb591545cf9d2acc18765a0ca5 |
| service_name | nova |
| service_type | compute |
| url | http://controller:8774/v2.1/%(tenant_id)s |
+--------------+------------------------------------------------+
root@controller:~# openstack endpoint create --region RegionOne compute
internal http://controller:8774/v2.1/%\(tenant_id\)s
. . .
root@controller:~# openstack endpoint create --region RegionOne compute
admin http://controller:8774/v2.1/%\(tenant_id\)s
. . .
root@controller:~#
```

It's time to install the Nova packages that will provide the API, the conductor, the console, and the scheduler services:

```
root@controller:~# apt install -y nova-api nova-conductor nova-consoleauth
nova-novncproxy nova-scheduler
```

The Nova packages we just installed provide the following services:

- `nova-api`: This service accepts and responds to user requests through a RESTful API. We use that for creating, running, and stopping instances, and so on.
- `nova-conductor`: This service sits between the `nova` database we created earlier and the `nova-compute` service, which runs on the compute nodes and creates the VMs and containers. We are going to install that service later in this chapter.
- `nova-consoleauth`: This service authorizes tokens for users that want to use various consoles to connect to the VMs or containers.
- `nova-novncproxy`: This service grants access to instances running VNC.

- `nova-scheduler`: This service, as mentioned previously, makes decisions on where to provision a VM or LXC container.

The following is a minimal functioning Nova configuration:

```
root@controller:~# cat /etc/nova/nova.conf
[DEFAULT]
dhcpbridge_flagfile=/etc/nova/nova.conf
dhcpbridge=/usr/bin/nova-dhcpbridge
log-dir=/var/log/nova
state_path=/var/lib/nova
force_dhcp_release=True
verbose=True
ec2_private_dns_show_ip=True
enabled_apis=osapi_compute,metadata
transport_url = rabbit://openstack:lxcpassword@controller
auth_strategy = keystone
my_ip = 10.208.132.45
use_neutron = True
firewall_driver = nova.virt.firewall.NoopFirewallDriver
[database]
connection = mysql+pymysql://nova:lxcpassword@controller/nova
[api_database]
connection = mysql+pymysql://nova:lxcpassword@controller/nova_api
[oslo_concurrency]
lock_path = /var/lib/nova/tmp
[libvirt]
use_virtio_for_bridges=True
[wsgi]
api_paste_config=/etc/nova/api-paste.ini
[keystone_authtoken]
auth_uri = http://controller:5000
auth_url = http://controller:35357
memcached_servers = controller:11211
auth_type = password
project_domain_name = default
user_domain_name = default
project_name = service
username = nova
password = lxcpassword
[vnc]
vncserver_listen = $my_ip
vncserver_proxyclient_address = $my_ip
[glance]
api_servers = http://controller:9292
root@controller:~#
```

With the config file in place, we can now populate the `nova` database:

```
root@controller:~# su -s /bin/sh -c "nova-manage api_db sync" nova
...
root@controller:~# su -s /bin/sh -c "nova-manage db sync" nova
...
root@controller:~#
```

Finally, start the compute services:

```
root@controller:~# service nova-api restart
root@controller:~# service nova-consoleauth restart
root@controller:~# service nova-scheduler restart
root@controller:~# service nova-conductor restart
root@controller:~# service nova-novncproxy restart
root@controller:~#
```

Since we are going to use a single node for this OpenStack deployment, we need to install the `nova-compute` service. In production, we usually have a pool of compute servers that only run that service.

```
root@controller:~# apt install -y nova-compute
```

Use the following minimal configuration file, which will allow running `nova-compute` and the rest of the Nova services on the same server:

```
root@controller:~# cat /etc/nova/nova.conf
[DEFAULT]
dhcpbridge_flagfile=/etc/nova/nova.conf
dhcpbridge=/usr/bin/nova-dhcpbridge
log-dir=/var/log/nova
state_path=/var/lib/nova
force_dhcp_release=True
verbose=True
ec2_private_dns_show_ip=True
enabled_apis=osapi_compute,metadata
transport_url = rabbit://openstack:lxcpassword@controller
auth_strategy = keystone
my_ip = 10.208.132.45
use_neutron = True
firewall_driver = nova.virt.firewall.NoopFirewallDriver
compute_driver = libvirt.LibvirtDriver
[database]
connection = mysql+pymysql://nova:lxcpassword@controller/nova
[api_database]
connection = mysql+pymysql://nova:lxcpassword@controller/nova_api
[oslo_concurrency]
lock_path = /var/lib/nova/tmp
```

```
[libvirt]
use_virtio_for_bridges=True
[wsgi]
api_paste_config=/etc/nova/api-paste.ini
[keystone_authtoken]
auth_uri = http://controller:5000
auth_url = http://controller:35357
memcached_servers = controller:11211
auth_type = password
project_domain_name = default
user_domain_name = default
project_name = service
username = nova
password = lxcpassword
[vnc]
enabled = True
vncserver_listen = $my_ip
vncserver_proxyclient_address = $my_ip
novncproxy_base_url = http://controller:6080/vnc_auto.html
[glance]
api_servers = http://controller:9292
[libvirt]
virt_type = lxc
root@controller:~#
```

Notice under the `libvirt` section how we specify LXC as the default virtualization type we are going to use. To enable LXC support in Nova, install the following package:

```
root@controller:~# apt install -y nova-compute-lxc
```

The package provides the following configuration file:

```
root@controller:~# cat /etc/nova/nova-compute.conf
[DEFAULT]
compute_driver=libvirt.LibvirtDriver
[libvirt]
virt_type=lxc
root@controller:~#
```

Restart the `nova-compute` service and list all available Nova services:

```
root@controller:~# service nova-compute restart
root@controller:~# openstack compute service list
+----+------------------+-------------+----------+--------+--------+--------
--------------------+
| ID | Binary | Host | Zone | Status | State | Updated At |
+----+------------------+-------------+----------+--------+--------+--------
--------------------+
```

```
| 4 | nova-consoleauth | controller | internal | enabled | up |
2016-12-02T20:01:19.000000 |
| 5 | nova-scheduler | controller | internal | enabled | up |
2016-12-02T20:01:25.000000 |
| 6 | nova-conductor | controller | internal | enabled | up |
2016-12-02T20:01:26.000000 |
| 8 | nova-compute | controller | nova | enabled | up |
2016-12-02T20:01:22.000000 |
+----+------------------+------------+----------+---------+-------+---------
--------------------+
root@controller:~#
```

Be sure to verify that all four services are `enabled` and `up`. With all the Nova services configured and running, now it's time to move to the networking part of the deployment.

Installing and configuring the networking service

The networking component of OpenStack, codenamed Neutron, manages networks, IP addresses, software bridging, and routing. In the previous chapters, we had to create the Linux bridge, add ports to it, configure DHCP to assign IPs to the containers, and so on. Neutron exposes all of these functionalities through a convenient API and libraries that we can use.

Let's start by creating the database, user, and permissions:

```
root@controller:~# mysql -u root -plxcpassword
MariaDB [(none)]> CREATE DATABASE neutron;
Query OK, 1 row affected (0.00 sec)
MariaDB [(none)]> GRANT ALL PRIVILEGES ON neutron.* TO
'neutron'@'localhost' IDENTIFIED BY 'lxcpassword';
Query OK, 0 rows affected (0.00 sec)
MariaDB [(none)]> GRANT ALL PRIVILEGES ON neutron.* TO 'neutron'@'%'
IDENTIFIED BY 'lxcpassword';
Query OK, 0 rows affected (0.00 sec)
MariaDB [(none)]> exit
Bye
root@controller:~#
```

Next, create the `neutron` user and add it to the `admin` role in Keystone:

```
root@controller:~# openstack user create --domain default --password-prompt
neutron
User Password:
Repeat User Password:
+-------------------------+----------------------------------+
| Field | Value |
```

```
+---------------------+-----------------------------------+
| domain_id | default |
| enabled | True |
| id | 68867f6864574592b1a29ec293defb5d |
| name | neutron |
| password_expires_at | None |
+---------------------+-----------------------------------+
root@controller:~# openstack role add --project service --user neutron
admin
root@controller:~#
```

Create the neutron service and endpoints:

```
root@controller:~# openstack service create --name neutron --description
"OpenStack Networking" network
+-------------+----------------------------------+
| Field | Value |
+-------------+----------------------------------+
| description | OpenStack Networking |
| enabled | True |
| id | 8bd98d58bfb5410694cbf7b6163a71a5 |
| name | neutron |
| type | network |
+-------------+----------------------------------+
root@controller:~# openstack endpoint create --region RegionOne network
public http://controller:9696
+-------------+----------------------------------+
| Field | Value |
+-------------+----------------------------------+
| enabled | True |
| id | 4e2c1a8689b146a7b3b4207c63a778da |
| interface | public |
| region | RegionOne |
| region_id | RegionOne |
| service_id | 8bd98d58bfb5410694cbf7b6163a71a5 |
| service_name | neutron |
| service_type | network |
| url | http://controller:9696 |
+-------------+----------------------------------+
root@controller:~# openstack endpoint create --region RegionOne network
internal http://controller:9696
...
root@controller:~# openstack endpoint create --region RegionOne network
admin http://controller:9696
...
root@controller:~#
```

With all the services and endpoints defined in the identity service, install the following packages:

```
root@controller:~# apt install -y neutron-server neutron-plugin-ml2
neutron-linuxbridge-agent neutron-l3-agent neutron-dhcp-agent neutron-
metadata-agent
```

The Neutron packages that we installed earlier provide the following services:

- `neutron-server`: This package provides API to dynamically request and configure virtual networks
- `neutron-plugin-ml2`: This is a framework that enables the use of various network technologies, such as the Linux bridge, Open vSwitch, GRE, and VXLAN, which we saw in earlier chapters
- `neutron-linuxbridge-agent`: This provides the Linux bridge plugin agent
- `neutron-l3-agent`: This performs forwarding and NAT functionality between software-defined networks by creating virtual routers
- `neutron-dhcp-agent`: This controls the DHCP service that assigns IP addresses to the instances running on the compute nodes
- `neutron-metadata-agent`: This is a service that passes instance metadata to Neutron

The following is a minimal working configuration file for Neutron:

```
root@controller:~# cat /etc/neutron/neutron.conf
[DEFAULT]
core_plugin = ml2
service_plugins = router
allow_overlapping_ips = True
transport_url = rabbit://openstack:lxcpassword@controller
auth_strategy = keystone
notify_nova_on_port_status_changes = True
notify_nova_on_port_data_changes = True
[agent]
root_helper = sudo /usr/bin/neutron-rootwrap /etc/neutron/rootwrap.conf
[cors]
[cors.subdomain]
[database]
connection = mysql+pymysql://neutron:lxcpassword@controller/neutron
[keystone_authtoken]
auth_uri = http://controller:5000
auth_url = http://controller:35357
memcached_servers = controller:11211
auth_type = password
project_domain_name = default
```

```
user_domain_name = default
project_name = service
username = neutron
password = lxcpassword
[matchmaker_redis]
[nova]
auth_url = http://controller:35357
auth_type = password
project_domain_name = default
user_domain_name = default
region_name = RegionOne
project_name = service
username = nova
password = lxcpassword
[oslo_concurrency]
[oslo_messaging_amqp]
[oslo_messaging_notifications]
[oslo_messaging_rabbit]
[oslo_messaging_zmq]
[oslo_policy]
[qos]
[quotas]
[ssl]
root@controller:~#
```

We need to define what network extension we are going to support and the type of network. All this information is going to be used when creating the LXC container and its configuration file, as we'll see later:

```
root@controller:~# cat /etc/neutron/plugins/ml2/ml2_conf.ini
[DEFAULT]
[ml2]
type_drivers = flat,vlan,vxlan
tenant_network_types = vxlan
mechanism_drivers = linuxbridge,l2population
extension_drivers = port_security
[ml2_type_flat]
flat_networks = provider
[ml2_type_geneve]
[ml2_type_gre]
[ml2_type_vlan]
[ml2_type_vxlan]
vni_ranges = 1:1000
[securitygroup]
enable_ipset = True
root@controller:~#
```

Define the interface that will be added to the software bridge and that the IP the bridge will be bound to. In this case, we are using the `eth1` interface and its IP address:

```
root@controller:~# cat /etc/neutron/plugins/ml2/linuxbridge_agent.ini
[DEFAULT]
[agent]
[linux_bridge]
physical_interface_mappings = provider:eth1
[securitygroup]
enable_security_group = True
firewall_driver =
neutron.agent.linux.iptables_firewall.IptablesFirewallDriver
[vxlan]
enable_vxlan = True
local_ip = 10.208.132.45
l2_population = True
root@controller:~#
```

We specify the bridge driver for the L3 agent as follows:

```
root@controller:~# cat /etc/neutron/l3_agent.ini
[DEFAULT]
interface_driver = neutron.agent.linux.interface.BridgeInterfaceDriver
[AGENT]
root@controller:~#
```

The configuration file for the DHCP agent should look similar to the following:

```
root@controller:~# cat /etc/neutron/dhcp_agent.ini
[DEFAULT]
interface_driver = neutron.agent.linux.interface.BridgeInterfaceDriver
dhcp_driver = neutron.agent.linux.dhcp.Dnsmasq
enable_isolated_metadata = True
[AGENT]
root@controller:~#
```

Finally, the configuration for the metadata agent is as follows:

```
root@controller:~# cat /etc/neutron/metadata_agent.ini
[DEFAULT]
nova_metadata_ip = controller
metadata_proxy_shared_secret = lxcpassword
[AGENT]
[cache]
root@controller:~#
```

We need to update the configuration file for the Nova services. The new complete files should look as follows this; replace the IP address as needed:

```
root@controller:~# cat /etc/nova/nova.conf
[DEFAULT]
dhcpbridge_flagfile=/etc/nova/nova.conf
dhcpbridge=/usr/bin/nova-dhcpbridge
log-dir=/var/log/nova
state_path=/var/lib/nova
force_dhcp_release=True
verbose=True
ec2_private_dns_show_ip=True
enabled_apis=osapi_compute,metadata
transport_url = rabbit://openstack:lxcpassword@controller
auth_strategy = keystone
my_ip = 10.208.132.45
use_neutron = True
firewall_driver = nova.virt.firewall.NoopFirewallDriver
compute_driver = libvirt.LibvirtDriver
scheduler_default_filters = RetryFilter, AvailabilityZoneFilter, RamFilter,
ComputeFilter, ComputeCapabilitiesFilter, ImagePropertiesFilter,
ServerGroupAntiAffinityFilter, ServerGroupAffinityFilter
[database]
connection = mysql+pymysql://nova:lxcpassword@controller/nova
[api_database]
connection = mysql+pymysql://nova:lxcpassword@controller/nova_api
[oslo_concurrency]
lock_path = /var/lib/nova/tmp
[libvirt]
use_virtio_for_bridges=True
[wsgi]
api_paste_config=/etc/nova/api-paste.ini
[keystone_authtoken]
auth_uri = http://controller:5000
auth_url = http://controller:35357
memcached_servers = controller:11211
auth_type = password
project_domain_name = default
user_domain_name = default
project_name = service
username = nova
password = lxcpassword
[vnc]
enabled = True
vncserver_listen = $my_ip
vncserver_proxyclient_address = $my_ip
novncproxy_base_url = http://controller:6080/vnc_auto.html
[glance]
```

```
api_servers = http://controller:9292
[libvirt]
virt_type = lxc
[neutron]
url = http://controller:9696
auth_url = http://controller:35357
auth_type = password
project_domain_name = default
user_domain_name = default
region_name = RegionOne
project_name = service
username = neutron
password = lxcpassword
service_metadata_proxy = True
metadata_proxy_shared_secret = lxcpassword
root@controller:~#
```

Populate the neutron database:

```
root@controller:~# su -s /bin/sh -c "neutron-db-manage --config-file
/etc/neutron/neutron.conf --config-file
/etc/neutron/plugins/ml2/ml2_conf.ini upgrade head" neutron
INFO [alembic.runtime.migration] Context impl MySQLImpl.
INFO [alembic.runtime.migration] Will assume non-transactional DDL.
Running upgrade for neutron ...
INFO [alembic.runtime.migration] Context impl MySQLImpl.
INFO [alembic.runtime.migration] Will assume non-transactional DDL.
...
OK
root@controller:~#
```

Finally, start all networking services and restart nova-compute:

```
root@controller:~# service nova-api restart
root@controller:~# service neutron-server restart
root@controller:~# service neutron-linuxbridge-agent restart
root@controller:~# service neutron-dhcp-agent restart
root@controller:~# service neutron-metadata-agent restart
root@controller:~# service neutron-l3-agent restart
root@controller:~# service nova-compute restart
```

Let's verify the Neutron services are running:

```
root@controller:~# openstack network agent list
+------------------------------------+------------------------+-------------+-
------------------+--------+-------+----------------------------+
| ID | Agent Type | Host | Availability Zone | Alive | State | Binary |
+------------------------------------+------------------------+-------------+-
```

```
--------------------+-------+--------+----------------------------+
| 2a715a0d-5593-4aba-966e-6ae3b2e02ba2 | L3 agent | controller | nova |
True | UP | neutron-l3-agent |
| 2ce176fb-dc2e-4416-bb47-1ae44e1f556f | Linux bridge agent | controller |
None | True | UP | neutron-linuxbridge-agent |
| 42067496-eaa3-42ef-bff9-bbbbcbf2e15a | DHCP agent | controller | nova |
True | UP | neutron-dhcp-agent |
| fad2b9bb-8ee7-468e-b69a-43129338cbaa | Metadata agent | controller | None
| True | UP | neutron-metadata-agent |
+----------------------------------+---------------------+-------------+--
--------------------+-------+--------+----------------------------+
root@controller:~#
```

Defining the LXC instance flavor, generating a key pair, and creating security groups

Before we can create an LXC instance, we need to define its flavour - CPU, memory, and disk size. The following creates a flavor named `lxc.medium` with one virtual CPU, 1 GB RAM, and 5 GB disk:

```
root@controller:~# openstack flavor create --id 0 --vcpus 1 --ram 1024 --
disk 5 lxc.medium
+----------------------------+-------------+
| Field | Value |
+----------------------------+-------------+
| OS-FLV-DISABLED:disabled | False |
| OS-FLV-EXT-DATA:ephemeral | 0 |
| disk | 5 |
| id | 0 |
| name | lxc.medium |
| os-flavor-access:is_public | True |
| properties | |
| ram | 1024 |
| rxtx_factor | 1.0 |
| swap | |
| vcpus | 1 |
+----------------------------+-------------+
root@controller:~#
```

In order to SSH to the LXC containers, we can have the SSH keys managed and installed during the instance provisioning, if we don't want them to be baked inside the actual image. To generate the SSH key pair and add it to OpenStack, run the following command:

```
root@controller:~# ssh-keygen -q -N ""
```

Enter the file in which to save the key (`/root/.ssh/id_rsa`):

```
root@controller:~# openstack keypair create --public-key ~/.ssh/id_rsa.pub
lxckey
+-------------+----------------------------------------------------+
| Field | Value |
+-------------+----------------------------------------------------+
| fingerprint | 84:36:93:cc:2f:f0:f7:ba:d5:73:54:ca:2e:f0:02:6d |
| name | lxckey |
| user_id | 3a04d141c07541478ede7ea34f3e5c36 |
+-------------+----------------------------------------------------+
root@controller:~#
```

To list the new key pair we just added, execute the following:

```
root@controller:~# openstack keypair list
+---------+-------------------------------------------------+
| Name | Fingerprint |
+---------+-------------------------------------------------+
| lxckey | 84:36:93:cc:2f:f0:f7:ba:d5:73:54:ca:2e:f0:02:6d |
+---------+-------------------------------------------------+
root@controller:~#
```

By default, once a new LXC container is provisioned, iptables will disallow access to it. Let's create two security groups that will allow ICMP and SSH, so we can test connectivity and connect to the instance:

```
root@controller:~# openstack security group rule create --proto icmp
default
+-------------------+--------------------------------------+
| Field | Value |
+-------------------+--------------------------------------+
| created_at | 2016-12-02T20:30:14Z |
| description | |
| direction | ingress |
| ethertype | IPv4 |
| headers | |
| id | 0e17e0ab-4495-440a-b8b9-0a612f9eccae |
| port_range_max | None |
| port_range_min | None |
| project_id | 488aecf07dcb4ae6bc1ebad5b76fbc20 |
| project_id | 488aecf07dcb4ae6bc1ebad5b76fbc20 |
| protocol | icmp |
| remote_group_id | None |
| remote_ip_prefix | 0.0.0.0/0 |
| revision_number | 1 |
| security_group_id | f21f3d3c-27fe-4668-bca4-6fc842dcb690 |
| updated_at | 2016-12-02T20:30:14Z |
```

```
+-------------------+-------------------------------------+
root@controller:~#
root@controller:~# openstack security group rule create --proto tcp --dst-
port 22 default
...
root@controller:~#
```

Creating the networks

Let's start by creating a new network called nat in Neutron:

```
root@controller:~# openstack network create nat
+-------------------------+-------------------------------------+
| Field | Value |
+-------------------------+-------------------------------------+
| admin_state_up | UP |
| availability_zone_hints | |
| availability_zones | |
| created_at | 2016-12-02T20:32:53Z |
| description | |
| headers | |
| id | 66037974-d24b-4615-8b93-b0de18a4561b |
| ipv4_address_scope | None |
| ipv6_address_scope | None |
| mtu | 1450 |
| name | nat |
| port_security_enabled | True |
| project_id | 488aecf07dcb4ae6bc1ebad5b76fbc20 |
| project_id | 488aecf07dcb4ae6bc1ebad5b76fbc20 |
| provider:network_type | vxlan |
| provider:physical_network | None |
| provider:segmentation_id | 53 |
| revision_number | 3 |
| router:external | Internal |
| shared | False |
| status | ACTIVE |
| subnets | |
| tags | [] |
| updated_at | 2016-12-02T20:32:53Z |
+-------------------------+-------------------------------------+
root@controller:~#
```

Next, define the DNS server, the default gateway, and the subnet range that will be assigned to the LXC container:

```
root@controller:~# openstack subnet create --network nat --dns-nameserver
8.8.8.8 --gateway 192.168.0.1 --subnet-range 192.168.0.0/24 nat
+--------------------+----------------------------------------+
| Field | Value |
+--------------------+----------------------------------------+
| allocation_pools | 192.168.0.2-192.168.0.254 |
| cidr | 192.168.0.0/24 |
| created_at | 2016-12-02T20:36:14Z |
| description | |
| dns_nameservers | 8.8.8.8 |
| enable_dhcp | True |
| gateway_ip | 192.168.0.1 |
| headers | |
| host_routes | |
| id | 0e65fa94-be69-4690-b3fe-406ea321dfb3 |
| ip_version | 4 |
| ipv6_address_mode | None |
| ipv6_ra_mode | None |
| name | nat |
| network_id | 66037974-d24b-4615-8b93-b0de18a4561b |
| project_id | 488aecf07dcb4ae6bc1ebad5b76fbc20 |
| project_id | 488aecf07dcb4ae6bc1ebad5b76fbc20 |
| revision_number | 2 |
| service_types | [] |
| subnetpool_id | None |
| updated_at | 2016-12-02T20:36:14Z |
+--------------------+----------------------------------------+
root@controller:~#
```

Update the subnet's information in Neutron:

```
root@controller:~# neutron net-update nat --router:external
Updated network: nat
root@controller:~#
```

As the `lxc` user, create a new software router:

```
root@controller:~# . rc.lxc
root@controller:~# openstack router create router
+-------------------------+-------------------------------------+
| Field | Value |
+-------------------------+-------------------------------------+
| admin_state_up | UP |
| availability_zone_hints | |
| availability_zones | |
```

```
| created_at | 2016-12-02T20:38:08Z |
| description | |
| external_gateway_info | null |
| flavor_id | None |
| headers | |
| id | 45557fac-f158-40ef-aeec-496de913d5a5 |
| name | router |
| project_id | b0cc5ccc12eb4d6b98aadd784540f575 |
| project_id | b0cc5ccc12eb4d6b98aadd784540f575 |
| revision_number | 2 |
| routes | |
| status | ACTIVE |
| updated_at | 2016-12-02T20:38:08Z |
+--------------------------+---------------------------------------+
root@controller:~#
```

As the admin user, add the subnet we created earlier as an interface to the router:

```
root@controller:~# . rc.admin
root@controller:~# neutron router-interface-add router nat
Added interface be0f1e65-f086-41fd-b8d0-45ebb865bf0f to router router.
root@controller:~#
```

Let's list the network namespaces that were created:

```
root@controller:~# ip netns
qrouter-45557fac-f158-40ef-aeec-496de913d5a5 (id: 1)
qdhcp-66037974-d24b-4615-8b93-b0de18a4561b (id: 0)
root@controller:~#
```

To show the ports on the software router and the default gateway for the LXC containers, run the following command:

```
root@controller:~# neutron router-port-list router
+-----------------------------------------+------+--------------------+--------
--+
| id | name | mac_address | fixed_ips |
+-----------------------------------------+------+--------------------+--------
--+
| be0f1e65-f086-41fd-b8d0-45ebb865bf0f | | fa:16:3e:a6:36:7c |
{"subnet_id": "0e65fa94-be69-4690-b3fe-406ea321dfb3", "ip_address":
"192.168.0.1"} |
+-----------------------------------------+------+--------------------+--------
--+
root@controller:~#
```

Provisioning LXC container with OpenStack

Before we launch our LXC container with OpenStack, let's double-check we have all the requirements in place.

Start by listing the available networks:

```
root@controller:~# openstack network list
+--------------------------------------+------+------------------------------------
-----------+
| ID | Name | Subnets |
+--------------------------------------+------+------------------------------------
-----------+
| 66037974-d24b-4615-8b93-b0de18a4561b | nat | 0e65fa94-be69-4690-
b3fe-406ea321dfb3 |
+--------------------------------------+------+------------------------------------
-----------+
root@controller:~#
```

Display the compute flavors we can choose from:

```
root@controller:~# openstack flavor list
+----+------------+------+------+-----------+-------+-------------+
| ID | Name | RAM | Disk | Ephemeral | VCPUs | Is Public |
+----+------------+------+------+-----------+-------+-------------+
| 0 | lxc.medium | 1024 | 5 | 0 | 1 | True |
+----+------------+------+------+-----------+-------+-------------+
root@controller:~#
```

Next, list the available images:

```
root@controller:~# openstack image list
+--------------------------------------+------------------+--------+
| ID | Name | Status |
+--------------------------------------+------------------+--------+
| 417e72b5-7b85-4555-835d-ce442e21aa4f | lxc_ubuntu_12.04 | active |
+--------------------------------------+------------------+--------+
root@controller:~#
```

Also, display the default security group we created earlier:

```
root@controller:~# openstack security group list
+--------------------------------------+---------+------------------------
-------------------------------------+
| ID | Name | Description | Project |
+--------------------------------------+---------+------------------------
-------------------------------------+
| f21f3d3c-27fe-4668-bca4-6fc842dcb690 | default | Default security group |
```

```
488aecf07dcb4ae6bc1ebad5b76fbc20 |
+---------------------------------------+----------+------------------------
+---------------------------------------+
root@controller:~#
```

Now load the **Network Block Device** (**NBD**) kernel module, as Nova expects it:

```
root@controller:~# modprobe nbd
```

Finally, to provision LXC container with OpenStack, we execute the following command:

```
root@controller:~# openstack server create --flavor lxc.medium --image
lxc_ubuntu_12.04 --nic net-id=66037974-d24b-4615-8b93-b0de18a4561b --
security-group default --key-name lxckey lxc_instance
...
root@controller:~#
```

Notice how we specified the instance flavor, the image name, the ID of the network, the security group, the key-pair name, and the name of the instance.

Make sure to replace the IDs with the output returned on your system.

To list the LXC container, its status, and assigned IP address, run the following command:

```
root@controller:~# openstack server list
+---------------------------------------+----------------+---------+------------
-------+--------------------+
| ID | Name | Status | Networks | Image Name |
+---------------------------------------+----------------+---------+------------
-------+--------------------+
| a86f8f56-80d7-4d36-86c3-827679f21ec5 | lxc_instance | ACTIVE |
nat=192.168.0.3 | lxc_ubuntu_12.04 |
+---------------------------------------+----------------+---------+------------
-------+--------------------+
root@controller:~#
```

As we saw earlier in this chapter, OpenStack uses the libvirt driver to provision LXC containers. We can use the virsh command we used in Chapter 2, *Installing and Running LXC on Linux Systems*, to list the LXC containers on the host:

```
root@controller:~# virsh --connect lxc:// list --all
Id Name State
---------------------------------------------------------
16225 instance-00000002 running
root@controller:~#
```

If we list the processes on the host, we can see that the `libvirt_lxc` parent process spawned the init process for the container:

```
root@controller:~# ps axfw
...
16225 ? S 0:00 /usr/lib/libvirt/libvirt_lxc --name instance-00000002 --
console 23 --security=apparmor --handshake 26 --veth vnet0
16227 ? Ss 0:00  \_ /sbin/init
16591 ? S 0:00  \_ upstart-socket-bridge --daemon
16744 ? Ss 0:00  \_ dhclient3 -e IF_METRIC=100 -pf
/var/run/dhclient.eth0.pid -lf /var/lib/dhcp/dhclient.eth0.leases -1 eth0
17692 ? S 0:00  \_ upstart-udev-bridge --daemon
17696 ? Ss 0:00  \_ /sbin/udevd --daemon
17819 ? S 0:00  |  \_ /sbin/udevd --daemon
18108 ? Ss 0:00  \_ /usr/sbin/sshd -D
18116 ? Ss 0:00  \_ dbus-daemon --system --fork --activation=upstart
18183 ? Ss 0:00  \_ cron
18184 ? Ss 0:00  \_ atd
18189 ? Ss 0:00  \_ /usr/sbin/irqbalance
18193 ? Ss 0:00  \_ acpid -c /etc/acpi/events -s /var/run/acpid.socket
18229 pts/0 Ss+ 0:00  \_ /sbin/getty -8 38400 tty1
18230 ? Ssl 0:00  \_ whoopsie
18317 ? Sl 0:00  \_ rsyslogd -c5
19185 ? Ss 0:00  \_ /sbin/getty -8 38400 tty4
19186 ? Ss 0:00  \_ /sbin/getty -8 38400 tty2
19187 ? Ss 0:00  \_ /sbin/getty -8 38400 tty3
root@controller:~#
```

The location of the container's configuration file and disk is as follows:

```
root@controller:~# cd /var/lib/nova/instances/
root@controller:/var/lib/nova/instances# ls -la
a86f8f56-80d7-4d36-86c3-827679f21ec5/
total 12712
drwxr-xr-x 3 nova nova 4096 Dec 2 20:52 .
drwxr-xr-x 5 nova nova 4096 Dec 2 20:52 ..
-rw-r--r-- 1 nova nova 0 Dec 2 20:52 console.log
-rw-r--r-- 1 nova nova 13041664 Dec 2 20:57 disk
-rw-r--r-- 1 nova nova 79 Dec 2 20:52 disk.info
-rw-r--r-- 1 nova nova 1534 Dec 2 20:52 libvirt.xml
drwxr-xr-x 2 nova nova 4096 Dec 2 20:52 rootfs
root@controller:/var/lib/nova/instances#
```

Let's examine the container's configuration file:

```
root@controller:/var/lib/nova/instances# cat
a86f8f56-80d7-4d36-86c3-827679f21ec5/libvirt.xml
<domain type="lxc">
```

```
<uuid>a86f8f56-80d7-4d36-86c3-827679f21ec5</uuid>
<name>instance-00000002</name>
<memory>1048576</memory>
<vcpu>1</vcpu>
<metadata>
  <nova:instance
    xmlns:nova="http://openstack.org/xmlns/libvirt/nova/1.0">
    <nova:package version="14.0.1"/>
    <nova:name>lxc_instance</nova:name>
    <nova:creationTime>2016-12-02 20:52:52</nova:creationTime>
    <nova:flavor name="lxc.medium">
      <nova:memory>1024</nova:memory>
      <nova:disk>5</nova:disk>
      <nova:swap>0</nova:swap>
      <nova:ephemeral>0</nova:ephemeral>
      <nova:vcpus>1</nova:vcpus>
    </nova:flavor>
    <nova:owner>
      <nova:user uuid="3a04d141c07541478ede7ea34f3e5c36">
      admin
      </nova:user>
      <nova:project uuid="488aecf07dcb4ae6bc1ebad5b76fbc20">
        admin
      </nova:project>
    </nova:owner>
    <nova:root type="image" uuid="417e72b5-7b85-4555-835d-ce442e21aa4f"/>
  </nova:instance>
</metadata>
<os>
  <type>exe</type>
  <cmdline>console=tty0 console=ttyS0 console=ttyAMA0</cmdline>
  <init>/sbin/init</init>
</os>
<cputune>
  <shares>1024</shares>
</cputune>
<clock offset="utc"/>
<devices>
  <filesystem type="mount">
    <source dir="/var/lib/nova/instances/
    a86f8f56-80d7-4d36-86c3-827679f21ec5/rootfs"/>
    <target dir="/"/>
  </filesystem>
  <interface type="bridge">
    <mac address="fa:16:3e:4f:e5:b5"/>
    <source bridge="brq66037974-d2"/>
    <target dev="tapf2073410-64"/>
  </interface>
```

```
        <console type="pty"/>
    </devices>
</domain>
root@controller:/var/lib/nova/instances#
```

We've seen similar configuration files for the libvirt containers we built in earlier chapters.

With the networking managed by Neutron, we should see the bridge and the container's interface added as a port:

```
root@controller:/var/lib/nova/instances# brctl show
bridge name          bridge id            STP enabled      interfaces
brq66037974-d2       8000.02d65d01c617    no               tap4e3afc26-88
                                                           tapbe0f1e65-f0
                                                           tapf2073410-64
                                                           vxlan-53
virbr0               8000.5254004e7712    yes              virbr0-nic
root@controller:/var/lib/nova/instances#
```

Let's configure an IP address on the bridge interface and allow NAT connectivity to the container:

```
root@controller:/var/lib/nova/instances# ifconfig brq66037974-d2
192.168.0.1
root@controller:~# iptables -A POSTROUTING -t nat -s 192.168.0.0/24 ! -d
192.168.0.0/24 -j MASQUERADE
root@controller:~#
```

To connect to the LXC container using SSH and the key pair we generated earlier, execute the following command:

```
root@controller:/var/lib/nova/instances# ssh ubuntu@192.168.0.3
Welcome to Ubuntu 12.04.5 LTS (GNU/Linux 4.4.0-51-generic x86_64)
ubuntu@lxc-instance:~$ ifconfig
eth0 Link encap:Ethernet HWaddr fa:16:3e:4f:e5:b5
inet addr:192.168.0.3 Bcast:192.168.0.255 Mask:255.255.255.0
inet6 addr: fe80::f816:3eff:fe4f:e5b5/64 Scope:Link
UP BROADCAST RUNNING MULTICAST MTU:1450 Metric:1
RX packets:290 errors:0 dropped:0 overruns:0 frame:0
TX packets:340 errors:0 dropped:0 overruns:0 carrier:0
collisions:0 txqueuelen:1000
RX bytes:35038 (35.0 KB) TX bytes:36830 (36.8 KB)
lo Link encap:Local Loopback
inet addr:127.0.0.1 Mask:255.0.0.0
inet6 addr: ::1/128 Scope:Host
UP LOOPBACK RUNNING MTU:65536 Metric:1
RX packets:0 errors:0 dropped:0 overruns:0 frame:0
TX packets:0 errors:0 dropped:0 overruns:0 carrier:0
```

```
collisions:0 txqueuelen:1
RX bytes:0 (0.0 B) TX bytes:0 (0.0 B)
ubuntu@lxc-instance:~$ exit
logout
Connection to 192.168.0.3 closed.
root@controller:/var/lib/nova/instances# cd
root@controller:~#
```

Finally, to delete the LXC container using OpenStack, run the following commands:

```
root@controller:~# openstack server delete lxc_instance
root@controller:~# openstack server list
root@controller:~#
```

Summary

In this chapter, we looked at an example of a basic OpenStack deployment using only the identity service Keystone for storing a catalog of services, and authentication and authorization, the Nova compute services for provisioning the LXC instance, the image service Glance, which stores the LXC container images, and the networking services with Neutron that created the bridge and assigned the IP address to our container.

A full production-ready deployment would consist of multiple controller nodes that run the aforementioned services, along with a pool of compute servers to provision the containers on.

OpenStack with LXC is a great way to create and manage multitenant cloud environments, running various software applications in a centralized and highly scalable way.

LXC Alternatives to Docker and OpenVZ

LXC is designed and ideally suited for running full system containers; this means that an LXC instance contains the filesystem of an entire operating system distribution, very similar to a virtual machine. Even though LXC can run a single process, or a replacement of the init system with a custom script, there are other container alternatives that are better suited for executing just a single, self-contained program. In this Appendix, we are going to look at two container implementation alternatives to LXC that can run side by side with LXC – Docker and OpenVZ.

Building containers with OpenVZ

OpenVZ is one of the oldest operating-system-level virtualization technologies, dating back to 2005. It is similar to LXC in the sense that it is geared toward running an entire operating system, rather than a single program such as Docker. Being a containerization technology, it shares the host OS kernel with no hypervisor layer. OpenVZ uses a patched version of the Red Hat kernel that is maintained separately from the Vanilla kernel.

Let's explore some of the OpenVZ features and see how they compare to LXC:

For this example deployment, we are going to use Debian Wheezy:

```
root@ovz:~# lsb_release -rd
Description:       Debian GNU/Linux 7.8 (wheezy)
Release:    7.8
root@ovz:~#
```

Start by adding the OpenVZ repository and key, then update the package index:

```
root@ovz:~# cat << EOF > /etc/apt/sources.list.d/openvz-rhel6.list
deb http://download.openvz.org/debian wheezy main
EOF
root@ovz:~#
root@ovz:~# wget ftp://ftp.openvz.org/debian/archive.key
root@ovz:~# apt-key add archive.key
root@ovz:~# apt-get update
```

Next, install the OpenVZ kernel:

```
root@ovz:~# apt-get install linux-image-openvz-amd64
```

If using GRUB, update the boot menu with the OpenVZ kernel; in this example, the kernel is added as menu item 2:

```
root@ovz:~# cat /boot/grub/grub.cfg | grep menuentry
menuentry 'Debian GNU/Linux, with Linux 3.2.0-4-amd64' --class debian --
class gnu-linux --class gnu --class os {
menuentry 'Debian GNU/Linux, with Linux 3.2.0-4-amd64 (recovery mode)' --
class debian --class gnu-linux --class gnu --class os {
menuentry 'Debian GNU/Linux, with Linux 2.6.32-openvz-042stab120.11-amd64'
--class debian --class gnu-linux --class gnu --class os {
menuentry 'Debian GNU/Linux, with Linux 2.6.32-openvz-042stab120.11-amd64
 (recovery mode)' --class debian --class gnu-linux --class gnu --class os {
root@ovz:~#

root@ovz:~# vim /etc/default/grub
...
GRUB_DEFAULT=2
...

root@ovz:~# update-grub
Generating grub.cfg ...
Found linux image: /boot/vmlinuz-3.2.0-4-amd64
Found initrd image: /boot/initrd.img-3.2.0-4-amd64
Found linux image: /boot/vmlinuz-2.6.32-openvz-042stab120.11-amd64
Found initrd image: /boot/initrd.img-2.6.32-openvz-042stab120.11-amd64
done
root@ovz:~#
```

We need to enable routing in the kernel and disable proxy ARP:

```
root@ovz:~# cat /etc/sysctl.d/ovz.conf
net.ipv4.ip_forward = 1
net.ipv6.conf.default.forwarding = 1
net.ipv6.conf.all.forwarding = 1
```

```
net.ipv4.conf.default.proxy_arp = 0
net.ipv4.conf.all.rp_filter = 1
kernel.sysrq = 1
net.ipv4.conf.default.send_redirects = 1
net.ipv4.conf.all.send_redirects = 0
root@ovz2:~#
root@ovz:~# sysctl -p /etc/sysctl.d/ovz.conf
...
root@ovz:~#
```

Now it's time to reboot the server, then check whether the OpenVZ is now loaded:

```
root@ovz:~# reboot
root@ovz:~# uname -a
Linux ovz 2.6.32-openvz-042stab120.11-amd64 #1 SMP Wed Nov 16 12:07:16 MSK
2016 x86_64 GNU/Linux
root@ovz:~#
```

Next, install the userspace tools:

```
root@ovz:~# apt-get install vzctl vzquota ploop vzstats
```

OpenVZ uses templates in a similar way to LXC. The templates are archived root filesystems and can be built with tools such as debootstrap. Let's download an Ubuntu template in the directory where OpenVZ expects them by default:

```
root@ovz:~# cd /var/lib/vz/template/
root@ovz:/var/lib/vz/template# wget
http://download.openvz.org/template/precreated/ubuntu-16.04-x86_64.tar.gz
root@ovz:/var/lib/vz/template#
```

With the template archive in place, let's create a container:

```
root@ovz:/var/lib/vz/template# vzctl create 1 --ostemplate ubuntu-16.04-
x86_64 --layout simfs
Creating container private area (ubuntu-16.04-x86_64)
Performing postcreate actions
CT configuration saved to /etc/vz/conf/1.conf
Container private area was created
root@ovz:/var/lib/vz/template#
```

We specify simfs as the type of the underlying container store, which will create the root filesystem on the host OS, similar to LXC and the default directory type. OpenVZ provides alternatives, such as Ploop, which creates an image file containing the containers filesystem.

Next, create a Linux bridge:

```
root@ovz:/var/lib/vz/template# apt-get install bridge-utils
root@ovz:/var/lib/vz/template# brctl addbr br0
```

To allow OpenVZ to connect its containers to the host bridge, create the following config file:

```
root@ovz:/var/lib/vz/template# cat /etc/vz/vznet.conf
#!/bin/bash
EXTERNAL_SCRIPT="/usr/sbin/vznetaddbr"
root@ovz:/var/lib/vz/template#
```

The file specifies an external script that will add the containers virtual interface to the bridge we created earlier.

Let's configure our container with a network interface, by specifying the name of the interfaces inside and outside the container, and the bridge they should be connected to:

```
root@ovz:/var/lib/vz/template# vzctl set 1 --save --netif_add
eth0,,veth1.eth0,,br0
CT configuration saved to /etc/vz/conf/1.conf
root@ovz:/var/lib/vz/template#
```

List the available containers on the host by executing the following command:

```
root@ovz:/var/lib/vz/template# vzlist -a
CTID       NPROC STATUS    IP_ADDR        HOSTNAME
  1          - stopped     -              -
root@ovz:/var/lib/vz/template# cd
```

To start our container, run the following command:

```
root@ovz:~# vzctl start 1
Starting container...
Container is mounted
Setting CPU units: 1000
Configure veth devices: veth1.eth0
Adding interface veth1.eth0 to bridge br0 on CT0 for CT1
Container start in progress...
root@ovz:~#
```

Then, to attach, or enter the container, execute the following commands:

```
root@ovz:~# vzctl enter 1
entered into CT 1
root@localhost:/# exit
logout
exited from CT 1
root@ovz:~#
```

Manipulating the available container resources can be done on the fly, without the need for restarting the container, very much like with LXC. Let's set the memory to 1 GB:

```
root@ovz:~# vzctl set 1 --ram 1G --save
UB limits were set successfully
CT configuration saved to /etc/vz/conf/1.conf
root@ovz:~#
```

Every OpenVZ container has a config file, which is updated when passing the `--save` option to the `vzctl` tool. To examine it, run the following command:

```
root@ovz:~# cat /etc/vz/conf/1.conf | grep -vi "#" | sed '/^$/d'
PHYSPAGES="0:262144"
SWAPPAGES="0:512M"
DISKSPACE="2G:2.2G"
DISKINODES="131072:144179"
QUOTATIME="0"
CPUUNITS="1000"
NETFILTER="stateless"
VE_ROOT="/var/lib/vz/root/$VEID"
VE_PRIVATE="/var/lib/vz/private/$VEID"
VE_LAYOUT="simfs"
OSTEMPLATE="ubuntu-16.04-x86_64"
ORIGIN_SAMPLE="vswap-256m"
NETIF="ifname=eth0,bridge=br0,mac=00:18:51:A1:C6:35,host_ifname=veth1.eth0,
host_mac=00:18:51:BF:1D:AC"
root@ovz:~#
```

With the container running, ensure the virtual interface on the host is added to the bridge. Note that the bridge interface itself is in a DOWN state:

```
root@ovz:~# brctl show
bridge name     bridge id               STP enabled     interfaces
br0             8000.001851bf1dac       no              veth1.eth0

root@ovz:~# ip a s
...
4: br0: <BROADCAST,MULTICAST> mtu 1500 qdisc noop state DOWN
    link/ether 00:18:51:bf:1d:ac brd ff:ff:ff:ff:ff:ff
```

```
6: veth1.eth0: <BROADCAST,MULTICAST,UP,LOWER_UP> mtu 1500 qdisc noqueue
state UNKNOWN
    link/ether 00:18:51:bf:1d:ac brd ff:ff:ff:ff:ff:ff
    inet6 fe80::218:51ff:febf:1dac/64 scope link
        valid_lft forever preferred_lft forever
root@ovz:~#
```

We can execute commands inside the container without the need to attach to it. Let's configure an IP address to the containers' interface:

```
root@ovz:~# vzctl exec 1 "ifconfig eth0 192.168.0.5"
root@ovz:~#
```

Bring the bridge interface on the host up and configure an IP address, so we can reach the container from the host:

```
root@ovz:~# ifconfig br0 up
root@ovz:~# ifconfig br0 192.168.0.1
```

Let's test connectivity:

```
root@ovz:~# ping -c3 192.168.0.5
PING 192.168.0.5 (192.168.0.5) 56(84) bytes of data.
64 bytes from 192.168.0.5: icmp_req=1 ttl=64 time=0.037 ms
64 bytes from 192.168.0.5: icmp_req=2 ttl=64 time=0.036 ms
64 bytes from 192.168.0.5: icmp_req=3 ttl=64 time=0.036 ms
--- 192.168.0.5 ping statistics ---
3 packets transmitted, 3 received, 0% packet loss, time 1999ms
rtt min/avg/max/mdev = 0.036/0.036/0.037/0.005 ms
root@ovz:~#
```

Let's enter the container and make sure the available memory is indeed 1 GB, as we set it up earlier:

```
root@ovz:~# vzctl enter 1
entered into CT 1
root@localhost:/# free -g
          total    used    free    shared   buff/cache    available
Mem:       1        0       0        0            0            0
Swap:      0        0       0
root@localhost:/# exit
logout
exited from CT 1
root@ovz:~#
```

Notice how the OpenVZ container uses `init` to start all other processes, just like a virtual machine:

```
root@ovz:~# ps axfww
...
3303 ?        Ss       0:00 init -z
3365 ?        Ss       0:00  \_ /lib/systemd/systemd-journald
3367 ?        Ss       0:00  \_ /lib/systemd/systemd-udevd
3453 ?        Ss       0:00  \_ /sbin/rpcbind -f -w
3454 ?        Ssl      0:00  \_ /usr/sbin/rsyslogd -n
3457 ?        Ss       0:00  \_ /usr/sbin/cron -f
3526 ?        Ss       0:00  \_ /usr/sbin/xinetd -pidfile /run/xinetd.pid -
stayalive -inetd_compat -inetd_ipv6
3536 ?        Ss       0:00  \_ /usr/sbin/saslauthd -a pam -c -m
/var/run/saslauthd -n 2
3540 ?        S        0:00  |   \_ /usr/sbin/saslauthd -a pam -c -m
/var/run/saslauthd -n 2
3542 ?        Ss       0:00  \_ /usr/sbin/apache2 -k start
3546 ?        Sl       0:00  |   \_ /usr/sbin/apache2 -k start
3688 ?        Ss       0:00  \_ /usr/lib/postfix/sbin/master
3689 ?        S        0:00  |   \_ pickup -l -t unix -u -c
3690 ?        S        0:00  |   \_ qmgr -l -t unix -u
3695 ?        Ss       0:00  \_ /usr/sbin/sshd -D
3705 tty1     Ss+      0:00  \_ /sbin/agetty --noclear --keep-baud console
115200 38400 9600 vt220
3706 tty2     Ss+      0:00  \_ /sbin/agetty --noclear tty2 linux
root@ovz:~#
```

We now know that all container implementations use cgroups to control system resources and OpenVZ is no exception. Let's see where the cgroup hierarchies are mounted:

```
root@ovz:~# mount | grep cgroup
beancounter on /proc/vz/beancounter type cgroup
(rw,relatime,blkio,name=beancounter)
container on /proc/vz/container type cgroup
(rw,relatime,freezer,devices,name=container)
fairsched on /proc/vz/fairsched type cgroup
(rw,relatime,cpuacct,cpu,cpuset,name=fairsched)
tmpfs on /var/lib/vz/root/1/sys/fs/cgroup type tmpfs
(ro,nosuid,nodev,noexec,size=131072k,nr_inodes=32768,mode=755)
cgroup on /var/lib/vz/root/1/sys/fs/cgroup/systemd type cgroup
(rw,nosuid,nodev,noexec,relatime,release_agent=/lib/systemd/systemd-
cgroups-agent,name=systemd)
cgroup on /var/lib/vz/root/1/sys/fs/cgroup/memory type cgroup
(rw,nosuid,nodev,noexec,relatime,memory)
cgroup on /var/lib/vz/root/1/sys/fs/cgroup/blkio type cgroup
(rw,nosuid,nodev,noexec,relatime,blkio,name=beancounter)
 root@ovz:~#
```

The container we created earlier has an ID of 1 as we saw in the earlier example. We can grab the PIDs of all processes running inside the container by running the following command:

```
root@ovz:~# cat /proc/vz/fairsched/1/cgroup.procs
3303
3304
3305
3365
3367
3453
3454
3457
3526
3536
3540
3542
3546
3688
3689
3690
3695
3705
3706
root@ovz:~#
```

We can also obtain the number of CPUs assigned to the container:

```
root@ovz:~# cat /proc/vz/fairsched/1/cpu.nr_cpus
0
root@ovz:~#
```

Let's assign two cores to the container with ID 1:

```
root@ovz:~# vzctl set 1 --save --cpus 2
UB limits were set successfully
Setting CPUs: 2
CT configuration saved to /etc/vz/conf/1.conf
root@ovz:~#
```

Then ensure the change is visible in the same file:

```
root@ovz:~# cat /proc/vz/fairsched/1/cpu.nr_cpus
2
root@ovz:~#
```

The container's configuration file should also reflect the change:

```
root@ovz:~# cat /etc/vz/conf/1.conf | grep -i CPUS
CPUS="2"
root@ovz:~#
```

Using the `ps` command or, by reading the preceding system file, we can get the PID of the `init` process inside the container, in this example, `3303`. Knowing that PID, we can get the ID of the container by running the following command:

```
root@ovz:~# cat /proc/3303/status | grep envID
envID:        1
root@ovz:~#
```

Since the root filesystem of the container is present on the host, migrating an OpenVZ instance is similar to LXC – we first stop the container, then archive the root filesystem, copy it to the new server, and extract it. We also need the config file for the container. Let's see an example of migrating OpenVZ container to a new host:

```
root@ovz:~# vzctl stop 1
Stopping container ...
Container was stopped
Container is unmounted
root@ovz:~#

root@ovz:~# tar -zcvf /tmp/ovz_container_1.tar.gz -C /var/lib/vz/private 1
root@ovz:~# scp  /tmp/ovz_container_1.tar.gz 10.3.20.31:/tmp/
root@ovz:~# scp /etc/vz/conf/1.conf 10.3.20.31:/etc/vz/conf/
root@ovz:~#
```

On the second server, we extract the root filesystem:

```
root@ovz2:~# tar zxfv /tmp/ovz_container_1.tar.gz --numeric-owner -C
/var/lib/vz/private
root@ovz2:~#
```

With the config file and the filesystem in place, we can list the container by running the following command:

```
root@ovz2:~# vzlist -a
stat(/var/lib/vz/root/1): No such file or directory
CTID      NPROC STATUS    IP_ADDR         HOSTNAME
1            - stopped    -               -
root@ovz2:~#
```

Finally, to start the OpenVZ instance and ensure it's running on the new host, execute the following command:

```
root@ovz2:~# vzctl start 1
Starting container...
stat(/var/lib/vz/root/1): No such file or directory
stat(/var/lib/vz/root/1): No such file or directory
stat(/var/lib/vz/root/1): No such file or directory
Initializing quota ...
Container is mounted
Setting CPU units: 1000
Setting CPUs: 2
Configure veth devices: veth1.eth0
Container start in progress...
root@ovz2:~# vzlist -a
CTID      NPROC STATUS    IP_ADDR         HOSTNAME
1         47 running      -               -
root@ovz2:~#
```

OpenVZ does not have a centralized control daemon, which provides easier integration with init systems such as upstart or systemd. It's important to note that OpenVZ is the foundation for the Virtuozzo virtualization solution offered by the Virtuozzo company, and its latest iteration will be an ISO image of an entire operating system, instead of running a patched kernel with a separate toolset.

 For more information on the latest OpenVZ and Virtuozzo versions, visit https://openvz.org.

Building containers with Docker

The Docker project was released in 2013 and gained popularity quickly, surpassing that of OpenVZ and LXC. Large production deployments now run Docker, with various orchestration frameworks, such as Apache Mesos and Kubernetes, offering Docker integration.

Unlike LXC and OpenVZ, Docker is better suited for running single applications in a minimal container setup. It uses Docker Engine daemon, which controls the containerd process for managing the life cycle of the containers, thus making it harder to integrate with other init systems such as systemd.

Docker exposes a convenient API that various tools use, and makes it easy to provision containers from prebuilt images, hosted either on remote public or private repositories/registries.

We can run LXC and Docker containers on the same host without any problems, as they have clear separation. In the next section, we are going to explore most of Docker's features, by examining the life cycle of a Docker container and seeing how it compares to LXC.

Let's start by updating our server and installing the repo and key:

```
root@docker:~# apt-get update && apt-get upgrade && reboot
...

root@docker:~# apt-key adv --keyserver hkp://ha.pool.sks-keyservers.net:80
--recv-keys 58118E89F3A912897C070ADBF76221572C52609D
Executing: /tmp/tmp.Au9fc0rNu3/gpg.1.sh --keyserver
hkp://ha.pool.sks-keyservers.net:80
--recv-keys
58118E89F3A912897C070ADBF76221572C52609D
gpg: requesting key 2C52609D from hkp server ha.pool.sks-keyservers.net
gpg: key 2C52609D: public key "Docker Release Tool (releasedocker)
<docker@docker.com>" imported
gpg: Total number processed: 1
gpg:              imported: 1  (RSA: 1)

root@docker:~# echo "deb https://apt.dockerproject.org/repo ubuntu-xenial
main" | sudo tee /etc/apt/sources.list.d/docker.list
deb https://apt.dockerproject.org/repo ubuntu-xenial main
root@docker:~# apt-get update
```

List the currently available package versions and install the latest candidate:

```
root@docker:~# apt-cache policy docker-engine
docker-engine:
  Installed: (none)
  Candidate: 1.12.4-0~ubuntu-xenial
  Version table:
     1.12.4-0~ubuntu-xenial 500
        500 https://apt.dockerproject.org/repo ubuntu-xenial/main amd64
Packages
     1.12.3-0~xenial 500
        500 https://apt.dockerproject.org/repo ubuntu-xenial/main amd64
Packages
     1.12.2-0~xenial 500
            500 https://apt.dockerproject.org/repo ubuntu-xenial/main amd64
Packages
     1.12.1-0~xenial 500
        500 https://apt.dockerproject.org/repo ubuntu-xenial/main amd64
```

```
Packages
    1.12.0-0~xenial 500
        500 https://apt.dockerproject.org/repo ubuntu-xenial/main amd64
Packages
    1.11.2-0~xenial 500
        500 https://apt.dockerproject.org/repo ubuntu-xenial/main amd64
Packages
    1.11.1-0~xenial 500
        500 https://apt.dockerproject.org/repo ubuntu-xenial/main amd64
Packages
    1.11.0-0~xenial 500
        500 https://apt.dockerproject.org/repo ubuntu-xenial/main amd64
Packages

root@docker:~# apt-get install linux-image-extra-$(uname -r) linux-image-
extra-virtual
root@docker:~# apt-get install docker-engine
```

Start the Docker services and ensure they are running:

```
root@docker:~# service docker start
root@docker:~# pgrep -lfa docker
24585 /usr/bin/dockerd -H fd://
24594 docker-containerd -l unix:///var/run/docker/libcontainerd/docker-
containerd.sock --shim docker-containerd-shim --metrics-interval=0 --start-
timeout 2m --state-dir /var/run/docker/libcontainerd/containerd --runtime
docker-runc
root@docker:~#
```

With the Docker daemon running, let's list all available containers, of which we currently have none:

```
root@docker:~# docker ps
CONTAINER ID        IMAGE               COMMAND             CREATED
STATUS              PORTS               NAMES
root@docker:~#
```

Let's find an Ubuntu image from the upstream public registry, by executing the following command:

```
root@docker:~# docker search ubuntu
NAME            DESCRIPTION             STARS       OFFICIAL
AUTOMATED
ubuntu   Ubuntu is a Debian-based Linux operating s...    5200        [OK]
ubuntu-upstart   Upstart is an event-based replacement for ...    69
[OK]
...
root@docker:~#
```

We pick the official Ubuntu image for our container; to create it, run the following command:

```
root@docker:~# docker create --tty --interactive ubuntu bash
Unable to find image 'ubuntu:latest' locally
latest: Pulling from library/ubuntu
af49a5ceb2a5: Pull complete
8f9757b472e7: Pull complete
e931b117db38: Pull complete
47b5e16c0811: Pull complete
9332eaf1a55b: Pull complete
Digest:
sha256:3b64c309deae7ab0f7dbdd42b6b326261ccd6261da5d88396439353162703fb5
Status: Downloaded newer image for ubuntu:latest
ec66fcfb5960c0779d07243f2c1e4d4ac10b855e940d416514057a9b28d78d09
root@docker:~#
```

We should now have a cached Ubuntu image on our system:

```
root@docker:~# docker images
REPOSITORY    TAG       IMAGE ID      CREATED       SIZE
ubuntu        latest    4ca3a192ff2a  2 weeks ago   128.2 MB
root@docker:~#
```

Let's list the available container on the host again:

```
root@docker:~# docker ps --all
CONTAINER ID    IMAGE      COMMAND      CREATED          STATUS
PORTS           NAMES
ec66fcfb5960    ubuntu     "bash"       29 seconds ago       Created
docker_container_1
root@docker:~#
```

Starting the Ubuntu Docker container is just as easy:

```
root@docker:~# docker start docker_container_1
docker_container_1
root@docker:~# docker ps
CONTAINER ID    IMAGE    COMMAND    CREATED          STATUS
PORTS      NAMES
ec66fcfb5960    ubuntu   "bash"     About a minute ago   Up 17 seconds
docker_container_1
root@docker:~#
```

By examining the process list, notice how we now have a single bash process running as a child of the `dockerd` and `docker-containerd` processes:

```
root@docker:~# ps axfww
...
24585 ?         Ssl    0:07 /usr/bin/dockerd -H fd://
24594 ?         Ssl    0:00  \_ docker-containerd -l
unix:///var/run/docker/libcontainerd/docker-containerd.sock --shim docker-
containerd-shim --metrics-interval=0 --start-timeout 2m --state-dir
/var/run/docker/libcontainerd/containerd --runtime docker-runc
26942 ?         Sl     0:00       \_ docker-containerd-shim
ec66fcfb5960c0779d07243f2c1e4d4ac10b855e940d416514057a9b28d78d09
/var/run/docker/libcontainerd/ec66fcfb5960c0779d07243f2c1e4d4ac10b855e940d4
16514057a9b28d78d09 docker-runc
26979 pts/1    Ss+    0:00           \_ bash
root@docker:~#
```

By attaching to the container, we can see that it is running a single bash process, unlike the full init system that LXC or OpenVZ use:

```
root@docker:~# docker attach docker_container_1
root@ec66fcfb5960:/# ps axfw
PID TTY     STAT   TIME   COMMAND
1   ?        Ss     0:00   bash
10  ?        R+     0:00   ps axfw

root@ec66fcfb5960:/# exit
exit
root@docker:~#
```

Notice that after exiting the container, it is terminated:

```
root@docker:~# docker attach docker_container_1
You cannot attach to a stopped container, start it first
root@docker:~# docker ps -a
CONTAINER ID        IMAGE                     COMMAND           CREATED
STATUS                    PORTS               NAMES
ec66fcfb5960        ubuntu                    "bash"
3 minutes ago       Exited (0) 26 seconds ago
docker_container_1
root@docker:~#
```

Let's start it back up again; we can either specify its name or ID, in the same manner as with OpenVZ, or libvirt LXC:

```
root@docker:~# docker start ec66fcfb5960
ec66fcfb5960

root@docker:~# docker ps
CONTAINER ID        IMAGE               COMMAND             CREATED
STATUS              PORTS
NAMES
ec66fcfb5960        ubuntu              "bash"
3 minutes ago       Up 2 seconds
docker_container_1
root@docker:~#
```

To update the container's memory, execute the following command:

```
root@docker:~# docker update --memory 1G docker_container_1
docker_container_1
root@docker:~#
```

Inspect the memory settings of the container to make sure the memory was successfully updated:

```
root@docker:~# docker inspect docker_container_1 | grep -i memory
    "Memory": 1073741824,
    "KernelMemory": 0,
    "MemoryReservation": 0,
    "MemorySwap": 0,
    "MemorySwappiness": -1,
root@docker:~#
```

Just like LXC and OpenVZ, the corresponding cgroup hierarchy was updated. We should be able to see the same memory amount in the cgroup file for the container ID:

```
root@docker:~# cat
/sys/fs/cgroup/memory/docker/ec66fcfb5960c0779d07243f2c1e4d4ac10b855e940d41
6514057a9b28d78d09/memory.limit_in_bytes
1073741824
root@docker:~#
```

Let's update the CPU shares:

```
root@docker:~# docker update --cpu-shares 512 docker_container_1
docker_container_1
root@docker:~#
```

Then, examine the setting in the cgroup file, replacing the container ID with the one running on your host:

```
root@docker:~# cat
/sys/fs/cgroup/cpu/docker/ec66fcfb5960c0779d07243f2c1e4d4ac10b855e940d41651
4057a9b28d78d09/cpu.shares
512
root@docker:~#
```

Docker provides few ways of monitoring the container status and resource utilization, very much like LXC:

```
root@docker:~# docker top docker_container_1
UID                     PID                     PPID                    C
STIME                   TTY                     TIME                    CMD
root                    27812                   27774                   0
17:41                   pts/1                   00:00:00                bash

root@docker:~# docker stats docker_container_1
CONTAINER               CPU %                   MEM USAGE / LIMIT    MEM %
NET I/O                 BLOCK I/O               PIDS
docker_container_1    0.00%                     1.809 MiB / 1 GiB    0.18%
648 B / 648 B           0 B / 0 B               1
^C
root@docker:~#
```

We can also run a command inside the containers' namespace without attaching to it:

```
root@docker:~# docker exec docker_container_1 ps ax
PID TTY       STAT    TIME COMMAND
1 ?           Ss+     0:00 bash
11 ?          Rs      0:00 ps ax
root@docker:~#
```

Copying a file from the host filesystem to that of the container is done with the following command; we saw similar examples with LXC and OpenVZ:

```
root@docker:~# touch /tmp/test_file
root@docker:~# docker cp /tmp/test_file docker_container_1:/tmp/
root@docker:~# docker exec docker_container_1 ls -la /tmp
total 8
drwxrwxrwt  2 root root 4096 Dec 14 19:39 .
drwxr-xr-x 36 root root 4096 Dec 14 19:39 ..
-rw-r--r--  1 root root    0 Dec 14 19:38 test_file
root@docker:~#
```

Moving the container between hosts is even easier with Docker; there's no need to manually archive the root filesystem:

```
root@docker:~# docker export docker_container_1 > docker_container_1.tar
root@docker:~# docker import docker_container_1.tar
sha256:c86a93369be687f9ead4758c908fe61b344d5c84b1b70403ede6384603532aa9

root@docker:~# docker images
REPOSITORY          TAG             IMAGE ID            CREATED             SIZE
<none>              <none>          c86a93369be6        6 seconds ago       110.7
MB
ubuntu              latest          4ca3a192ff2a        2 weeks ago         128.2
MB
    root@docker:~#
```

To delete local images, run the following command:

```
root@docker:~# docker rmi c86a93369be6
Deleted:sha256:c86a93369be687f9ead4758c908fe61b344d5c84b1b70403ede638460353
2aa9
Deleted:sha256:280a817cfb372d2d2dd78b7715336c89d2ac28fd63f7e9a0af2228966021
4d32
root@docker:~#
```

The Docker API exposes a way to define the software networks, similar to what we saw with libvirt LXC. Let's install the Linux bridge and see what is present on the Docker host:

```
root@docker:~# apt-get install bridge-utils
root@docker:~# brctl show
bridge name     bridge id           STP    enabled interfaces
docker0         8000.0242d6dd444c   no         vethf5b871d
root@docker:~#
```

Notice the docker0 bridge, created by the Docker service. Let's list the networks that were automatically created:

```
root@docker:~# docker network ls
NETWORK ID          NAME            DRIVER          SCOPE
a243008cd6cd        bridge          bridge          local
24d4b310a2e1        host            host            local
1e8e35222e39        none            null            local
root@docker:~#
```

To inspect the `bridge` network, run the following command:

```
root@docker:~# docker network inspect bridge
[
    {
        "Name": "bridge",
        "Id":"a243008cd6cd01375ef389de58bc11e1e57c1f3
         e4965a53ea48866c0dcbd3665",
        "Scope": "local",
        "Driver": "bridge",
        "EnableIPv6": false,
        "IPAM": {
            "Driver": "default",
            "Options": null,
            "Config": [
            {
                "Subnet": "172.17.0.0/16"
             }
            ]
        },
        "Internal": false,
        "Containers": {
          "ec66fcfb5960c0779d07243f2c1e4d4ac10b8
            55e940d416514057a9b28d78d09": {
                "Name": "docker_container_1",
                "EndpointID":"27c07e8f24562ea333cdeb5c
                11015d13941c746b02b1fc18a766990b772b5935",
                "MacAddress": "02:42:ac:11:00:02",
                "IPv4Address": "172.17.0.2/16",
                "IPv6Address": ""
            }
        },
        "Options": {
            "com.docker.network.bridge.default_bridge": "true",
            "com.docker.network.bridge.enable_icc": "true",
            "com.docker.network.bridge.enable_ip_masquerade":
            "true",
            "com.docker.network.bridge.host_binding_ipv4":
            "0.0.0.0",
            "com.docker.network.bridge.name": "docker0",
            "com.docker.network.driver.mtu": "1500"
        },
        "Labels": {}
    }
]
root@docker:~#
```

Finally, to stop and delete the Docker container, execute the following command:

```
root@docker:~# docker stop docker_container_1
docker_container_1
root@docker:~#  docker rm docker_container_1
```

Running unprivileged LXC containers

Let's briefly touch on security with LXC. Starting with LXC version 1.0, support for unprivileged containers was introduced, allowing for unprivileged users to run containers. The main security concern running LXC containers as root is that UID 0 inside the container is the same as UID 0 on the host; thus, breaking out of a container will grant you root privileges on the server.

In `Chapter 1`, *Introduction to Linux Containers*, we talked in detail about the user namespace and how it allows for a process inside the user namespace to have a different user and group ID than that of the default namespace. In the context of LXC, this allows for a process to run as root inside the container, while having the unprivileged ID on the host. To take advantage of this, we can create a mapping per container that will use a defined set of UIDs and GIDs between the host and the LXC container.

Let's look at an example of setting up and running a LXC container as an unprivileged user.

Start by updating your Ubuntu system and installing LXC:

```
root@ubuntu:~# apt-get update&& apt-get upgrade
root@ubuntu:~# reboot
root@ubuntu:~# apt-get install lxc
```

Next, create a new user and assign it a password:

```
root@ubuntu:~# useradd -s /bin/bash -c 'LXC user' -m lxc_user
root@ubuntu:~# passwd lxc_user
Enter new UNIX password:
Retype new UNIX password:
passwd: password updated successfully
root@ubuntu:~#
```

Make a note of what the range of UIDs and GIDs on the system is for the new user we created:

```
root@ubuntu:~# cat /etc/sub{gid,uid} | grep lxc_user
lxc_user:231072:65536
lxc_user:231072:65536
root@ubuntu:~#
```

Note the name of the Linux bridge that was created:

```
root@ubuntu:~# brctl show
bridge name bridge id          STP enabled interfaces
lxcbr0              8000.000000000000 no
root@ubuntu:~#
```

Specify how many virtual interfaces can be added to the bridge for a user, in this example, 50:

```
root@ubuntu:~# cat /etc/lxc/lxc-usernet
# USERNAME TYPE BRIDGE COUNT
lxc_user veth lxcbr0 50
root@ubuntu:~#
```

Next, as the `lxc_user`, create the directory structure and config files as follows:

```
root@ubuntu:~# su - lxc_user
lxc_user@ubuntu:~$ pwd
/home/lxc_user
lxc_user@ubuntu:~$ mkdir -p .config/lxc
lxc_user@ubuntu:~$ cp /etc/lxc/default.conf .config/lxc/
lxc_user@ubuntu:~$ cat .config/lxc/default.conf
lxc.network.type = veth
lxc.network.link = lxcbr0
lxc.network.flags = up
lxc.network.hwaddr = 00:16:3e:xx:xx:xx
lxc.id_map = u 0 231072 65536
lxc.id_map = g 0 231072 65536
lxc_user@ubuntu:~$
```

The preceding `id_map` options will map the range of virtual IDs for the `lxc_user`.

We can now create the container as usual:

```
lxc_user@ubuntu:~$ lxc-create --name user_lxc --template download
...
Distribution: ubuntu
Release: xenial
Architecture: amd64
Downloading the image index
Downloading the rootfs
Downloading the metadata
The image cache is now ready
Unpacking the rootfs
...
lxc_user@ubuntu:~$
```

The container is in the stopped state; to start it, run the following command:

```
lxc_user@ubuntu:~$ lxc-ls -f
NAME       STATE    AUTOSTART GROUPS IPV4 IPV6
user_lxc STOPPED 0          -       -    -
lxc_user@ubuntu:~$ lxc-start --name user_lxc
lxc_user@ubuntu:~$ lxc-ls -f
NAME       STATE    AUTOSTART GROUPS IPV4 IPV6
user_lxc RUNNING 0          -       -    -
lxc_user@ubuntu:~$
```

Notice that the processes in the container are owned by the `lxc_user` instead of root:

```
lxc_user@ubuntu:~$ ps axfwwu
lxc_user  4291  0.0  0.0  24448  1584 ?         Ss   19:13   0:00
/usr/lib/x86_64-linux-gnu/lxc/lxc-monitord /home/lxc_user/.local/share/lxc
5
lxc_user  4293  0.0  0.0  32892  3148 ?         Ss   19:13   0:00 [lxc
monitor] /home/lxc_user/.local/share/lxc user_lxc
231072    4304  0.5  0.0  37316  5356 ?         Ss   19:13   0:00  \_
/sbin/init
231072    4446  0.1  0.0  35276  4056 ?         Ss   19:13   0:00        \_
/lib/systemd/systemd-journald
231176    4500  0.0  0.0 182664  3084 ?         Ssl  19:13   0:00        \_
/usr/sbin/rsyslogd -n
231072    4502  0.0  0.0  28980  3044 ?         Ss   19:13   0:00        \_
/usr/sbin/cron -f
231072    4521  0.0  0.0   4508  1764 ?         S    19:13   0:00        \_
/bin/sh /etc/init.d/ondemand background
231072    4531  0.0  0.0   7288   816 ?         S    19:13   0:00        |
\_ sleep 60
231072    4568  0.0  0.0  15996   856 ?         Ss   19:13   0:00        \_
/sbin/dhclient -1 -v -pf /run/dhclient.eth0.pid -lf
```

```
/var/lib/dhcp/dhclient.eth0.leases -I -df
/var/lib/dhcp/dhclient6.eth0.leases eth0
231072    4591  0.0  0.0  15756  2228 pts/1     Ss+  19:13    0:00         \_
/sbin/agetty --noclear --keep-baud pts/1 115200 38400 9600 vt220
231072    4592  0.0  0.0  15756  2232 pts/2     Ss+  19:13    0:00         \_
/sbin/agetty --noclear --keep-baud pts/2 115200 38400 9600 vt220
231072    4593  0.0  0.0  15756  2224 pts/0     Ss+  19:13    0:00         \_
/sbin/agetty --noclear --keep-baud pts/0 115200 38400 9600 vt220
231072    4594  0.0  0.0  15756  2228 pts/2     Ss+  19:13    0:00         \_
/sbin/agetty --noclear --keep-baud console 115200 38400 9600 vt220
231072    4595  0.0  0.0  15756  2232 ?         Ss+  19:13    0:00         \_
/sbin/agetty --noclear --keep-baud pts/3 115200 38400 9600 vt220
lxc_user@ubuntu:~$
```

The root filesystem and config file location is different when running the container as a non root user:

```
lxc_user@ubuntu:~$ ls -la .local/share/lxc/user_lxc/
total 16
drwxrwx---  3    231072 lxc_user 4096 Dec 15 19:13 .
drwxr-xr-x  3 lxc_user lxc_user 4096 Dec 15 19:13 ..
-rw-rw-r--  1 lxc_user lxc_user  845 Dec 15 19:13 config
drwxr-xr-x 21    231072    231072 4096 Dec 15 03:59 rootfs
-rw-rw-r--  1 lxc_user lxc_user    0 Dec 15 19:13 user_lxc.log
lxc_user@ubuntu:~$ cat .local/share/lxc/user_lxc/config | grep -vi "#" |
sed '/^$/d'
lxc.include = /usr/share/lxc/config/ubuntu.common.conf
lxc.include = /usr/share/lxc/config/ubuntu.userns.conf
lxc.arch = x86_64
lxc.id_map = u 0 231072 65536
lxc.id_map = g 0 231072 65536
lxc.rootfs = /home/lxc_user/.local/share/lxc/user_lxc/rootfs
lxc.rootfs.backend = dir
lxc.utsname = user_lxc
lxc.network.type = veth
lxc.network.link = lxcbr0
lxc.network.flags = up
lxc.network.hwaddr = 00:16:3e:a7:f2:97
lxc_user@ubuntu:~$
```

Summary

In this chapter, we saw examples on how to deploy containers with alternative technologies to LXC such as OpenVZ and Docker.

OpenVZ is one of the oldest container solutions, and as of this writing it's being rebranded to Virtuozzo. The main difference between LXC and OpenVZ is the custom Linux kernel that OpenVZ runs on. It's based on the Red Hat kernels and soon will be shipped as a single installation ISO as compared to the packaged kernel and userspace tools we used in the earlier examples.

Docker is the de-facto standard and an adoption leader in the containerized world. Being one of the newer containerization technologies, its ease of use, and available API makes it an ideal solution for running microservices in a mass scale. Docker does not need a patched kernel to work, and the availability of centralized registries to store container images makes it a great choice in many scenarios.

We ended the chapter by showing an example of how to run unprivileged LXC containers. This feature is relatively new, and it's a step in the right direction when it comes to container security.

Index

www.ingramcontent.com/pod-product-compliance
Lightning Source LLC
Chambersburg PA
CBHW062055050326
40690CB00016B/3096